Basic
Tagalog

for Foreigners and Non-Tagalogs

In memory of my father, Lope K. Santos

Publisher's note:

While the national language of the Philippines has come to be known as Filipino within the Philippines, we refer to it in this book as TAGALOG, as this remains the basis for the language and the name by which it is known internationally.

Basic Tagalog

for Foreigners and Non-Tagalogs

SECOND EDITION

By Paraluman S. Aspillera

Revised and updated by Yolanda Canseco Hernandez

TUTTLE PUBLISHING
Tokyo • Rutland, Vermont • Singapore

Acknowledgments

We are grateful to the following persons who have helped in the publication of this revised edition of **Basic Tagalog**: Dr. Monita Manalo, University of Wisconsin-Madison for reviewing the updated manuscript; Dr. Isagani R. Cruz and Dr. Luis P. Gatmaitan for granting us permission to include their materials in this book; Leo Angelito C. Alvarado of Ilustrador ng Kabataan (Illustrators for Children) [INK] for providing illustrations for this book.

Published by Tuttle Publishing, an imprint of Periplus Editions (HK) Ltd, with editorial offices at 364 Innovation Drive, North Clarendon, Vermont 05759 and 61 Tai Seng Avenue #02-12 Singapore 534167.

LCC Card No. 2007933898
ISBN 13: 978-0-8048-3837-5
ISBN 10: 0-8048-3837-2

First Tuttle edition, 1969
First Tuttle paperback edition, 1993
Revised edition, 2007

Distributed by:

North America, Latin America & Europe
Tuttle Publishing
364 Innovation Drive
North Clarendon, VT 05759-9436
Tel: (802) 773 8930; Fax: (802) 773 6993
Email: info@tuttlepublishing.com
www.tuttlepublishing.com

Asia Pacific
Berkeley Books Pte. Ltd.
61 Tai Seng Avenue #02-12
Singapore 534167
Tel: (65) 6280 1330; Fax: (65) 6280 6290
Email: inquiries@periplus.com.sg
www.periplus.com

Japan
Tuttle Publishing
Yaekari Building, 3F
5-4-12 Osaki, Shinagawa-ku
Tokyo 141-0032, Japan
Tel: (81) 3 5437-0171; Fax: (81) 3 5437-0755
Email: tuttle-sales@gol.com
www.tuttlepublishing.com

10 09 08 07   6 5 4 3 2 1

Printed in Singapore

Table of Contents

Preface to the Revised Edition

More than 500 new words and expressions have been added to this completely updated and expanded version of **Basic Tagalog**. These are spread throughout the 44 lessons, the Appendices and the exercises as well as in the Tagalog-English/English-Tagalog vocabulary lists at the back of this book. The added vocabulary is meant to keep learners abreast of changes that have occurred in the language since the first edition of **Basic Tagalog** which was published in 1969.

This edition has retained all the grammar lessons and the tried-and-tested teaching methodology developed by the author, **Paraluman S. Aspillera**, for the original version. Her method has proven to be extremely effective for tens of thousands of foreigners and non-Tagalogs who have used this book to learn Tagalog, including many who have successfully learned to speak and write Tagalog through self-study on their own without a teacher. An audio CD has also been added to facilitate the correct pronunciation of Tagalog words and phrases. A succinct introduction to the language and a description of the character of Filipinos will hopefully provide learners with a better understanding of the language they are learning.

The lessons in this book are intended for a three-month period of intensive study followed by another three months of applied oral communication of at least two hours per day. In six months (or about 250 hours), it is expected that an average learner should be able to speak, write and understand simple, everyday, conversational Tagalog as spoken by most Filipinos.

I hope that the new and expanded edition of this book will further encourage both non-Tagalogs and non-Filipinos to speak the Tagalog language better. Only then shall they appreciate the individuality of the language that reflects the resilience and flexibility of Filipinos all around the world. In the end, such learning will improve daily interactions and communications between non-Filipinos and Filipinos—whether in business, educational, social or civic endeavors.

Yolanda Canseco Hernandez

INTRODUCTION
Tagalog—A Living Language

What is a living language? It is defined as a language that is "currently in use or valid." Thus, it is alive, it is dynamic, it is vibrant.

Language is a system through which people express their thoughts, feelings and sentiments, either orally or in writing. It mirrors the kind of society they live in, their customs and traditions, and their aspirations as a nation.

Tagalog is a living language. It is the basis of the national language of the Philippines as mandated by the 1987 Constitution of the Republic of the Philippines under Article XIV, Section 6, on "Language." The provision states: "The national language of the Philippines is Filipino. As it evolves, it shall be further developed and enriched on the basis of existing Philippine and other languages. Subject to provisions of law and as the Congress may deem appropriate, the Government shall take steps to initiate and sustain the use of Filipino as a medium of official communication and as a language of instruction in the education system."

While still considered a young but nonetheless maturing national language, Filipino is constantly beng developed through its usage in various fields of endeavor. As the nation develops and progresses, Filipino also grows linguistically and lexically with the assimilation of new words, concepts and ideas into the language brought about by technological advances, changes in lifestyles, globalization trends and contacts with foreign cultures, political and religious upheavals, and media developments, among others.

Historical Influences and Contacts

Tagalog as a language has very ancient roots going back thousands of years, and even had its own writing system in ancient times, borrowed from the Sanskritic writing systems of the region. According to Filipino anthropologist F. Landa Jocano, "Writing as a system of communication was fairly well-developed in many parts of the archipelago when the Spaniards came during the early part of the 16th century."

Alibata, also known as **Baybayin**, the Sanskritic alphabet that was in use in the Philippines in earlier times.

Documents unearthed by Spanish chroniclers Pedro Chirino and Francisco Colin show different types of alphabets or syllabary writing. The writing had vowel and consonant syllable signs which, according to anthropologist Robert Fox, conform "to a common phonemic pattern of Philippine (contemporary languages)."

Comparisons with other Asian language groups indicate that the Tagalog language along with other Philippine languages belong to the Malayan branch of the great Malayo-Polynesian or Austronesian linguistic family, which includes hundreds of languages now spread across almost half the globe from Taiwan through the Philippine Islands to Hawaii, Fiji and New Zealand in the Pacific, across the islands of Indonesia and the Malay peninsula to Madagascar.

Filipino linguist Juan Francisco cited many Indian influences on Philippine language and literature. He found about 336 terms derived from Sanskrit, out of which 150 were identified and used in the Philippine languages, specifically in the names of plants and animals. Many of these appear to have been borrowed from Malay.

Loan words from China have also crept into the Philippine vocabulary, particularly standard Tagalog. Linguist Arsenio E. Manuel, in his study *Chinese Elements in the Tagalog Language* (1948), compiled a "list of 381 Tagalog words of Chinese origins, excluding variants, derivatives and compounds." These words pertain to food, abstract ideas or terms, metal smithing, kinship, and words concerning agriculture, business, tools, industries and games.

The few Arabic words in Tagalog came in with the arrival of Islam from the southern Philippine islands where the religion has had a foothold since 1380. However, the defeat of a sultan in Manila in 1571 meant the subsequent extinction of the faith in Tagalog-speaking areas and many Arabic words fell into disuse.

The Spanish has contributed a great deal to the Philippine languages, and many Spanish loan words have now been thoroughly naturalized. These include religious, governmental, social, legal and abstract terms, including many terms for foreign articles and luxuries. Contacts with traders during the Spanish period also led to a few Mexican words, mainly Nahuatl or Aztec, creeping into the Tagalog lexicon. Other parts of the country, specifically in the Zamboanga provinces in the Mindanao region, the dominant language of the Zamboangueño people has evolved from the marriage of Spanish and Cebuano into what is now known as Chavacano or Philippine Creole Spanish.

In his 1,027-page *Diksyunaryo Tesauro Pilipino Ingles* posthumously published in 1973, Dr. Jose Villa Panganiban—who was a professor, linguist, and former director of the Institute of National Language in Manila—included 27,069 main word entries, containing almost 217,500 lexical items. He listed 12,000 loan words derived from Spanish, English, Chinese and Indo-European languages. He also included synonyms, antonyms, and homonyms with other languages along with identities and cognacies between Tagalog and 12 other Philippine languages.

While the colonization of the Philippines by the Spaniards for more than 300 years had a profound impact on the lifestyles of the Filipinos, other colonizers especially the Americans left their marks on Philippine culture and society by introducing their own brand of education and government. English words which had no exact equivalent have been adapted into the Philippine languages and given a regional treatment for suitability in the language. Although most are still quoted, some are used and spelled as they are especially with the recent modification of the Filipino alphabet. The Japanese also occupied the islands in the 1940s but seemed to have furnished no words to the Tagalog lexicon. After all these occupations, however, the construction of Tagalog does not seem to have been influenced by any of the colonizers' languages. It has retained its essentially Malayo-Polynesian structure.

A National Language Is Born

The adoption of a national language for Filipinos came during the Commonwealth years (1935 to 1946) under the American regime. It was not easy for proponents of a national language to push Tagalog as the basis for a language that was to be used from Luzon to the Visayas and all the way down to Mindanao. The three main island groupings in the Philippines each has its own distinct identity as the archipelagic nature of the country gave rise to a wide variety of cultures and languages separated by seas and strengthened by history.

Populated then by an estimated 16 million inhabitants, the Philippines had a diverse collection of 172 languages of which three are already extinct. Eight major languages (Tagalog, Cebuano, Ilocano, Hiligaynon, Bicolano, Waray, Kapampangan and Pangasinan) all belong to the Malayo-Polynesian linguistic family but no two are mutually comprehensible. In the 1980s, these eight languages and their dialects were spoken by 90% of the population (see Language Map of the Philippines on page 12). Even though they are separate languages, they are closely related (like French, Italian and Spanish), and some languages are much closer than others—for example, Ilocano and Pangasinan speakers might find little difficulty in learning each other's languages in contrast to learning any of the Visayan languages. The same can be said for Visayan speakers of Cebuano, Hiligaynon and Waray with regards to learning each other's languages and the opposite for learning the Northern Luzon languages.

It is thus understandable that fierce opposition from certain non-Tagalog legislators and rabid advocates of the English language delayed somewhat the entire process of adopting a national language. In the end, however, Tagalog prevailed when President Manuel L. Quezon proclaimed the creation of a national language based on Tagalog on December 31, 1937. The body which was responsible for the adoption of the national language was the National Language Institute created by President Quezon. It was composed of non-Tagalogs and Tagalog representatives from different regions in the country. The Chairman was Jaime C. de Veyra from Samar, Leyte, with the following as members: Santiago A. Fonacier (Ilocano); Filomeno Sotto (Cebu, Visayas); Casimiro T. Perfecto (Bicol); Felix Sales Rodriguez (Panay, Visayas); Madji Butin (Mindanao) and Dr. Cecilio Lopez (Tagalog).

Tagalog was chosen as the basis for the Philippines' national language for the following reasons:

1. **Tagalog is the most widely spoken** and the most widely understood language in all regions of the Philippines. By 1989, 25% of the Philippine population spoke Tagalog as their mother tongue. They are scattered across the Tagalog regions, or **Katagalugan**, stretching from the central to the southern parts of Luzon island and covering 10 major provinces—Nueva Ecija, Aurora, Bataan, Batangas, Bulacan, Cavite, Laguna, Metro Manila (or the National Capital Region), Quezon and Rizal—as well as parts of the islands of Marinduque and Mindoro. Further away from these regions, there has been less exposure to Tagalog and one finds a lower competency level in the language.

   Compared to Tagalog, the second most widely-spoken Philippine language—Cebuano—was spoken by 24% of the population in 1989 but is mostly understood only by its own speakers. Other major languages including Ilocano, Hiligaynon, Bicol and Waray are spoken by 5% to 9% of the total population. Many other languages or dialects are spoken by the remaining 22% of the population. Recent 2000 census figures reveal that around 29% of the total population speak Tagalog as their first language and 65% speak or understand the language with varying degrees of proficiency.

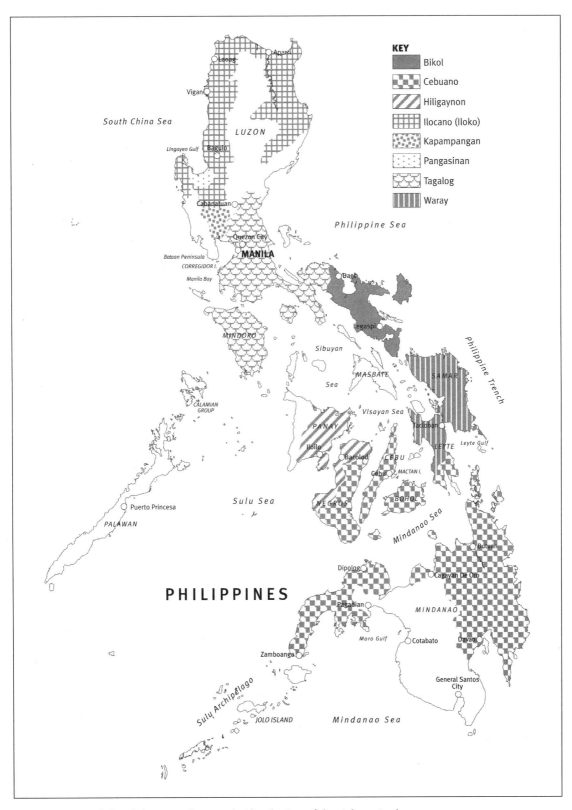

KEY

- Bikol
- Cebuano
- Hiligaynon
- Ilocano (Iloko)
- Kapampangan
- Pangasinan
- Tagalog
- Waray

Language Map of the Philippines showing the distribution of the eight major languages

2. **It is not divided into dialects** unlike the Visayan languages. There are three major Visayan languages: Cebuano, Hiligaynon and Waray. Cebuano is spoken in many parts of the Visayan and Mindanao regions but residents from various provinces have their own distinct Cebuano sub-languages or dialects. There may be variations in the Tagalog language but these are still comprehensible to all native Tagalog speakers.

3. **Tagalog has the richest literature**. More books are written and published in Tagalog than in any other native language.

4. **Tagalog has always been the language of Manila,** the country's capital city, even long before the Spanish came. As the capital city, Manila houses all the major government offices from Malacanang Palace down to the administration's smallest bureaus. At present, economic and political decisions are decided in Manila and its surrounding provinces and cities, which also speak Tagalog. Historically, though, Cebu is the first and oldest city in the Philippines. It is also an alternate gateway to the nation from abroad.

5. **Tagalog was the language of the Revolution and the Katipunan,** two major events in Philippine history.

On June 18, 1938, the Philippine National Assembly created the Institute of National Language (this institute was different from the National Language Institute which was eventually dissolved). Two years after the institute was established, two monumental language books in Tagalog were presented to President Quezon: the *Tagalog-English Dictionary* authored by Dr. Cecilio Lopez and the *Balarila ng Wikang Pambansa*, a grammar book written by Lope K. Santos, then acknowledged as the Dean of Tagalog Writers and Father of the National Language. The publication of these books paved the way for the introduction of the national language beginning with the school year 1940-41 during the fourth year of all high schools and in the second year of both public and private normal schools in the whole country.

"Pilipino" Emerges

On July 4, 1946 under Commonwealth Act No. 570, independence was granted to the Philippines by the United States of America. It provided for the use of the national language as one of the official languages of the Philippines (the others being Spanish and English) in government offices. Soon, adherents of the Tagalog-based national language increased rapidly all over the islands.

In 1954, the national language was given a further boost by President Ramon Magsaysay when he proclaimed the celebration of a **Linggo ng Wika** (National Language Week) and the national observance annually of the birthday of Francisco Balagtas, a great Tagalog poet.

In 1961, the Office of the Secretary of Education introduced the term "Pilipino" when referring to the national language. It gained wide acceptance in schools and among the general public, thus the Tagalog-based national language was soon called Pilipino. By 1974, the Pilipino movement stirred the public to "think Pilipino." School teachers were encouraged to attend seminars in Pilipino, the Department of Education started issuing memos, circulars and bulletins enjoining school organs to include sections in Pilipino in their publications, translate English and other foreign materials into Pilipino, use Pilipino on school diplomas and certificates, and sing the national anthem only in Pilipino. In schools, Pilipino was introduced at the tertiary level and in the teaching of civics and culture at lower levels. In 1990, then Philippine President Corazon Aquino ordered government offices to use Pilipino as a medium of communication. The government was encouraged to use Pilipino in naming their departments and buildings, and to print Pilipino text on their letterheads, seals and signages. Government employees were also enjoined to attend seminars on Pilipino to broaden their knowledge and skill in the use of the national language.

The Medium of Instruction and Communication

The Department of Education and the schools have continuously promoted Pilipino, now called Filipino, as a medium of instruction and communication. Other supportive forces have joined them in the propagation and enrichment of the language. Radio and television, for instance, use Filipino in a majority of their programs to reach out to the masses. Of late, more dubbing and subtitling of foreign-produced programs has been done in Filipino and has contributed much to the promotion of the language.

In the print media, the number of publishers who produce and circulate books, magazines, comics, broadsheets and tabloids in Filipino is increasing. Songs in Filipino are also "in" and played over the airwaves, sung in concerts and in theatrical performances. Composers in Filipino are now enjoying recognition and patronage from a growing audience.

Masses and services in Catholic and Christian churches are now said in Filipino. There are Filipino versions of the bible and other religious books. And when it comes to campaigning during elections, Filipino has become the language to attract voters and certainly the language that an ordinary citizen on the street is most comfortable with. At present, Filipino as a subject is taught all over the country from pre-school (3 years) up to grade school (6 years) and high school (4 years). Considering that the basic literacy rate in 2003 is high at nearly 90% (wherein 9 out of 10 Filipinos are able to read and write), it is not a surprise that Filipino is understood and spoken by most Filipinos now.

Enriching the National Language

More positive moves are being undertaken to strengthen and enrich Filipino as a national language. National language advocates and institutions like the Commission on the Filipino Language, **Sentro ng Wikang Filipino** of the University of the Philippines, along with many teachers, administrators, researchers, writers, authors and linguists are working hard to improve the quality of the Filipino language. They host and sponsor seminars, workshops, forums and conferences to discuss ways of translating works, produce adequate and well-researched Filipino books for schools, enrich and infuse Filipino with more words and terms from other major Philippine languages like Cebuano, Ilocano, Hiligaynon, Waray, Kapampangan and others, that are fast becoming part of the Filipino vocabulary. With their concerted efforts, these formidable groups will certainly help enliven the use of Filipino in the daily lives of the people and keep alive a national language that fosters genuine nationalism and unity among Filipinos.

Understanding the Filipino Character

Learning Tagalog becomes more enjoyable and meaningful if one understands the culture of the Philippines as well as the temperament and character of its people. The Philippines is populated by more than 80 million people living on 7,101 islands, which are abundantly blessed by nature. Pristine beaches, verdant mountains and rainforests, a treasure-trove of exotic fauna and flora attract tourists and locals alike. Colorful customs and traditions in the country are brought to the forefont when people celebrate their lively and spectacular fiestas and showcase their innate creativity, spirituality, culinary skills and well-renowned hospitality.

In the book *Living in the Philippines* (1980) published by the American Chamber of Commerce in the Philippines and intended for the use of foreign business representatives, expatriates and their families, it is stated that "one of the best things about the Philippines is the Filipino people themselves; reams have been written about their warmth and hospitality—all of it is true." The book also presented the Filipinos as a versatile and talented people, stating that "nowhere is this evident than in the music and the arts. Museums and galleries abound, and even the smallest pub features a talented musician."

Filipinos are very friendly, loving and caring people. They go out of their way to help others in time of disaster and in crisis they manage to keep their sense of humor and survive despite the economic and political challenges that face them. Filipinos, however, have their own idiosyncracies. Their strengths may also often be their weaknesses. An indepth study made by a Philippine senator in 1998 detailed the strengths and weaknesses of the Filipino character as follows:

1. **Pakikipagkapwa-tao** (a basic sense of justice and concern for others)
2. Family orientation
3. Joy and humor
4. Flexibility, adaptability and creativity
5. Hard work and industry
6. Faith and religiosity
7. Resiliency (or the ability to survive)

Filipino weaknesses which surfaced were: extreme personalism; extreme family centeredness; lack of discipline; passivity; colonial mentality; **kanya-kanya** syndrome (selfishness or to each his own—the literal translation is *his-his* or *hers-hers*); and lack of analysis and self-reflection.

A trait which puzzles a lot of foreigners in the country and which affects relationships, negatively, is the relaxed attitude toward time. Coming late for appointments, not meeting deadlines, and not starting parties or programs on time all result in irritation and even embarrassment not only among foreigners but also among fellow Filipinos who observe punctuality.

As to dealing with Filipinos, language learners should learn to read the body language and movements of the locals. What do they really mean when they say *yes* or *no* or *perhaps*? What are the meanings of some peculiar signs and sounds they make? All these certainly represent a big challenge to the learner or student of Tagalog. For the appreciation of the language student and for the better understanding of the Filipino character, more Filipino traits and characteristics will be discussed in the subsequent lessons and exercises.

The Tagalog Alphabet

In the 1930s, when Tagalog was chosen as the basis for the national language, there were 20 letters in the alphabet consisting of five vowels and 15 consonants. These were:

a	e	i	o	u		
b	k	d	g	h	l	m
n	ng	p	r	s	t	w	y

The consonants were originally referred to with the vowel **a** appended to each letter so that these were pronounced **ba**, **ka**, **da**, and so on. The **ng** consonant was pronounced as **nang**.

In the 1980s, eight more consonants were added to the alphabet. These are **c**, **f**, **j**, **ñ**, **q**, **v**, **x** and **z**. This was done to facilitate the writing of new words and terms borrowed from other languages. The letters of the Tagalog alphabet are now referred to in the same way as the letters in the English alphabet except for **ng** and **ñ** (pronounced *en-ye*) which is of Spanish origin.

Generally, the eight additional consonants are used for proper nouns (names of persons, places, buildings, brand names, the like) such as Fe, Carlos, Santo Niño, Leyte Gulf, Jones Bridge, Jollibee and Louis Vuitton. They are also used for borrowed terms like **zakat** (almsgiving, the third pillar of Islam), indigenous or native terms like **carayab** (an Igorot costume made of tree bark), and medical and scientific terms like zinc and amoxicillin.

There are conventions in the pronunciation of the consonants **ñ** and **ng**. Tagalog words with **ñ** are pronounced as if there is a combination of **n** and **y** consonants instead of one consonant. The first half is the **n** part which takes the sound of the vowel before it while the second half is the **y** part which takes the sound of the vowel after it. For example, the word **Niño** in Santo Niño is pronounced **nin-yo**. Note that **ñ** is between **i** and **o**, thus **n** takes the initial sound of the vowel **i** while **y** takes the sound of the vowel **o**.

The pronunciation of the consonant **ng** is very difficult for foreigners particularly when it appears at the beginning of a word. To produce the sound **ng**, push the tongue back and up—making sure that the back part of the tongue is curled and almost touches the molars and the roof of your mouth to produce a nasal sound, and then add the sound of the vowel after it. The syllable before **ng** usually rides on the nasal **ng** sound.

Another Tagalog consonant that may pose some difficulty for foreigners is the consonant **r**. Unlike the English *r* where the tongue does not touch the sides of the mouth, the Tagalog **r** is produced by quickly tapping the tip of the tongue on the gum ridge behind the upper teeth (like a Spanish *r* but not rolled or trilled).

A Tagalog word is pronounced just as it is spelled, and each syllable is pronounced separately and distinctly. Except for certain vowel and semi-vowel combinations (diphthongs) such as **ay**, **aw**, **ey**, **iw**, **oy**, and **uy**, foreigners will have minimal difficulty in pronouncing most Tagalog words. However, foreigners may find the **iw** and **uy** combinations a bit hard to pronounce and may likely break up the combinations especially when they appear at the end of words. Some Tagalog examples of these diphthongs are:

agiw	**a-giw**	cobweb	**áway**	**a-way**	fight
bítiw	**bi-tiw**	let go	**láway**	**la-way**	saliva
kasúy	**ka-suy**	cashew	**reyna**	**rey-na**	queen
badúy	**ba-duy**	dowdy	**káhoy**	**ka-hoy**	wood
mabábaw	**ma-ba-baw**	shallow	**amóy**	**a-moy**	scent
áyaw	**a-yaw**	do not like			

Foreign Words in Tagalog

When a foreign word is borrowed or assimilated into Tagalog, it is written according to the conventions of Tagalog phonetics. However, the names of persons and places need not be changed. Many foreign words (mostly Spanish and English) have been absorbed into the Tagalog vocabulary and remain foreign when their original spelling and pronunciation is retained. But when changed to conform with the Tagalog alphabet, they become Tagalog words. Although many new English loan words have come into the language in recent years (especialy technical and scientific terms), there are still many common, everyday words in the language that were borrowed from Spanish in earlier times. Between the English word *telephone* and the Spanish equivalent *telefono*, for example, the Tagalogs have adopted the latter and write it as **teléponó**.

In writing and pronouncing Spanish loan words in Tagalog, be guided by the following:

			SPANISH	TAGALOG	ENGLISH
hard *c*	is changed to **k**	as in	calesa	**kalésa**	rig
soft *c*	is changed to **s**	as in	circo	**sírko**	circus
ch	is changed to **ts**	as in	lechon	**litsón**	roast pig
f	is changed to **p**	as in	final	**pinál**	final
soft *j*	is changed to **h**	as in	cajon	**kahón**	box, drawer
	or **s**	as in	jabon	**sabón**	soap
ll	is changed to **ly**	as in	calle	**kálye**	street
q	is changed to **k**	as in	maquina	**mákina**	machine
v	is changed to **b**	as in	vapor	**bapór**	ship
z	is changed to **s**	as in	lapiz	**lápis**	pencil

English words also undergo changes when they are assimilated into the Tagalog language. Some words may bear some resemblance to the original English words although others have an added hint of Spanish influence. Still others undergo odd, sometimes comical changes when English sounds are given the nearest Tagalog equivalent such as **kwaliti** for *quality*. Since **kalidád** is another Tagalog loan word (from Spanish), an English word may often have more than one Tagalog equivalent.

A current but debatable issue on the Filipinization of English words has also led to the use of words such as **efektiv** from the English word *effective*, the Tagalog equivalent of which is **mabísa**. Another example is **varayti** from *variety* (or **urí** in Tagalog).

The following lists a few of the rules:

			ENGLISH	TAGALOG
soft *c*	is changed to **s**	as in	cinema	**sine**
hard *c*	is changed to **k**	as in	academic	**akadémik**
ck	is changed to **k**	as in	gimmick	**gímik**
ct	is changed to **k**	as in	addict	**ádik**
qua or *q*	are changed to **kwa**	as in	quality	**kwáliti**
long *i*	is changed to **ay**	as in	driver	**dráyber**
f	is changed to **p**	as in	traffic	**trápik**
v	is changed to **b**	as in	believe	**bilíb**
long *o*	is changed to **u**	as in	approve	**aprúb**
cle	is changed to **kel**	as in	tricycle	**tráysikel**
tion	is changed to **syon**	as in	institution	**institusyón**
x	is changed to **ks**	as in	boxing	**bóksing**
j	is changed to **dy**	as in	janitor	**dyánitor**
beginning *s*	is changed to **is**	as in	sport	**ísport**
soft *ch*	is changed to **ts**	as in	teacher	**títser**
hard *ch*	is changed to **k**	as in	school	**iskúl**

Students should also learn how to write the following foreign words in Tagalog that are very common in everyday conversation. Needless to say, correct pronunciation is very important. Learn to pronounce these words as true Tagalog words by taking particular notice of the accent marks and stresses (these will be discussed in Lesson Two). Repeat the words aloud and take note of the vowels.

alkohól	alcohol	**klub**	club	**silyá**	chair
piyáno	piano	**sinehán**	movie house	**kompyúter**	computer
rádyo	radio	**pelíkula**	movie	**pasapórte**	passport
kótse	car	**bentiladór**	electric fan	**tiangge**	bazaar
telépono	telephone	**otél**	hotel	**tindáhan**	store
bangkô	bench	**tabáko**	tobacco	**papél**	paper
kapé	coffee	**tenis**	tennis	**plástik**	plastic
restawrán	restaurant	**sigarílyo**	cigarette	**telebísyon**	television

DAYS OF THE WEEK

Lúnes	Monday	**Biyérnes**	Friday
Martés	Tuesday	**Sábado**	Saturday
Miyérkules	Wednesday	**Linggó**	Sunday
Huwébes	Thursday		

MONTHS OF THE YEAR

Enéro	January	**Húlyo**	July
Pebréro	February	**Agósto**	August
Márso	March	**Setyémbre**	September
Abríl	April	**Oktúbre**	October
Máyo	May	**Nobyémbre**	November
Húnyo	June	**Disyémbre**	December

Syllables and Stress in Tagalog

I. SYLLABLES IN TAGALOG

A knowledge of the different kinds of syllables (word divisions) in Tagalog will help the learner to articulate the words correctly. There are four kinds of syllables in Tagalog, namely:

1. The simple syllable consisting of only one vowel (V)

as	**o**	in	**tá-o**	person
as	**a**	in	**pa-á**	foot
as	**i**	in	**i-yák**	cry
as	**u**	in	**ú-lo**	head

2. The consonant + vowel syllable (CV)

as	**ba** or **sa**	in	**ba-sa**	read
as	**ta**	in	**tá-o**	person
as	**na**	in	**i-ná**	mother
as	**lo**	in	**ú-lo**	head

3. The vowel + consonant syllable (VC)

as	**an**	in	**an-táy**	wait
as	**am**	in	**am-bón**	shower / drizzle
as	**ak**	in	**ak-yát**	climb
as	**it**	in	**ma-pa-ít**	bitter

4. The consonant + vowel + consonant syllable (CVC)

as	**tak**	in	**tak-bó**	run
as	**lak**	in	**bu-lak-lák**	flower
as	**lon**	in	**ta-lón**	jump
as	**law**	in	**í-law**	light

When pronouncing Tagalog words, there are no hard and fast rules to help you know how to break the syllables (in other words, to know where each syllable starts and ends). An understanding though of the types of syllables that exist and the possible combinations of vowels and consonants that are formed through exposure to the Tagalog language will help the learner pronounce words correctly after some time. In the beginning, however, it is best to simply memorize the stress accents along with the words as you learn them.

Look out as well for prefixes and suffixes which "grab" vowels and consonants from the root word (see Lesson 14 on the **-um-** and **mag-** verbs, and similar discussions on other affixes). An example is **bu-lak-lák** (*flower*) which becomes **bu-lak-lá-kin** (flowery) where the suffix **-in** grabs the final consonant of the root.

A useful rule to remember is not to apply the pronunciation of English words to Tagalog words—for example saying **ku-must-á** rather than **ku-mus-tá** (*how are you*)—since the maximum number of letters in a Tagalog syllable does not exceed three (keeping in mind that **ng** is treated as a single letter). Thus, there is no **must** in **kumustá** although there is **pang** in **pang-ápat** (*fourth*) and **ngin** in **hángin** (*wind*). The syllables **pang** and **ngin** are only made up of three sounds as **ng** is considered a single consonant or letter in the Tagalog alphabet.

Another useful rule for foreigners is not to separate an intial consonant from a vowel, leaving a VC syllable in the middle of a word, as in **bu-má-nat** or *to strike* (which should not be pronounced **bu-má-nat**). VC syllables are mostly found at the beginning of words such as **an-táy** (*wait*) and **ak-yát** (*climb*). VC syllables may also be found at the end of words if the previous syllables end in a vowel as in **pa-ít** (*bitter*) and **la-ot** (*sea*).

As a general rule for the proper pronunciation of Tagalog words, remember to deliver these words in a faster, sharper and less breathy manner than in English (more in the manner of Spanish pronunciation). Do not make any audible breaths (aspirations) in pronouncing the *p*'s, *k*'s, *t*'s and other consonants. Otherwise, you will be branded a "slang," the local term for anyone who speaks Tagalog with an American accent or with too many long *a*'s, long *e*'s and long *o*'s.

Exercises

Break the following words correctly into their individual syllables. The first syllable of each word has been given.

1. **magandá**	ma - _____ - _____		beautiful
2. **páaralán**	pa - _____ - _____ - _____		school
3. **pagkáin**	pag- _____ - _____		food
4. **inilutò**	i- _____ - _____ - _____		was cooked
5. **ialís**	i- _____ - _____		to be removed
6. **inalís**	i- _____ - _____		was removed
7. **hángin**	ha- _____		wind
8. **linísin**	li- _____ - _____		to be cleaned
9. **tatló**	tat- _____		three
10. **álaála**	a- _____ - _____ - _____		gift, remembrance
11. **kailángan**	ka- _____ - _____ - _____		needed
12. **násaán**	na- _____ - _____		where
13. **ngayón**	nga- _____		now, today
14. **awítin**	a- _____ - _____		to sing
15. **mabaít**	ma- _____ - _____		good
16. **pangálan**	pa- _____ - _____		name
17. **maliit**	ma- _____ - _____		small
18. **paalám**	pa- _____ - _____		goodbye
19. **maaárì**	ma- _____ - _____ - _____		can be
20. **nag-áaral**	nag- _____ - _____ - _____		studying

Pronounce the words listed in the Exercises on page 19 slowly, syllable by syllable, then repeat them pronouncing each word a bit faster.

II. STRESS

In Tagalog, the use of stress on a particular syllable in a word can make a difference in meaning. **Stress** is the vocal emphasis of a particular syllable. In this book, an accent mark is placed over the vowel of a syllable to indicate which syllable is to be stressed and how the stress is to be sounded.

1. Principal types of stresses
There are four principal types of stresses and in this book, they are marked in the following ways:

a. End Stress
An acute accent mark (´) is placed over the vowel of the last syllable of the word if this syllable receives a stronger emphasis than the others.

anák	a-NAK	child
amá	a-MA	father
iná	i-NA	mother
bulaklák	bu-lak-LAK	flower
malakás	ma-la-KAS	strong

b. Penultimate Stress
An acute accent mark (´) is also used to indicate a stress on the next to last syllable of a word, by placing the accent above the vowel of that syllable.

babáe	ba-BA-e	woman
laláki	la-LA-ki	man
maínit	ma-I-nit	hot
malínis	ma-LI-nis	clean
táo	TA-o	person

c. Penultimate Stress with a Glottal Catch
A grave accent mark (`) is used above the vowel of the last syllable to indicate a strong emphasis on the next to last syllable. The vowel at the end is pronounced with a glottal catch, which is produced by an abrupt closing of the throat to block the air stream in both the mouth and voice box. The glottal catch is hard to hear and beginners often mistake the sound as that of *k*.

For this particular lesson, however, we shall indicate the pronunciation of the glottal catch with the letter **Q**. Note that this is only a representation of the glottal catch and should not be interpreted as the literal pronunciation of the words (Please refer to the audio CD to hear how the words are pronounced).

punò	PU-noQ	tree
kandilà	kan-DI-laQ	candle
pusà	PU-saQ	cat
susì	SU-siQ	key
batà	BA-taQ	child

d. **End Glottal Catch** (no stress)

The circumflex mark (ˆ) is used above the vowel of the last syllable when it is pronounced without a stress but with a glottal catch at the end. The difference with the preceding stress type is that words that fall under this category are pronounced faster and the stress on the last syllable seems lost with the glottal catch.

punô	**pu-noQ**	full
sampû	**sam-puQ**	ten
bakyâ	**bak-yaQ**	wooden shoes
masamâ	**ma-sa-maQ**	bad
gintô	**gin-toQ**	gold

Note that longer words may have more than one stressed syllable such as **pinagkákaguluhán** (being mobbed) and **mapágsamantalâ** (opportunistic).

2. On the use of stress and accents

There are some important facts that the language learner should also remember about the use of stress and accents in Tagalog. These are the following:

a. A difference in stress can cause a difference in meaning, as in the following examples:

kaibígan	**ka-i-BI-gan**	friend
kaibigán	**ka-i-bi-GAN**	desire
káibigán	**KA-i-bi-GAN**	have mutual understanding with
kaíbigan	**ka-I-bi-gan**	sweetheart
makaalís	**ma-ka-a-LIS**	to be able to leave
makáalis	**ma-KA-a-lis**	to leave unintentionally
matúlog	**ma-TU-log**	to sleep
matulóg	**ma-tu-LOG**	to fall asleep unintentionally

b. The glottal catch is lost when a suffix is added after the final vowel.

batà	**BA-taQ**	child
kabatáan	**ka-ba-TA-an**	youth
luhà	**LU-haQ**	tears
luhaán	**lu-ha-AN**	miserable
punô	**pu-noQ**	full
punuín	**pu-nu-IN**	to fill with
susì	**SU-siQ**	key
susián	**su-si-AN**	keyhole

c. Monosyllabic words often take on the stress of a preceding word, and the stress in that word is lost. The stress is thus "transferred" to the following single-syllable word.

kumáin	Kumain ká.	Ku-ma-in KA.	You may eat.
hindî	Hindi pá.	Hin-di PA.	Not yet.
ganitó	Ganito bá?	Ga-ni-to BA?	Like this?
malápit	Malapit ná.	Ma-la-pit NA.	It is near.
hindî	Hindi pô.	Hin-di PO.	No, sir / madam.

d. To avoid mispronunciation, a hyphen separates the prefix that ends in a consonant and with a glottal stop from the root that follows which starts with a vowel.

pag-ása	pagQ-A-sa	hope
mag-alís	magQ-a-LIS	to remove
mag-isá	magQ-i-SA	alone
pag-íbig	pagQ-I-big	love

Exercises

Practice pronouncing the following words by paying careful attention to the four types of stress and accent marks used to indicate them.

anák	a-NA	child
amá	a-MA	father
iná	i-NA	mother
bulaklák	bu-lak-LAK	flower
malakás	ma-la-KAS	strong
babáe	ba-BA-e	woman
laláki	la-LA-ki	man
maínit	ma-I-nit	hot
táo	TA-o	person
punò	PU-noQ	tree
kandilà	kan-DI-laQ	candle
pusà	PU-saQ	cat
susì	SU-siQ	key
batà	BA-taQ	child
punô	pu-noQ	full
sampû	sam-puQ	ten
bakyâ	bak-yaQ	wooden shoes
masamâ	ma-sa-maQ	bad
gintô	gin-toQ	gold

LESSON THREE
Greetings and Common Expressions

Aside from the borrowed *Hi* and *Hello*, Tagalogs have other forms of greetings—peppered with speech suffixes that define courtesy and deference.

I. POLITE FORMS OF ADDRESS—**PÔ** AND **HÔ**

Tagalog politeness is a trait worthy to be discussed and taught to learners of the language. Younger generations and junior employees include the terms **pô** or **hô** at the start or end of their greetings and responses to express respect for older people—parents, older relatives, and other senior individuals—or persons with honorific titles or authority—clergy, teachers, community leaders, employers,. and policemen—regardless of age. **Pô** and **hô** approximately mean *sir* or *madam* in English and reflect the speaker's good manners and his respect to the one spoken to.

Pô is not used by an older person when talking to a younger person such as a father talking to his son or daughter. Neither do equals, such as siblings or friends, use the term.

Short positive responses can be just **oo** or *yes* when speaking to a younger person or a peer in a familiar manner, but when speaking to an older person, you must use either **o-pô** or **o-hô**, both of which are the formal or polite versions of *yes*.

II. GREETINGS—GOOD DAY, ETC.

Greetings usually start with **magandá**, which means *beautiful*. The complete greeting is **Magandá ang áraw**—often shortened to **Magandáng áraw**—which literally means *beautiful day*. The most common greetings from morning to evening, in their polite forms, are:

Magandáng áraw pô.	Good day, sir/madam.
Magandáng umága pô.	Good morning, sir/madam.
Magandáng tanghálì pô.	Good afternoon, sir/madam.
Magandáng hápon pô.	Good afternoon, sir/madam.
Magandáng gabí pô.	Good evening, sir/madam.

Note that **tanghálì** is *noon* or *midday*. The period covers lunch time, from around 11 in the morning to 1 o'clock in the afternoon. This is the time when most Tagalog families prepare and have their lunch.

Vocabulary List

tanghálì = noon or midday	**magandá** = beautiful	**salámat** = thank you
kapílya = chapel	**gabí** = night	**hápon** = afternoon
pangálan = name	**Kumustá?** = How are you?	**áraw** = morning
mabúti = fine	**paálam** = goodbye	**opô** (or **ohô**) = yes (formal)

For equals, it is fine to drop **pô** and just say:

Magandáng umága.	Good morning.
Magandáng hápon.	Good afternoon.

In addition to the use of **pô** or **hô**, another polite way of greeting people is to address them in the plural form by adding **sa inyó**, which means *to you* (plural), and **sa kanilá**, which means *to them*, at the end of the greeting. In English, however, a greeting with **sa kanilá** at the end still translates to *to you* in Tagalog and not literally *to them*. The plural forms emphasize the greeter's acknowledgment of the seniority or authority of the person being greeted. On the other hand, equals use **sa iyó** or *to you* (singular).

Magandáng umága pô sa inyó.	Good morning to you, sir/madam.
Magandáng hápon pô sa kanilá.	Good afternoon to you, sir/madam.
Magandáng umága sa iyó.	Good morning to you.

The usual responses of both older or senior individuals and equals contain **rin** and **namán**, which mean *too*, indicating that the one who received the greeting meant the greeter to have a similar good day.

Magandáng umága rin sa iyó.	Good morning to you, too.
Magandáng umága namán.	Good morning, too.
Magandáng tanghálì rin pô.	Good afternoon, too, sir/madam.

III. GREETINGS—HOW ARE YOU?

The influence of Spanish is evident in the way Filipinos, particularly Tagalogs, greet people. Derived from the Spanish "como esta," Tagalogs use a similar greeting when they meet a friend, a relative or an acquaintance of about their age or stature. Older people also use this greeting toward younger people.

Kumustá ka?	How are you?

The Tagalog quivalent for the singular pronoun *you* is **ikáw**; it becomes **ka** when the pronoun is used in an inverted word order (Refer to discussions on sentence formation and pronouns in Lessons Five and Six).

But when greeting an elder or superior, Tagalogs use the plural **kayó** and **silá** instead of **ka**. This is the polite way of greeting and asking how one is. **Kayó** and **silá** are the plural pronouns for *you* and *they*, respectively. **Pô** may be dropped if **kayó** and **silá** are used.

Kumustá pô kayó?	How are you, sir/madam?
Kumustá silá?	How are you, sir/madam?

Take note that it is not unusual for Tagalogs to ask about one's family—parents, spouse, children, and everyone else in the family—when they see each other, whether the speaker is young, old or at about the same age as the person spoken to. Other cultures should see this as a reflection of the thoughtful nature of Filipinos, young and old alike.

The responses to these greetings usually include **mabúti** which means *fine*, **salámat** which means *thank you*, as well as **rin** and **namán**.

Mabúti namán (pô). Salámat (pô).	Fine, too, sir/madam.
Mabúti rin (pô). Salámat.	Thank you, sir/madam.

Salámat is optional at the end of the sentence, thus **pô** or **hô** may be attached to the first half of the response. However, it is never wrong to say **pô** again when **salámat** is retained. Foreigners and Tagalog alike could never go wrong with an overuse of the term but will only endear them to older or senior people.

Another peculiarity of the Tagalog is the use of the questions *Where are you going?* or *Where have you been?* in the same context as **Kumustá ka?** when meeting people they know. These very common greetings among Tagalogs should not be taken literally by foreigners. Filipinos are not really asking your itinerary—these are the equivalent of the English *How is it going?* and is simply another way of saying *Hello!* and striking up a conversation.

Saán ka púpuntá? (informal)	Where are you going?
Saán kayó púpuntá? (formal)	Where are you going, sir/madam?

Saán ka nanggáling? (informal)	Where have you been?
Saán kayó nanggáling? (formal)	Where have you been, sir/madam?

The usual response is **Diyán lámang (pô)** which means *Just nearby (sir/madam)*. However, you may be specific about the place and say, for example, **Sa Quezon City (pô)** which means either *I'm going to Quezon City (sir/madam)* or *I've been to Quezon City (sir/madam)*.

IV. VARIOUS WAYS OF SAYING EXCUSE ME

There is no exact equivalent for *excuse me* in Tagalog. However, there are five different ways of expressing it depending on the situation.

1. **Paumanhín pô** is used when one apologizes or asks to be excused, or if one bumps into someone else accidentally.
2. **Pakiraán pô** is used when one asks for permission to pass through.

3. **Mawaláng-gálang pô** is used when one requests to be heard.

4. **Patáwad pô** is used when one apologizes for causing physical injury or emotional hurt to someone else.

5. **Pasintábi pô** is used when one gives a warning of something that may be offensive or distasteful to others.

In which situations can each of the above be used?

1. When a small group is having a formal discussion or meeting and you need to leave, you may say in a modest tone of voice to the nearest person or to the one presiding the meeting, **Paumanhin (pô), aalis na ako** or **Paumanhin (pô), lálabas lamang ako sandalî.** The statements mean *Excuse me (sir/madam), I will leave now* or *Excuse me (sir/madam), I will go out for a while.* One does not have to say **Paumanhin (pô)** in a big meeting where one's absence is not obvious, unless one is the special guest.

   Another situation that calls for **Paumanhin (pô)** is when one bumps into someone unintentionally such as at a party or in a crowded area like a shopping mall. This statement is also equivalent to *I'm sorry.*

2. When you want to pass through a passage way or hall that is blocked by two persons talking to one another, you say **Pakiraán pô** (*Please let me pass.*) then pass.

3. When you are in a meeting and wish to voice requests or opinions, or interrupt the speaker to make a comment, you say **Mawaláng-gálang pô** and proceed to make the statement. The phrase literally means *May I lose my courtesy?* but translates as *I beg your pardon.*

   This is also appropriate when one wants to ask directions from somebody who is talking to another person, **Mawaláng-gálang pô, paano pumuntá sa Ayala Avenue** (*Excuse me, how do I get to Ayala Avenue?*)?

4. When someone is deeply hurt—either physically or emotionally—by another, the one at fault who realizes his mistake should say **Patawad pô** or **Patawárin ninyó akó,** which means *Forgive me.*

5. Some people cannot withstand unpleasant stories or photos. To warn them of a forthcoming offensive situation, one should say **Pasintabi pô**. This is commonly used by news reporters when a gruesome film footage is about to be shown on television. The phrase literally means *Please set aside*.

Can one of the above expressions sometimes be used in place of another?

Yes, **Mawaláng-gálang pô** may be used for situations 1 and 2 but not for 4.

Can one use **Paumanhin pô** instead of **Patawad pô**?

No, **Paumanhin pô** may mean *Sorry* but it is is too mild to use in cases of physical or emotional injury.

V. OTHER COMMON EXPRESSIONS

Tagalogs have common everyday expressions that should be memorized by students of this language. The following expressions have shortened forms that are used in everyday speech just as the shortened form of the English *Let's* is used in place of *Let us*. More shortened forms are listed in Lesson Forty-Three.

Saan kayó nakatirá?	Where do you live?
Anó ang pangálan mo?	What is your name?
Aywan ko. (shortened: **Èwan ko.**)	I don't know.
Hindí ko alám. (shortened: **Di ko alám.**)	I don't know.
Ayaw akó. (shortened: **Ayòko.**)	I don't like.
Bahála na!	Come what may!
Kauntî lámang. (shortened: **Lang**)	Just a little.
Kung mínsan.	Once in a while.
Gísing na!	Wake up!
Hindî bale!	Never mind!
Hindî namán.	Not so.
Hintáy ka! (shortened: **Teka!**)	Wait for a moment.
Huwag na. Salámat.	No more. Thank you.
Bahálà ka.	It is up to you.
Magmadali ká. (shortened: **Dali ka!**)	Hurry up! (literally: *Be quick, you!*)
Mámayá na.	For a while.
Salámat.	Thank you.
Maráming salámat.	Thank you very much.
Anó pô? (or **Anó?**)	What did you say, sir/madam?
Saká na.	Later.
Sandalî lámang. (shortened: **Lang**)	Just a moment.
Síge na!	Go on!
Sáyang!	What a pity. What a loss.
Tahímik kayó.	Be silent.
Táma na.	It is all right. It is enough.
Táyo na. (shortened: **Tena.**)	Let's go.
Totoó ba? (shortened: **Totoò?**)	Is it true?

Túlog na.	Go to sleep.
Maráhil.	Maybe.
Sigúro.	Maybe or definitely.

Note that the meaning of **sigúro** depends on the response to the question being asked. For example, there may be three responses to the question **Siguro ka?** or *Are you sure?*:

Oô, sigúro ako.	Yes, I am sure (or *Yes, definitely*).
Hindî ako sigúro.	I am not sure.
Sigúro.	Maybe.

Remember to include **pô** or appropriately change **ka** into **kayó** or **silá** to all the above expressions whenever possible to show respect.

Kataká-taká!	It seems incredible!
Magalíng!	Outstanding! (literally: Skilled)
Nakayáyamót!	It is annoying!
Mabúhay!	Welcome! (literally: *May you live long!*)

Mabuhay, the official greeting of Filipinos to foreign visitors, has also become an expression of collective joy and pride for any occasion, especially when Filipinos are proud of an achievement whether in politics or sports; may also be used to greet newly weds, **Mabuhay ang bagong kasal!** or literally, *May the newlyweds live long!*

Maligáyang batì (pô)!	Congratulations (sir/madam)! (literally: *Happy greetings!* The phrase has now come to be associated with birthday celebrations.)

Exercises

Match a situation from Column B to the appropriate response from column A.

COLUMN A	COLUMN B
Magalíng!	1. Your mother calls out that dinner is ready. You are still tidying up your study table as you have just finished doing your homework.
Anó pô?	2. Your 2-year old nephew sings the song *Brother John* from start to finish.
Magandáng hápon din pô.	3. Your grandmother asks a question but you did not understand half of the words she was saying.
Sandalí lang pô.	4. You are looking for a building along Ayala Avenue. While looking up at one tall building, you bump into somebody.
Paumanhín pô.	5. The town mayor is leaving the municipal hall just as you were entering. He greets you good afternoon.

The Articles **Si** and **Ang**

Any noun that is used as the subject of a sentence—including names of persons, places, and things—is always preceded by an article, except in direct conversation and in imperative statements.

I. THE ARTICLES **SI** AND **SINÁ**

The singular article **si** is used before the name of a person and the plural article **siná** is used before the names of two or more persons.

Si Ruth ay babáe.	Ruth is a woman.
Si Peter ay laláki.	Peter is a man.
Si Helen ay batáng babáe.	Helen is a young girl.
Si Tom ay batáng laláki.	Tom is a young boy.
Si Ruth ay magandá.	Ruth is pretty.
Si Peter ay marúnong.	Peter is intelligent.
Sina Helen at Tom ay mababaít.	Helen and Tom are good.
Sina Helen at Tom ay mga batà.	Helen and Tom are children.

Note that Tagalog sentences follow a plurality rule where either the subject or predicate may be made plural. However, the pluralization of both subject and predicate is optional. In the last sentence above, the article **sina** indicates that the subject is plural while **mga** (a plural marker that has no meaning on its own) before **batà** indicates that the noun is plural. Adjectives form their plural by duplicating the first syllable of the root word. For example, **mabaít** (or *kind*, root word is **baít**) becomes **mababaít**.

II. THE ARTICLES **ANG** AND **ANG MGA**

The article **ang** is used before the name of a single thing or place while **ang mga** (pronounced **ma-nga**) is used before the names of two or more things or places.

Ang batà ay mabait.	The child is good.
Ang áso ay mabait.	The dog is good.
Ang batà at ang áso ay mababaít.	The child and the dog are good.
Ang mga batà at ang mga áso ay mababaít.	The children and the dogs are good.
Ang mga sapátos ay malilínis.	The shoes are clean.

Vocabulary List

marúnong = intelligent	**magkapatìd** = siblings	**lugár** = place
batá = young (adj.); child (n.)	**malínis** = clean	**mahál** = expensive
lungsód = city	**sapátos** = shoes	

Ang barò at ang sapátos ay malilínis.   The dress and the shoes are clean.

Ang mga barò at ang mga sapátos ay malilínis. The dresses and the pairs of shoes are clean.

The article **ang** must always precede the name of a place. However, the article **mga** may be placed before the adjective, which must then take on a plural form if there is more than one name of place in the subject, or before the noun (see underlined words in the examples below).

Ang Pilipínas ay maliít.   The Philippines is small.

Ang Estados Unídos ay malakí.   The United States is big.

Ang Maynilà ay isang lungsod ng Pilipínas.   Manila is a city of the Philippines.

Ang Washington D.C. ay púnong-lungsód ng   Washington D.C. is the capital city of

   Estados Unídos.   the United States.

<u>Ang Maynilà</u> at <u>ang Washington D.C.</u> ay <u>mga lungsód</u>.   Manila and Washington D.C. are cities.

<u>Ang Baguio</u> at <u>ang Tagaytáy</u> ay <u>mga malalamíg na lugár</u>.

<u>Ang Baguio</u> at <u>ang Tagaytáy</u> ay <u>malalamíg na mga lugár</u>.   Baguio and Tagaytay are cool places.

Note that it is acceptable to delete the second **ang** before the second name of a place and the meaning of the sentence will not change.

<u>Ang Maynilà at Washington D.C.</u> ay mga lungsód.

<u>Ang Baguio at Tagaytáy</u> ay malalamíg na mga lugár.

Exercises

Fill in the blanks with the correct articles:

1. _____ **áso at _____ batà ay malilínis.**

2. _____ **batà at áso ay mababaít.**

3. _____ **Ruth at Peter ay magkapatíd.**

4. _____ **Amérika at Aprika ay malalakí.**

5. _____ **Peter at _____ Ruth ay mababaít at marurúnong.**

6. _____ **Helen, Tom, Mary at John ay malilínis.**

7. _____ **batà at _____ Helen ay magagandá.**

8. _____ **Tom ay mababaít** (plural form). Tom and companions are good.

9. _____ **Helen, John, at Peter at _____ áso ay mababaít.**

10. _____ **Amerika at Aprika ay malalakí.**

From the lists of subjects and predicates below, make 15 sentences in the subject-predicate word order (with the subject first and the predicate last). Use **ay** to join the subject and predicate, and add the correct articles before the subject.

SUBJECTS		PREDICATES	
babáe	woman	**magandá**	beautiful
laláki	man	**marúnong**	intelligent
batà	child	**matabâ**	fat
báhay	house	**mabaít**	kind; good (of character)
bansá	nation	**mabúti**	good (of condition or quality)
túbig	water	**maliít**	small
pagkáin	food	**malakí**	big
bulaklák	flower	**maínit**	hot
mésa	table	**malamíg**	cold
sílya	chair	**malínis**	clean
páaralán	school	**bágo**	new
kótse	car	**múra**	cheap
lápis	pencil	**mahál**	dear; expensive
papél	paper	**masaráp**	delicious; delightful
kapé	coffee	**malusóg**	healthy
isdâ	fish	**lumà**	old (inanimate)
áraw	sun; day	**matandâ**	old (animate)
hángin	wind	**mataás**	high
aklát	book	**mababà**	low
simbahan	church	**mahírap**	poor; difficult

All sentences in this lesson use the subject-predicate word order. The succeeding lessons will discuss how to make sentences using the inverted word order where the predicate comes before the subject. The inverted word order is more commonly used in everyday speech by Tagalogs.

LESSON FIVE

Sentence Formation

There are two basic ways to form a sentence in Tagalog. These are the **subject-predicate word order** where the subject appears at the beginning of the sentence and the **inverted or transposed word order** where the predicate is at the beginning and the subject is at the end of the sentence (or may be omitted). Tagalog speakers tend to use the inverted word order more often in everyday speech.

I. THE SUBJECT-PREDICATE SENTENCE ORDER

A sentence is in this order when the subject is the most important element in the sentence and it comes first within the sentence. In this order, the word **ay** (equivalent to the English *is* and *are*) is used.

1. **Ang báhay ay malakí.**   The house is big.
2. **Si Peter ay mabaít.**   Peter is good.
3. **Sina Peter at Mary ay mga batà.**   Peter and Mary are children.
4. **Ang batà ay kumákain.**   The child is eating.
5. **Ang babáe at ang laláki ay naglúlutò.**   The woman and the man are cooking.

The emphasis in this type of sentence is on the subject—meaning that the speaker wishes to focus attention on the subject. The word **ay** in sentences 1, 2, and 3 links the subject to what is said about the subject and is used here as a linking verb. The **ay** in sentences 4 and 5 is a helping verb that accompanies the principal verb, which represents the chief action in the sentence.

II. THE INVERTED OR TRANSPOSED SENTENCE ORDER

A sentence is in the inverted or transposed word order when the predicate comes at the beginning of the sentence before the subject. The word **ay** is not used in the inverted word order sentence.

1. **Malakí ang báhay.**   Big, the house is. (The house is big.)
2. **Kumákain ang batà.**   Eating, the child is. (The child is eating.)
3. **Mabaít si Peter.**   Good, Peter is. (Peter is good.)

The focus or emphasis in such sentences is on the predicate rather than on the subject. In inverted word order sentences having plural nouns as their subjects, the word **mga**—not **ang mga**—comes before the first nouns.

Vocabulary List

báhay = house	**kumákain** = is/are eating	**pusà** = cat
aso = dog	**maínit** = hot	**naglúlutò** = is/are cooking

Mga batà sina Peter at Mary.	Children, Peter and Mary are.
	Peter and Mary are children.
Mga lungsód ang Maynila at Cebu.	Cities, Manila and Cebu are.
	Manila and Cebu are cities.
Mga babáe sina Helen.	Women, Helen and companions are.
	Helen and companions are women.
Mga háyop ang áso't pusà.	Animals, the dog and cat are.
	The dog and cat are animals.

Note that in the last example above, the connective **at** (which means *and* in English) may be shortened to **'t** and attached to a preceding word that ends in a vowel such as **áso**.

Exercises

The sentences below from Lesson Four are all in the subject-predicate order. Rewrite them in the inverted or transposed order.

1. **Si Peter ay laláki.**
2. **Si Helen ay bátang babáe.**
3. **Si Ruth ay magandá.**
4. **Si Peter ay marúnong.**
5. **Sina Helen at Tom ay mababaít.**
6. **Sina Helen at Tom ay mga batà.**
7. **Ang batà at ang áso ay mababaít.**
8. **Ang mga batà at ang mga áso ay mababaít.**
9. **Ang mga sapátos ay malilínis.**
10. **Ang barò at ang sapátos ay malilínis.**
11. **Ang mga barò at ang mga sapátos ay malilinis.**
12. **Ang Estados Unidos ay malakí.**
13. **Ang Washington D.C. ay púnong-lungsód ng Estados Unidos.**
14. **Ang Maynilà at Washington D.C. ay mga lungsód.**
15. **Ang Baguio at Tagaytay ay malalamíg na lugar.**

The list below is from the second set of exercises in Lesson Four. Change the 15 subject-predicate sentences you made from this list into the inverted order.

SUBJECTS		PREDICATES	
babáe	woman	**magandá**	beautiful
laláki	man	**marúnong**	learned
batà	child	**matabâ**	fat
báhay	house	**mabaít**	kind; good (of character)
bansá	nation	**mabúti**	good (of condition or quality)
túbig	water	**maliít**	small

SUBJECTS		PREDICATES	
pagkáin	food	**malakí**	big
bulaklák	flower	**maínit**	hot
mésa	table	**malamíg**	cold
sílya	chair	**malínis**	clean
páaralán	school	**bágo**	new
kótse	car	**múra**	cheap
lápis	pencil	**mahál**	dear; expensive
papél	paper	**masaráp**	delicious; delightful
kapé	coffee	**malusóg**	healthy
isdâ	fish	**lumà**	old (inanimate)
áraw	sun; day	**matandâ**	old (animate)
hángin	wind	**mataás**	high
aklát	book	**mababà**	low
simbahan	church	**mahírap**	poor; difficult

Personal and Demonstrative Pronouns

A pronoun replaces a noun in a Tagalog sentence to make the sentence less repetitive. Two important types of Tagalog pronouns that are often used are personal pronouns (**akó**, **kamí**, **táyo**, **ikáw**, **kayó**, **siyá** and **silá**) and demonstrative pronouns (**itó**, **iyán** and **iyón**).

I. PERSONAL PRONOUNS

The following pronouns are nominative in form and can only be used as the subject of a verb in a sentence.

1. The personal pronoun **akó** (meaning *I*)

The pronoun **akó** is the equivalent of the English pronoun *I* and, when used as a subject, can come at the beginning of the sentence before the verb or, in the inverted word order, after the predicate, as in the following examples:

Akó ay si John.	I am John.
Akó ay laláki.	I am a man.
Masípag akó.	Industrious I am. (I am industrious.)
Malusóg akó.	Healthy I am. (I am healthy.)

Akó is linked by **ay** to the predicate in the first two sentences above using the subject-predicate word order. Note that in this type of sentence, **ay** may be shortened to '**y** when the preceding word ends in a vowel. The shortened form '**y** is also used after **kamí** (*we* including *he/she*, and *I*), **táyo** (*we* including *you, he/she*, and *I*), and other pronouns ending in vowels.

Ako'y si John.	I am John.
Ako'y laláki.	I am a man.
Ako'y nag-áaral.	I am studying.

2. The personal pronouns **kamí** and **táyo** (meaning *we*)

The pronoun *we* is expressed by **kamí** and **táyo** in Tagalog. **Kamí** means *we* in the sense of *he/she* and *I* excluding the person spoken to, whereas **táyo** means *we* in the sense of *you, he/she*, and *I*, or *you* (the person spoken to) and *I*.

Kamí ay sina John at Helen.	We are John and Helen.
Kamí'y magkapatid.	We are brothers and sisters.

Vocabulary List

masípag = industrious	**magkápatid** = siblings	**marámi** = plenty
magkaibígan = friends	**mahírap** = poor	**naníniwala** = believe

Mababaít kamí.	Good we are. (We are good.)
Mahihírap kamí.	Poor we are. (We are poor.)

It is important to remember that pronouns may come at the beginning of the sentence before the verb or at the end of the sentence after the predicate depending on the word order.

Táyo ay sina John at Mary.	We are John and Mary.
Táyo'y magkaibígan.	We are friends.
Mababaít táyo.	Good we are. (We are good.)
Masisípag táyo.	Industrious we are. (We are industrious.)

3. The personal pronouns **ikáw** and **kayó** (meaning *you*)

The pronoun **ikáw** is used to express *you* when it is used at the beginning of the sentence, however in the inverted word order where the subject comes after the predicate, it is shortened to **ka**.

Ikáw ay si Mary.	You are Mary.
Ikáw ay babáe.	You are a woman.
Masípag ka.	Industrious you are. (You are industrious.)
Malusóg ka.	Healthy you are. (You are healthy.)

Kayó is the plural form of **ikáw** excluding the speaker.

Kayó ay sina John at Helen.	You are John and Helen.
Kayó ay magkápatid.	You are brother and sister. (or siblings)
Malulusóg kayó.	Healthy you are. (You are healthy.)

4. The personal pronouns **siyá** and **silá** (meaning *he/she* and *they*)

The pronoun **siyá** is singular meaning *he* or *she*.

Siyá ay si Peter.	He is Peter.
Siyá'y isang batà.	He is a child.
Marúnong siyá.	Intelligent he is. (He is intelligent.)
Mabaít siya.	Good she is. (She is good.)

The plural form of **siyá** is **silá** meaning *they*.

Silá ay sina John at Mary.	They are John and Mary.
Silá ay magkaibígan.	They are friends.
Marurúnong silá.	Intelligent they are. (They are intelligent.)

In a polite or formal situation, either one of the plural pronouns **kayó** and **silá** may replace the singular pronoun **ikáw** or **ka** in sentences and questions to indicate respect (see Lesson Three on Greetings and Common Expressions.)

Kayó pô ba ay guro?	Are you a teacher, sir/madam?
Silá pô ba ay guro?	Are you a teacher, sir/madam?
Kayó ay mabaít.	You (plural) are kind.

Exercises

Fill in the blanks with the proper pronouns in the third sentence in each set of sentences by combining the pronouns mentioned in the first two sentences. For example, the answer in the first set of sentences is the combination of **kayó** + **akó**.

1. **Kayó ay bumilí ng pagkáin. Akó ay bumilí ng pagkáin. _____'y bumilí ng pagkáin.**
2. **Mabaít ka. Mabaít siyá. Mabaít _____.**
3. **Nag-áral si María. Nag-áral si Tíno. Nag-áral _____.**
4. **Akó'y naniniwála kay Delia. Silá'y naniniwála kay Delia. _____'y naniniwála kay Delia.**
5. **Nakákasúlat na si Gizelle. Nakákasúlat na akó. Nakákasúlat na _____.**

Translate the following sentences into Tagalog:

1. We (exclusive) are studying Tagalog.
2. I am Mary. He is John.
3. We (inclusive) are clean and good.
4. They are healthy and intelligent.
5. You are a teacher. (polite)
6. You (plural) are Filipinos.
7. She is playing. (**naglalaró**)
8. I believe (**naníniwala**) you.

II. THE DEMONSTRATIVES **ITÓ**, **IYÁN** AND **IYÓN**

The English demonstrative pronouns *this* and *that* have equivalents in the Tagalog language: **itó**, **iyán**, and **iyón**.

1. The demonstrative **itó** (*this*)

The demontrative **itó** (pronounced **i-TO**) is used to refer to a thing that is very near or close to the person speaking. It is followed by the linking verb **ay** in a subject-predicate sentence word order. The linking verb **ay** may be shortened to **'y** as it follows the word **itó**. In an inverted word order sentence where the predicate comes at the beginning, such as the sentence **Maliít itó**, the linking verb **ay** is dropped.

Itó ay si John.	This is John.
Ito'y si John.	This is John.
Itó'y batà.	This is a child.
Itó'y pagkáin.	This is food.
Maliít itó.	This is small.
Malakí itó.	This is big.

2. The demonstrative **iyán** (*that*)

The demonstrative **iyán** (pronounced **i-YAN**) is used to refer to a thing that is near the person spoken to. It is followed by **ay**.

Iyán ay si Mary.	That is Mary.
Iyán ay pagkáin.	That is food.
Iyán ay pagkáin ni Mary.	That is Mary's food.
Marámi iyán.	That is plenty.
Maínit iyán.	That is hot.

3. The demonstrative **iyón** (*that, over there*)

The demonstrative **iyón** (pronounced **i-YON**) is used to refer to a thing that is far from both the person speaking and the one spoken to.

Iyón ay Ílog Pasig.	That is Pasig River.
Iyón ay mahabà.	That is long.
Iyón ay malínis at mahabà.	That is clean and long.
Malínis iyón.	That is clean.
Mahabà iyón.	That is long.

4. Plural forms of **itó**, **iyán** and **iyón**

Note that since Tagalog sentences follow a plurality rule and either or both the subject or predicate may be made plural, sentences containing the plural forms of **itó**, **iyán**, and **iyón** may be marked by the plural marker **ang mga**. The singular forms of **itó**, **iyán**, and **iyón** are not preceded by **ang**; but the plural forms of these words are preceded by the plural article **ang mga**. *This* and *that* thus become *these* and *those*.

Ang mga itó ay mababaít.	These are good.
Ang mga iyán ay malalakí.	Those are big.
Ang mga iyón ay malilínis.	Those are clean.

As discussed in Lesson Four, the pluralization of both subject and predicate is optional, and will still produce correct sentences (as in the three sentences above). However, the third sentence may be restructured into **Ang mga iyón ay malínis** (plural subject) or **Iyón ay malilínis** (plural predicate).

5. *This* and *that* as modifiers

The demonstratives **itó**, **iyán**, and **iyón** can also be used as modifiers to point out or specify the subject of a sentence. It is interesting to note that when used as modifiers, these demonstratives are placed before the noun and may also be repeated for emphasis before the linking verb **ay** in a subject-predicate sentence (see first example) or at the end of an inverted word order sentence (see second example below). Either sentence structure is acceptable but the first one is more formal and the second is more colloquial.

Ang mésang itó ay malínis.
Itóng mésang itó ay malínis.

This table is clean.

Malakí ang báhay na iyón.
Malakí iyóng báhay na iyón.

That house is big.

Magandá ang suót mong iyán.
Magandá iyáng suót mong iyán.

Your clothes are beautiful.

Observe the use of **-ng**, **-g** and **na** in the following phrases:
   ** itó<u>ng</u> mésa<u>ng</u> itó**
   iyá<u>ng</u> suót mo<u>ng</u> iyán
   iyóng báhay <u>na</u> iyon

In these phrases, the connective **-ng** is attached to the modifier **itó**, the noun **mésa**, and the pronoun **mo**; the connective **-g** is attached to the modifiers **iyán** and **iyón**; and the connective **na** comes after the noun **bahay**.

The purpose of these three connectives or ligatures, to be discussed in the next lesson is to connect the following:
   — a demonstrative and a noun (**itó<u>ng</u> mésa, iyá<u>ng</u> suót, iyó<u>ng</u> báhay)**
   — a noun and a demonstrative (**báhay <u>na</u> iyon, mésa<u>ng</u> itó)**
   — a possessive pronoun and a demontrative (**mo<u>ng</u> iyán)**

In a sentence containing the demonstratives **itó**, **iyán**, and **iyón** and the marker **sa** (which means *in, at, on* or *to*, and is used to denote the location of an action), the demontratives **itó**, **iyán**, or **iyón** always appear after the noun at the end of the sentence.

Ang báta ay kumáin <u>sa mésang itó</u>.   The child ate <u>on this table</u>.
Pumunta kamí <u>sa báhay na iyán</u>.   We went <u>to that house</u>.
Súmakay silá <u>sa bus na iyón</u>.   They rode <u>on that bus</u>.

Exercises

You are in front of the class behind the teacher's desk pointing out where things are in the classroom. Show where the following things are by filling in the blanks below with the proper singular or plural forms of the demontratives **itó**, **iyán**, or **iyón**.

1. _____ **ang áking lamésa.** (table)

2. (Pointing to a student's seat) _____ **ay upúan ng estudyánte.**

3. **Sa likód** (at the back) **ay ang malakíng pisára** (blackboard). _____ **ay susulátan ko ng mga takdáng-aralín** (homeworks).

4. **Sa kánan** (to the right) **ay mga libró.** _____ **ay babasáhin nátin.**

5. **Sa káliwa** (to your left) **ninyó ay mga bintanà.** _____ **ay paláging nakábukás.** (always open)

Make five sentences each using **itó**, **iyán**, and **iyón** following the sample sentence patterns given.

1. **Itó** as the subject at the beginning of the sentence.
   Sentence pattern: **Itó'y aklat ko.** This is my book.

2. **Iyán** as the subject at the beginning of the sentence.
   Sentence pattern: **Iyán ay báhay na malakí.** That is a big house.

3. **Iyón** as the subject at the beginning of the sentence.
   Sentence pattern: **Iyón ay paáralan ko.** That is my school.

Make five sentences with **itó**, **iyán**, and **iyón** as a modifier of a subject in both subject-predicate and inverted word order sentences.

   Sentence patterns:
   Ang aklát na itó ay mabúting basáhin.   This book is good to read.
   Mabúti ang aklát na itó.

Words That Link and Describe

A peculiar but noteworthy feature of the Tagalog language is the use of connectives or ligatures to "link together" two adjacent words. The ligature suffixes **-ng** and **-g** are attached to the end of the first word in a sequence whereas the ligature word **na** is placed between the two words.

These ligatures have no particular meaning of their own, but merely indicate that there is a close relationship between the two words and that, generally, one modifies the other.

I. THE RULES FOR USING EACH TYPE OF LIGATURE

1. The suffix ligature **-ng**

The ligature **-ng** is attached as a suffix to the end of words that end in vowels.

Ang malakíng báhay ay isáng páaralan.　　(**malaki + -ng + bahay**)
The big house is a school.　　big house

Marunong ang bátang mabaít.　　(**batà + -ng + mabaít**)
The good child is intelligent.　　good child

2. The suffix ligature **-g**

The ligature **-g** is attached as a suffix to the end of words that end in the consonant **n**.

Ang mayámang laláki ay mapagbigáy.　　(**mayáman + -g + laláki**)
The rich man is generous.　　rich man

Ang hánging malakás ay malamíg.　　(**hángin + -g + malakás**)
The strong wind is cold.　　wind strong

3. The ligature **na**

The ligature word **na** is used after words that end in consonants other than **n**.

Kumáin siyá ng <u>maásim na manggà</u>.　　(**maásim + na + manggà**)
He/She ate a sour mango.　　sour mango

Vocabulary List

mapagbigáy = generous	**sariwá** = fresh	**matápang** = brave
hangál = fool	**maásim** = sour	**bundók** = mountain
pagód = tired	**tahímik** = quiet	
inapí = maltreated	**malínaw** = clear	

Magandá ang <u>tahímik na batà</u>.   (**tahímik** + **na** + **batà**)
The quiet child is beautiful.   quiet child

Note that the above sequences are made up of adjective + noun or noun + adjective. In a series of more than one adjective before a noun, only the last adjective has a ligature, for example, **mabaít at masunúring áso**.

II. OTHER WORD SEQUENCES THAT NEED LIGATURES

1. Noun + noun
Ang <u>batàng babáe</u> ay natúlog.   The <u>young girl</u> slept.
Ang lólo ko ay <u>matandàng laláki</u>.   My grandfather is an <u>old man</u>.

2. Noun + verb (or verb + noun)
Ang <u>íbong lumílipad</u> ay binaríl.   The flying bird was shot.
Ang <u>lumílipad na ibon</u> ay binaríl.

3. Adjective + verb (or verb + adjective)
<u>Pagód na dumatíng</u> si tátay sa báhay.   My father arrived home tired.
<u>Dumatíng na pagód</u> si tátay sa báhay.

4. Verb + adverb (or adverb + verb)
<u>Kumáing mabilís</u> si Pablo.   Pablo ate quickly.
<u>Mabilís na kumáin</u> si Pablo.

5. Noun + adverb (or adverb + noun)
Iwásan ang <u>pag-aáway na matagál</u>.   Avoid the long feud.
Iwásan ang <u>matagál na pag-aáway</u>.

6. Adjective + adverb (or adverb + adjective)
<u>Mahál na totoó</u> ang reló mo.   Your watch is truly expensive.
<u>Totoóong mahál</u> ang reló mo.

7. Conjunction + adverb
<u>Samantálang walâ</u>, mágtiis táyo.   While [we have] none, let us be patient.
<u>Sakáling dúmating</u>, paghintayín ang mensahéro. If he/she comes, make the messenger wait.

However, the conjunctive **kung** (which means *if*) does not need a ligature.
Kung walâ pa ako, máuna na kayó.   If I am not around yet, you may go ahead.

8. Verb + verb
<u>Hinayáang umalís</u> ang batà.   The child was allowed to leave.
<u>Namatáy na lumalában</u> ang sundálo.   The soldier died fighting.

Exceptions to this rule include the following:

a. Verb-verb sequences that result in an adjectival expression

Mamatáy-mabúhay ang reló ko.   My watch stops periodically.
(literally, dies and lives)

b. Helping verb and main verb sequences

Áyaw kumáin ng máysakit.   The sick person does not want to eat.

9. Adverb + adverb sequences where the adverb is repeated for emphasis

Gabíng-gabí na siyá umuwî.   He/She came home very late.
Búkas na búkas talaga ay bábalik ako.   I shall certainly return tomorrow.

10. Adjective + adjective sequences where the adjective is repeated to create a superlative

Malínaw na malínaw ang útos niya.   His/her command is very clear.
Mabaít na mabaít ang gurò ko.   My teacher is very kind.

11. Noun + pronoun (or pronoun + noun)

Ang báhay na iyán ay ákin.   That house is mine.
Itó ang áking lúpa.   This is my land.

An exception to this sequence is the noun + possessive pronoun (**ko**, **námin**, **nila** and others) combination as the possessive pronoun changes forms when it is placed after nouns. Examples include **aklát ko**, **báhay námin**, and **lúpa nila**.

12. Pronoun + adjective (or adjective + pronoun)

Ikáw na marúnong ay magsalitâ.   You who are learned should speak.
Ang hangál na itó ay umíiyak.   This fool is crying.

An exception to the pronoun + adjective or adjective + pronoun sequence is the adjective + nominative pronoun sequence. A nominative pronoun such as **ka** and **kayó** is a personal pronoun (see Lesson Six) that can be used as the subject of a sentence.

Marúnong ka.   You are intelligent (or learned).
Mababaít kayó.   You (plural) are kind.

13. Verb + pronoun (or pronoun + verb)

Tatawáging anó ang batà?   By what name shall the child be called?
Táyong kaniláng inapí ay natúto.   We, whom they maltreated, learned.

The verb + pronoun (or pronoun + verb) sequence below is the exception to the list of rules as most combinations of this type do not need ligatures, such as:

Liligáya táyo.   We shall be happy.
Kinúha ko itó.   I took this.

14. Pronoun + pronoun

Kinúha nínyo <u>yaóng amín</u>.   You took that which is ours.

<u>Táyong kaniláng inapí</u> ay natúto.   We, whom they maltreated, learned.

(**kaniláng inapí** is also an example of a pronoun + verb sequence)

Exceptions to the above sequence include those in sentences in the subjunctive mood (see first sentence) as well as two successive pronouns that form a complete sentence by themselves.

Kung <u>akó</u> [ay] <u>íkaw</u>, áalis áko.   If I were you, I will leave.

Kaniyá itó.   This is his/hers.

Observe that, generally, the exceptions in the last four sequences contain either a possessive personal pronoun that comes after a noun such as **ko**, **mo**, **niyá**, **námin**, **nátin**, **ninyó**, **nilá** or a nominative personal pronoun (see list in Lesson Six) that changes form when used in an inverted word order sentence such as **ka**, **kayó**, **kamí**, **táyo**, **siyá**, and **silá**. Some sequences not mentioned above also do not need a ligature and these will will be pointed out later.

Also note that changing the sequence of nouns, adjectives, verbs and adverbs does not change the meaning of the phrases or the position of the ligatures, which still come after the first word. And the resulting sequences still follow the rules for using the ligatures **-ng**, **-g**, and **na**.

batàng babáe or **babáeng batà**	young girl
matabáng lalakí or **lalakíng matabá**	fat man
íbong lumílipad or **lumílipad na íbon**	flying bird
pagód na dumatíng or **dumatíng na pagód**	arrived tired
kumáing mabilís or **mabilís na kumáin**	ate quickly
matagál na pag-aáway or **pag-aáway na matagál**	long feud
mahál na totoó or **totoóng mahál**	truly expensive

Below are more examples of subjects and modifiers:

NOUNS		MODIFIERS	
binatà	bachelor	**marámi**	many; much
dalága	unmarried woman	**masípag**	industrious
damít	cloth; dress	**mabilís**	fast
gabí	night	**marumí**	dirty
áraw	day; sun	**madilím**	dark
gamót	medicine	**lutò**	cooked
gúlay	vegetable	**mayáman**	rich
gurò	teacher	**mahúsay**	efficient
ibon	bird	**sariwà**	fresh
isdâ	fish	**payát**	thin
lamók	mosquito	**matabâ**	fat
túbig	water	**maitím**	black
pagkáin	food	**maputí**	whitish
dágat	sea	**matápang**	brave

NOUNS

lángit	sky
bundók	mountain
dahon	leaf
bulaklák	flower

MODIFIERS

maíngay	noisy
tahímik	quiet
tamád	lazy
matamís	sweet (food)

Exercises

Give the formula for attaching ligatures to the following pairs of words. The first one has been given as an example.

1. rich man   **mayámang laláki (mayáman + -g + lalaki**
                                 laláking mayáman (laláki + -ng + mayáman)
2. clean food
3. poor woman
4. dirty shoes
5. strong boy

From the nouns and the descriptive words in the previous page, construct 15 sentences in the inverted word order. Use the words in the second column as modifiers of the subjects, not as predicates. This is to practice the correct use of ligatures. Note that in the inverted order, there is no **ay**.

Translate each of the following pairs of English words into Tagalog in two different ways (noun + adjective, then adjective + noun) and use them in sentences.

fresh fish	new dress	pretty girl
small child	good teacher	small flower
noisy Manila		

LESSON EIGHT
Words That Show Possession

Certain words in Tagalog are used to indicate possession. These include the words **ni** and **ng**; possessive pronouns such as **ákin**; as well as **nitó**, **niyán** and **niyón**, which are the possessive counterparts of the demonstratives *this* and *that*.

I. THE POSSESSIVE WORDS **NI** AND **NG**

To indicate ownership, the possessive word **ni** is placed before a proper noun such as Maria or Pedro while the word **ng** is placed before a common noun such as **gurò** (teacher) or **babaé** (woman). **Ni** and **ng** both mean *of* in English. Note that in Tagalog sentences, the object that is possessed must always come before the owner as in the following examples:

ang báhay ni Maria	the house of Maria or Maria's house
ang barò ni Juan	the shirt of Juan or Juan's shirt
ang lápis ni Helen	the pencil of Helen or Helen's pencil
ang sapátos ni Berto	the shoes of Berto or Berto's shoes
ang aklát ni Paulo	the book of Paulo or Paulo's book
ang báhay ng laláki	the house of the man or man's house
ang barò ng sanggól	the dress of the baby or baby's dress
ang lápis ng gurò	the pencil of the teacher or teacher's pencil
ang sapátos ng batà	the shoes of the child or the child's shoes
ang aklát ng babáe	the book of the woman or the woman's book

Based on the plurality rule, when the owner or the thing that is possessed is more than one, the plural forms of **ni** and **ng** are used. The plural form of **ni** is **niná** while that of **ng** is **ng mga**.

ang báhay niná Maria at Pedro	the house of Maria and Pedro
ang lápis niná Helen	the pencil of Helen and company
ang bahay ng mga laláki	the house of the men
ang mga damít ng mga batà	the clothes of the children

Vocabulary List

damít = clothes	**pagkáin** = food	**malamíg** = cold
kotse = car	**lúma** = old	**madumí** = dirty
gamót = medicine	**paáralan** = school	

Exercises

Give six things or qualities each possessed by a mother (**iná**) and a book (**libró**). Afterwards, give the plural forms.

1. _____ **iná**

2. _____ **iná**

3. _____ **iná**

4. _____ **iná**

5. _____ **iná**

6. _____ **iná**

7. _____ **libró**

8. _____ **libró**

9. _____ **libró**

10. _____ **libró**

11. _____ **libró**

12. _____ **libró**

II. THE POSSESSIVE PRONOUNS **ÁKIN**, **IYÓ**, **KANIYÁ**, ETC.

The following possessive pronouns are used in Tagalog:

Table 1.   List of possessive pronouns

	Singular	Plural
First person	**ákin** (*my*)	**ámin** or *our* in the sense of *his/her* and *mine* (excluding the person spoken to) **átin** or *our* in the sense of *yours, his/her* and *mine* (including the speaker and person spoken to)
Second person	**iyó** (*your*)	**inyó** (*your*)
Third person	**kaniyá** (*his/her*)	**kanilá** (*their*)

These possessive pronouns are used either (1) before a noun or (2) after a noun. When the pronouns are used before a noun, note that the ligatures **-ng**, **-g** and **na** are needed. Possessive pronouns placed after the noun change their forms as seen in the examples below.

1. **Ákin(g)** becomes **ko** when placed after the noun.
Ang áking báhay ay malakí.   My house is big.
Ang báhay ko ay malakí.

2. **Iyó(ng)** becomes **mo** when placed after the noun.
Ang iyóng báro ay bágo.   Your dress is new.
Ang báro mo ay bágo.

3. **Kaniyá(ng)**, which may be shortened to **kanyá**, becomes **niyá** when placed after the noun.
Malínis ang kaniyáng sapátos.   His/Her shoes are clean.
Malínis ang sapátos niyá.

4. **Ámin(g)** (or *his/her* and *mine*) becomes **námin** when placed after the noun.
Lúma ang áming kótse.   Our car is old.
Lúma ang kótse námin.

5. **Átin(g)** (or *yours*, *his/her*, and *mine*) becomes **nátin** when placed after the noun.

Malakí ang áting bahay.   Our house is big.
Malakí ang bahay nátin.

6. **Inyó(ng)** becomes **ninyó** when placed after the noun.
Ang inyóng ama ay masípag.   Your father is industrious. (plural)
Ang ama ninyó ay masípag.

7. **Kanilá(ng)** becomes **nilá** when placed after the noun.

Mahába ang kaniláng lápis.   Their pencil is long.
Mahába ang lápis nilá.

Remember the following changes when pronouns are placed after nouns:

Table 2.   Changes in possessive pronouns

	Singular	Plural
First person	**ákin** becomes **ko**	**ámin** becomes **námin** **átin** becomes **nátin**
Second person	**iyó** becomes **mo**	**inyó** becomes **ninyó**
Third person	**kaniyá** becomes **niyá**	**kanilá** becomes **nilá**

In cases where two pronouns are used in a sentence, a combination of the two styles (possessive pronouns used before and after the nouns) instead of only one style for both pronouns, will produce a better sentence. For example, the sentence *Her mother went to her house* uses the pronoun *her* twice. Sticking to one style will produce the following awkward sentences:

Not Good: **Ang kanyáng iná ay pumuntá sa kanyáng báhay.**
Not Good: **Ang iná niyá ay pumuntá sa báhay niyá.**

The two sentences above use similar possessive pronouns, thus producing redundant sounds of either **niyá** or **kaniyá**.

However, a combination of two different possessive pronouns, one placed before the first noun and another placed after the second noun, will produce better sounding sentences.

Good: **Ang iná niyá ay pumuntá sa kanyáng báhay.**
Good: **Ang kanyáng iná ay pumuntá sa báhay niyá.**

Each sentence above uses two different versions of the possessive pronoun to avoid the repetition of either **niyá** or **kanyá** in the same sentence. However, the first sentence has the tongue-twisting phrase **iná niyá**. The second sentence sounds better as it eliminates the phrase by pairing **iná** with **kanyá** and **báhay** with **niyá**. Both sentences, however, are correct.

In other words, it is better if the same form of a possessive pronoun is not used twice in the same sentence. In this case, Tagalog speakers prefer to use two different forms of the same possessive pronoun (one appearing before and one after the nouns they modify).

In the case of plural nouns, the possessive personal pronouns are placed between **ang** and **mga**. Similarly, the adjectives should be in their plural forms as well.

Right: <u>**Ang áking mga** anák ay mababaít.</u>
Wrong: <u>**Ang mga áking** anák ay mababaít.</u>
              My children are good.

Exercises

Fill in the blanks with the appropriate possessive pronouns.

1. **Kakúlay ng _____ báro ang pitáka _____.** (*you*, singular)
   Your dress has the same color as your wallet.

2. **Pumuntà sa _____ báhay ang gurò _____.** (*our* excluding listener) Our teacher
   went to our house.

3. **Naghanáp ang _____ anák na babáe ng regálo para sa _____ kapatìd na babáe.**
   (*my*) My daughter looked for my gift for her sister. (literal)

4. **Mahába ang pasénsiya _____ sa _____ amá.** (*their*) They have long patience for
   their father.

5. **Ang pang-unáwa _____ ay mas mahalagà sa _____ abúloy.** (*you*, plural) Your
   understanding is more important than your contribution.

Translate the following sentences into Tagalog using both the subject-predicate word order and the
inverted or transposed order.
1. The man's shoes are new.
2. Their house is big.
3. The child's dress is dirty.
4. Peter's book is clean.
5. Your food is cold.

III. THE POSSESSIVES **NITÓ**, **NIYÁN** AND **NIYÓN**

Itó, **iyán** and **iyón** are similar to *this* and *that*; they indicate where an obejct is in relation to the speaker. As possessives, they change into **nitó** (*of this person*), **niyán** and **niyón** (*of that person*) and point to a possession belonging to a person near or far from the speaker or persons spoken to. When **nitó**, **niyán**, and **niyón** are used, the speaker assumes that the person he/she is talking to also recognizes the owner.

Note that in contrast with the preceding examples using possessive personal pronouns, the possessives **nitó**, **niyán**, and **niyón** are always used in the same place after the noun, even in an inverted sentence.

Ang báhay nitó ay malakí.
Malakí ang báhay nitó.
The house of this (person) is big.
(Owner of house is near the speaker)

Ang báhay niyán ay malíít.
Malíít ang báhay niyán.
The house of that (person) is small.
(Owner of the house is near the person spoken to)

Ang báhay niyón ay malíít.
Malíít ang báhay niyón.
The house of that (person) is small.
(Owner of the house is far from the persons talking)

As previously mentioned in Lesson Four, Tagalog sentences follow the plurality rule. In the case of possessive pronouns, their plural forms are formed by adding **ng mga** to the demonstratives **itó**, **iyán**, **iyón**; and not to the possessives **nitó**, **niyán** and **niyón**. As **ng** is already a possessive word, **ng mga niyán**, for example is both wrong and redundant.

ang báhay ng mga itó	the house of these people
ang báhay ng mga iyán	the house of those people
ang báhay ng mga iyón	the house of those people

Exercises

Translate the following sentences into Tagalog using the subject-predicate word order to indicate that the owner is near, far from the listener, and far from both you and the listener. Follow the sentence patterns of the first sentence.

1. Robert's dog is intelligent.
   Ang áso nitó ay matalino.
   Ang áso niyán ay matalino.
   Ang áso niyón ay matalino.

2. The baby's medicine is effective. (**mabísa**)
3. The girl's dress is pretty.
4. Peter's book is clean.
5. Her school is big.
6. The man's shoes are new.

Convert all your Tagalog sentences above into inverted sentences.

Asking Questions

I. QUESTION WORDS IN TAGALOG

There are 14 different question words in the Tagalog language that correspond to the English question words *who*, *what*, *which*, *how*, *why*, *when*, *where* and *whose*. These are:

síno	who	**Sino ba kayó?**
		Who are you?

anó	what	**Anó ba ang pangálan ninyó?**
		What is your name?

alín	which	**Alín ba ang iyóng gustó?**
		Which do you like?

gaáno	how	**Gaáno kalakí ang Pilipinas?**
		How large is the Philippines?

(requires a response expressing degree or quality)

paáno	how	**Paáno mo malaláman?**
		How will you know?

(requires a response detailing a process)

bakit	why	**Bakit siyá galít?**
		Why is he/she angry?

kailán	when	**Kailán kayó dumatíng sa Pilipinas?**
		When did you arrive in the Philippines?

nasaán	where	**Nasaán siyá?**
		Where is he/she?

(when asking for the location of a person or thing)

Vocabulary List

maláman = to know	**simbáhan** = church	**táo** = person
gustó = to like	**galít** = angry	**película** = movie
nakatirá = live/reside	**dumatíng** = arrived	

saán	where	**Saán kayó nakatirá?**
		Where do you live?
	(when asking for the location of an action)	

ilán	how many	**Ilán ang anák ninyó?**
		How many children do you have?

magkáno	how much	**Magkáno ang aklát?**
		How much is the book?

kaníno	whose	**Kaníno ang báhay na iyán?**
		Whose house is that?

Questions beginning with **kaníno** require responses that point to **ákin** (*mine*), **kaniyá** (*his* or *her*), **kanilá** (*their*) or other possessive pronouns.

para sa kaníno	for whom	**Para sa kaníno iyán?**
		For whom is that?

sa kaníno	with/to whom	**Sa kaníno iyán?**
		To whom does that belong?

II. THE PLURAL FORMS OF QUESTION WORDS

In Lesson Four, the pluralization of either or both the predicate and subject of a sentence has been pointed out. Plural markers such as **siná**, **niná**, **ng mga** and **ang mga** have also been introduced. Question words are not exempt from the plurality rule either.

The plural forms of these interrogatives are formed by duplicating the question words or certain syllables of the question words based on the following rules:

1. When a word is composed of two syllables, the whole word is duplicated:
    alín becomes **alín-alín**   **síno** becomes **sínu-síno**

2. When a word has three or more syllables, only the first two syllables are duplicated:
    kaníno becomes **kaní-kanino**   **magkano** becomes **magka-magkano**

3. The **o** in the last syllable becomes **u** in the first half of the new duplicated word.
    anó becomes **anu-anó**   **síno** becomes **sinu-síno**

The plural forms of these interrogative words are used when more than one thing is being referred to and when an answer in the plural form is expected. The interrogatives **nasaán** and **bakit** are never duplicated for the simple reason that nothing or no one can be in more than one place at the same time nor can there be more than one explanation for an event or action.

The following are examples of questions using duplicated interrogatives.

Sínu-síno ang inyóng mga anák?	Which of the children are yours?
Anú-anó ang mga pangálan ninyó?	What are your names?
Kaní-kaníno ang mga báhay na iyán?	Whose houses are those?
Saán-saán kayó nakatirá?	Where do you (plural) live?
Magká-magkáno ang mga aklát?	How much are each of the books?
Ilán-ilán ang mga anák nilá?	How many children do they have?

In the **ilán-ilán** question above, the speaker is referring to the total number of children of more than one couple or parent. The question may be translated to *Between those two (or three) couples (or parents), how many children do they have in all?*

Kaí-kailán kayó dumatíng sa Pilipinas?
When (plural, referring to several dates) did you (plural) arrive in the Philippines?

Note that **kaí-kailán** is very infrequently used nowadays and is mostly confined in rural Tagalog areas or regions.

III. CONTRACTED FORMS OF QUESTIONS

Contracted and shortened forms of a word or two words together are very common in spoken Tagalog, as in English. In the case of interrogatives, ligatures may produce another version of a question. Both **iyán** and **itó** may also be shortened to '**yan** and '**to**. They lose the stresses on the second syllable as both become monosyllabic modifiers. Note the differences in the following Tagalog questions.

Síno ang táong iyán?	Who is that person?
Sínong táo iyán?	
Síno 'yan?	Who is that (person)?
(Speaker is pointing to someone)	

Kaníno ang aklát na itó?	Whose book is this?
Kanínong aklát ito?	
Kaníno 'to?	Whose (book) is this?
(Speaker is pointing to or holding a book)	

Anó ang simbáhang iyán?	What church is that?
Anóng simbáhan iyán?	
Anó 'yan?	What (church) is that?
(Speaker is pointing to a church)	

IV. COMMON EVERYDAY QUESTIONS

Other common questions aside from the ones mentioned above that need to be commited to memory are the following. Note the presence of **ba** (the use of **ba** is discussed in the next lesson) in these questions.

Kilála mo ba siyá?	Do you know her/him?
Sásama ka ba?	Are you coming along?
Gustó mo ba itó?	Do you like this?
Uuwì ka na ba?	Are you going home already?
Gustó mo bang manóod ng síne?	Do you like to watch a movie?
Táma ba itó?	Is this correct?
Táma ba ako?	Am I right?
Anó ba 'yan?	What's that?
Anó'ng gustó mo?	What do you like?
Saan ka pupuntá?	Where are you going?
Síno ba siyá?	Who's she/he?
Nasaán siyá?	Where's she/he?

Exercises

Answer the first seven questions from the previous page with complete sentences. The *yes* and *no* responses have been preselected.

1. **Óo,** _____.

2. **Hindì,** _____.

3. **Óo,** _____.

4. **Hindì,** _____.

5. **Óo,** _____.

6. **Hindì,** _____.

7. **Óo,** _____.

Create fictional answers to these questions.

1. **Anó ba 'yan?**	What's that?
2. **Anó'ng gustó mo?**	What do you like?
3. **Saan ka pupuntá?**	Where are you going?
4. **Síno ba siyá?**	Who's she/he?
5. **Nasaan siyá?**	Where's she/he?

The Question Word **Ba**

Certain words unique to the Tagalog language give a particular meaning or sentiment that a speaker may wish to convey in his/her sentences and questions. These words spice up the language. Curiosity, frustration, irritation and other emotions pepper everyday Tagalog speech and a learner of this language will do well to understand these nuances.

One example is the question word **ba**. The word has no specific meaning and cannot be translated in English except that it serves as a spoken question mark to indicate clearly that the speaker is asking a question.

Questions do not necessarily need **ba** but without the **ba**, a question may be mistaken for a statement, especially when pronounced wrongly, as in the following examples:

Silá ay aalís na.	They will leave now.
Silá ba ay aalís na?	Are they leaving now?
	(Remember to raise the tone of voice at the end of a question to differentiate it from a statement.)

The question above may be written as **Aalís na ba silá?** to emphasize that the action **aalís** as being confirmed or awaited by the speaker. In **Silá ba ay aalís na?**, the focus is on the subject, which is **silá**, rather than on the action of leaving.

What are the rules for using **ba**?

1. To change a sentence in the subject-predicate word order into a question, place **ba** immediately after the subject and just before **ay**. The sequence **ba** + **ay** is then often shortened into **ba'y**.

Silá ay aalís na.	They will leave already.
Silá ba ay aalís na?	Are they leaving now?
Silá ba'y aalís na?	

Ang babáe ay mabaít.	The woman is good.
Ang babáe ba ay mabaít?	Is the woman good?
Ang babáe ba'y mabaít?	

Si Pedro ay marúnong.	Pedro is intelligent.
Si Pedro ba ay marúnong?	Is Pedro intelligent?
Si Pedro ba'y marúnong?	

Vocabulary List

aalís = is/are leaving	**matápang** = brave	**rádyo** = radio
magkáno = how much	**kasáma** = companion	**marumí** = dirty
kaibígan = friend	**magsalitâ** = to speak up	

2. To change a sentence in the inverted or transposed word order into a question, place **ba** immediately after the predicate.

Aalís silá.	They will leave.
Aalís ba silá?	Will they leave?
Mabaít ang babáe.	The woman is good
Mabaít ba ang babáe?	Is the woman good?
Kákain akó.	I shall eat.
Kákain ba akó?	Shall I eat?

3. In questions that start with interrogatives, always place **ba** immediately after the interrogative pronoun. This sequence is not answerable by *yes* or *no* unlike the examples in the first two rules in using **ba**.

Síno ba ang kasáma mo?	Who is your companion?
Anó ba ang gustó mo?	What do you like?
Saán ba kayo pupuntá?	Where are you going?
Kailán ba kayó aalís?	When are you leaving?
Magkáno ba itó?	How much is this?

There are cases where monosyllabic words—such as the personal pronouns **ka**, **ko**, and **mo** as well as the Tagalog particles **na**, **pa**, **din**, **daw**, **pô**, **hô**, **ngâ**, and others—are inserted for emphasis. They follow the interrogatives and push **ba** further toward the end of the question.

Ba actually belongs to the same group as the Tagalog particles **na**, **pa**, **din**, **daw**, and others, which are optional in sentences and questions but gives emphasis to statements. The other monosyllabic particles have the following meanings:

— **Na**   means *already* or *now*, and expresses finality
— **Pa**   means *still*, *yet* or *more*
— **Din** means *too* and *also*; placed after words ending in consonants (**Ikáw din ba?** *You too?*); **rin** is placed after words ending in vowels (**Akó rin ba?** *Me too?*)
— **Daw** means *they say* or *reportedly*; expresses that the information relayed by the speaker is from another source; placed after words ending in consonants (**Ikáw daw.** *They say it is you.*); **rin** is placed after words ending in vowels (**Akó raw.** *They say it is I.*)
— **Nga** means *indeed*, also puts emphasis to the word before it

Aalís na ba silá?	Will they leave already?
Aalís ka na ba?	Will you leave already?
Magandá rin ba ang babáe?	Is the woman pretty too?
Malinís daw ba ang batà?	Is the child clean as they say?
Marumí raw ba ang batà?	Is the child dirty as they say?
Marumí pa ba siyá?	Is he/she still dirty?

4. In questions that start with pseudo verbs such as **gustó**, **áyaw**, **íbig**, **puwéde**, **maáari**, and others, which help the main verb to express moods (see Lesson Seventeen on Pseudo Verbs), place **ba** between the pseudo verb and the main verb and attach the ligature **-ng** to **ba**.

Gustó bang kumáin ng batà?	Does the child like to eat?
Íbig bang umalís ng laláki?	Does the man like to leave?
Áyaw bang umalís ng babáe?	Doesn't the woman want to leave?

However, if a pronoun comes before the main verb (usually an **-um-** or **mag-** verb, see Lesson Fourteen), the ligature **-ng** is attached to the pronouns **siyá**, **kámi**, **silá** and **táyo** rather than to **ba**.

Dápat ba <u>siyáng</u> magsalitâ?	Should he/she speak?
Puwéde ba <u>akong</u> umalís?	Can I go?
Maáarì ba <u>kamíng</u> magtiwalà sa iyó?	Should we trust you?

Note that in some Tagalog-speaking provinces, **bagá** is used instead of **ba**. In asking questions, raise your voice at the end if the answer is either *yes* or *no*; if not, bring down the voice at the end.

<u>**Aalís ka ba?**</u> **Oô/Hindî.**	Are you leaving? Yes/No.
<u>**Síno ka ba?**</u> **Áko si Mary.**	Who are you? I am Mary.

Exercises

Form questions using the following statements by inserting **ba** in the appropriate places.

1. **Ang kaibígan ko ay si Herbert.**
2. **Silá ay pupuntá sa kapílya.**
3. **Akó ay gurò.**
4. **Marúnong ng Tagalog si Peter.**
5. **Siya ay mabaít na batà.**
6. **Ang magagandáng báhay ay kanilá.**
7. **Silá ay magsásalitâ sa rádyo.**
8. **Ang mga mababaít ay siná Helen at Mary.**
9. **Kákain ka na.**
10. **Mabaít din si Robert.**

Answer the following questions.

1. **Anó ba ang inyóng pangálan?** (formal)
2. **Saán ba kayó nakatirá?** (formal)
3. **Sino ba ang inyóng kaibigan dito?** (formal)
4. **Mabaít ba siyá?**
5. **Siyá ba ay Amerikáno?**
6. **Saán-saán kayó pumunta** (went)**?**
7. **Malakí ba ang báhay nila?**
8. **Marúnong ba si Rizál?***
9. **Si Bonifacio* ba ay matápang?**
10. **Gustó ba ninyó sa Pilipinas?**

* Jose P. Rizal (1861–1896) is the national hero of the Philippines. He is a writer, poet, physician, sociologist and nationalist, among others. Andres Bonifacio (1863–1896) is the father of the revolutionary movement called **Katipunan** and led the revolt of the masses against Spain.

Making Comparisons

People and things have qualities or attributes that may be compared to one another. These qualities are expressed by an adjective, which can indicate if two people or things are equal or not equal, or if a person or thing has a high degree of of a certain quality—if not the highest among all others.

In the Tagalog language, as in English, there are various ways of comparing things according to the different levels or degrees.

I. EQUALITY (A = B)

To express equality between two nouns (A and B) in terms of one quality, either attach the prefixes **kasíng-** or **magkasíng-,** which by themselves mean *as*, to the root word of an adjective; or use the words **parého, katúlad** or **gáya,** all of which mean *similar to* or *like*.

1. A is as [adjective] as B

Formula: A prefix **kasíng-** + adjective + **ni** (or **ng**) B
This phrase means *as* + adjective + *as* as seen in the following examples, and the order can also be reversed with **kasíng-** + adjective at the beginning of the sentence.

Si Maria ay kasínggandá ni Elena.	Maria is <u>as beautiful as</u> Elena.
Kasínggalíng ni Rizal si Bonifacio.	<u>As good as</u> Rizal, Bonifacio is. (lit.)
	Bonifacio is as good as Rizal.

2. A and B are equally [adjective]

Formula: prefix **magkasíng-** + adjective
Unlike the previous formula, subjects being compared using **magkasíng-** are mentioned side by side. An optional pronoun or article introducing the name or names of subject or subjects is needed if **magkasíng-** is placed at the beginning of the sentence (see second and third sentences).

Sina Maria at Elena ay magkasínggandá.	Maria and Elena <u>are equally beautiful</u>.
Magkasínggalíng sina Rizal at Bonifacio.	Rizal and Bonifacio <u>are equally good</u>.
Magkasíntaás kamí.	We are equally tall.

Note how the following prefixes are attached to the adjectives:

a. **kasíng-** or **magkasíng-** is attached to roots that begin in **a, e, i, o, u, k, g, h, m, n, w,** and **y** (for example: **kasíngkulót** meaning *as curly as*)

Vocabulary List

makabágo = modern	**parého, gáya** = similar to, like
lálo, higít na, mas = more	**gáya ng pusà** = like a cat

b. **kasín-** or **magkasín-** is attached to roots that begin with **d, l, r, s,** and **t** (for example: **kasíndumí** meaning *as dirty as*)

c. **kasím-** or **magkasím-** is attached to roots that begins with **b** and **p** (for example: **magkasímbahò** meaning *as foul-smelling as*)

Remember also that names of people must be preceded by the articles **ni/nina** and **si/sina** while names of things or places use the articles **ng/ng mga**.

3. A is [adjective] like B

Formula: A + adjective + **parého ni/ng**, **katúlad ni/ng** or **gáya ni/ng** + B
These phrases mean *similar to* or *like* on their own and but translate to the first formula (*as* + adjective + *as*) when used to compare the qualities of nouns.

Si Maria ay magandá parého ni Elena.
Si Maria ay magandá gáya ni Elena.
Maria is beautiful like (as beautiful as) Elena.

II. INEQUALITY (A ≠ B)

1. A is better than B

To express that something is better than something else, the formula is:
A + **lalóng** (or **higít na** or **mas**) + [adjective] + **káysa kay** (or **káysa sa**) + B

The first noun is usually the one with the higher degree of quality. **Lalóng** (**laló** + the ligature **-ng**), **higít na** (**higít** + the ligature **na**) or **mas** all mean *more* while **káysa** means *than*. Similar to the possessive words **ni** and **ng**, **káysa kay** is followed by the name of a person while **káysa sa** is followed by the name of a place or thing. **Káysa sa** may be shortened to **kesa**.

Si Peter ay lalóng marúnong káysa kay John.
Higít na marúnong si Peter káysa kay John.
Peter is brighter than John.

Ang matandá ay lalóng masípag káysa sa batà.
Mas masipag ang matandá káysa sa batà.
The old is more diligent than the young.

2. A is worse than B

To express a lower quality or lesser degree, the formula is:
A + **hindi kasíng-** + [adjective] + **ni /ng** + B

The resulting phrase *not as* [adjective] *as* means that the quality of the first noun is lower or lesser than that of the second noun.

Si John ay hindi kasíndúnong ni Peter.   John is not as bright as Peter.
Ang aking anák ay hindî kasímbaít ng anák niyá.   My child is not as good as his/her child.

III. INTENSIVES: A IS VERY [ADJECTIVE]

The intensive degree expresses a quality of a noun in a more forceful and emphatic way by using a phrase that starts with *very*. There are many ways to express the intensity of the qualities in Tagalog but the most common are the following:

1. By duplicating the adjective and attaching an appropriate ligature (**-ng**, **-g** or **na**):

magandáng-magandá	very beautiful
matandáng-matandâ	very old
pángit na pángit	very ugly
masípag na masípag	very industrious

2. By attaching the prefix **nápaka-** (which means *very*) to the adjective:

nápakapangit	very ugly
nápakasipag	very industrious
nápakatandâ	very old
nápakagandá	very beautiful

IV. SUPERLATIVES: A IS THE MOST [ADJECTIVE]

Superlatives express the quality of something to the highest degree (the greatest, the best, the most). It uses the prefix **pinaká-** (which means *most*) attached to adjectives, resulting in such words as the following:

pinakápángit	the ugliest
pinakámalinís	cleanest
pinakámasípag	most industrious
pinakámatandâ	oldest
pinakámagandá	most beautiful

Exercises

Compare the singing skills of two famous singers you like based on the following criteria using the different degrees of adjectives you have just learned. Use the adjectives given for each category to describe the similarity of or the differences in their skills.

1. rhythm (**indáyog**)   **mabilís**   fast
2. style (**istílo**)   **makabágo**   modern
3. voice (**boses** or **tono**) **malawak**   broad
4. kind of music (**urì ng tugtúgin**) **magandá** beautiful

Describe a quality or feature of the following nouns, using the superlative form.

1. **báhay**   house   6. **yélo**   ice
2. **babáe**   woman   7. **bundók**   mountain
3. **áraw**   sun   8. **ílog**   river
4. **gabí**   night   9. **rádyo**   radio
5. **simbáhan**   church   10. **lángit**   sky

Use the following adjectives and write down examples for each of the levels discussed in this lesson.

1. **baít**
2. **tabâ**
3. **dunong**
4. **samâ**
5. **lakí**
6. **hirap**
7. **sípag**
8. **yaman**
9. **ayos**

Using **May** and **Mayroón**

Sentences with the words **may** or **mayroón** (pronounced as **may-ro-on**) point to the existence (*there is* or *there are*) or possession (*has* or *have*) of things. Although both can mean *there is/there are* and *has/have*, the two words cannot be used interchangeably as there are certain rules to follow.

I. HOW TO USE **MAY** (THERE IS/THERE ARE, HAS/HAVE)

1. **May** is followed immediately by a noun, in either the subject-predicate or inverted order sentence, to show possession or existence (see last sentence). **May** sentences often do not explicitly mention the possessor.

   Akó ay may <u>kaibígan</u> sa Quezon City.   I have a friend in Quezon City.
   May <u>kaibígan</u> ako sa Quezon City.

   Kami ay may <u>báhay</u> sa Maynilà.   We have a house in Manila.
   May <u>báhay</u> kami sa Maynilà.

   May <u>táo</u> sa labás.   There is someone outside.

2. **May** is followed immediately by an adjective or numeral in either type of word order sentence, to indicate possession or existence.

   Siya'y may <u>magandáng</u> báhay.   He/She has a nice house.
   May <u>dálawang</u> áso sa kúlúngan.   There are two dogs in the cage.

3. When referring to more than one thing in possession or in existence, **may** is followed immediately by **mga** then the noun.

   May <u>mga</u> púnong-kahoy silá.   They have trees.
   May <u>mga</u> tao sa labás.   There are men outside.

4. **May** is followed immediately by a verb to indicate the existence of someone or something.

   May <u>natutúlog</u> na táo sa silíd.   There is a person sleeping in the room.

Vocabulary List

silíd = room	**másarap** = delicious	**mayroón** = has/have
bágo = new	**púnongkahoy** = trees	**walâ** = none

II. HOW TO USE **MAYROÓN** (HAS/HAVE)

1. **Mayroón** is followed by monosyllabic words like **ka**, **na**, **nang**, **pa**, **ba**, **din** and **daw** (see Lesson Ten for a discussion of these words). Ligatures are then attached to the monosyllabic words nearest to the nouns or adjectives. **Mayroón** may be shortened to **meron**.

Mayroón <u>pang</u> trabáho si Lucio.	Lucio still has a job.
Meron ka <u>bang</u> bágong aklát?	Do you have a new book?

2. **Mayroón** is followed by a personal pronoun such as **akó**, **ka**, **tayó**, **kamí**, **kayó**, and **silá** in inverted sentences to indicate possession. The suffix ligature **-ng** is attached to these pronouns as they end in vowels. To change a **may** sentence into a **mayroón** sentence, simply rearrange the **may** + noun + possessive pronoun sequence into a **mayroón** + possessive pronoun + **-ng** sequence.

May báhay kamí sa Maynilà.	We have a house in Manila.
Mayroón <u>kamí</u>ng báhay sa Maynilà.	

3. **Mayroón** alone is an answer to a question. The word **oo** (*yes*) at the start of a sentence as well as the noun or pronoun after **mayroón** is optional.

May bágong sapátos ba si Bob? (Oo),	Does Bob have a new pair of shoes? (Yes), he has.
mayroón (siyá).	

The **ma-** prefix that is attached to root words to form other words is actually a contracted form of **may**—for example, **marámi** (many) is **may damí** (there are many), **mataás** (tall) is **may taás** (literally, there is height) and **malinís** (clean) is **may linís** (there is clean).

In short, with abstract nouns, **ma-** means *there is/are*. With concrete nouns, **ma-** means *having many*, such as **mabutó** (bony; literally, having many bones).

III. HOW TO USE **WALÂ** (THERE IS/THERE ARE NO, DO/DOES NOT HAVE, NONE)

To negate the existence or possession of a thing, replace **may** and **mayroón** with the word **walâ**, which contradicts possession or existence. **Walâ** changes *there is/are* into <u>*there is/there are no*</u> and changes *has/have* into <u>*does not/do not have*</u>. **Walâ** also means *none* on its own or as a response to a **mayroón** question. To use **walâ**, follow these three simple rules based on the **may** and **mayroón** rules:

1. **Walâ** is usually used at the beginning of a sentence and is followed by a possessive pronoun or a monosyllabic word. The suffix ligature **-ng** is added to the pronoun or the monosyllabic word or the monosyllabic word that come after it.

Walâ <u>akó</u>ng kaibígan sa Quezon.	I do not have a friend in Quezon.
Walâ <u>silá</u>ng mga púnong-kahoy.	They do not have trees.
Walá <u>pang</u> bágong aklát.	There is no new book yet.
Walá <u>nang</u> trabáho si Lucio.	Lucio does not have a job now (or anymore).

2. **Walâ** with the suffix ligature **-ng** is used before numerals or adjectives, nouns, the article **mga** and verbs.

Walâng <u>dálawa</u>ng áso sa kúlúngan.	There are no two dogs in the cage.
Walâng <u>táo</u> sa labás.	There is no one outside.

Walâng <u>mga</u> táo sa labás.	There are no men outside.
Waláng <u>natutúlog</u> na táo sa silíd.	No one is sleeping in the room.

3. **Walâ** by itself is a negative response to a question using **may** or **mayroón** and means *none*. **Hindî** (or *no*) is an incorrect answer to this type of question. **Walâ** also changes a positive question into a negative one.

May bágong sapátos ba si Bob? Walâ.	Does Bob have a new pair of shoes? None.
May kótse ba silá? Walâ.	Do they have a car? None.
Mayroón ka bang pagkáin?	Do you have food?
Walâ ka bang pagkáin?	Don't you have food?

Exercises

Fill in the blanks with **may**, **mayroón** or **walâ**. Note that **walâ** may be used in most of the sentences.

1. **Ako ay _____ mabaít na anák.**

2. **Si Mary ay _____ magandáng bulaklák.**

3. **_____ bang aklát si John?**

4. **_____ pera ba kayó?**

5. **_____ damít ang batàng mahírap.**

6. **Ang mga táo ay _____ masayáng Pasko.**

7. **Ang báhay ay _____ lamók.**

8. **_____ kamíng masayáng búhay.**

9. **_____ kumakáing batà sa silíd** (room).

10. **Ako ay _____ aklát sa Tagálog.**

Translate the following sentences into Tagalog.

1. Yes, I have.
2. We have good boys and girls in school.
3. Do you have delicious food there?
4. None. We do not have delicious food.
5. I have a pretty sister.
6. They have many books in the library (**sa aklatan**).

LESSON THIRTEEN

Numbers

When learning the Tagalog names of numbers, it is also useful to learn the Spanish ones as well (spelled according to the conventions of Tagalog phonetics) since these are still commonly used, especially among the older generations. So in this lesson, we give the Spanish equivalents of numbers if they are commonly used by Filipinos.

I. CARDINAL NUMBERS

Tagalog numbers have equivalents in Spanish (written according to Tagalog orthography) and these are commonly used by older people, especially in buying and selling.

	TAGALOG	SPANISH		TAGALOG	SPANISH
1	**isá**	uno	25	**dalawampú't limá**	beynte sinko
2	**dalawá**	dos	30	**tatlumpú**	treynta
3	**tatló**	tres	36	**tatlumpú't ánim**	treynta'y seis
4	**ápat**	kuwatro	40	**apatnapú**	kuwarenta
5	**limá**	sinko	47	**apatnapú't pitó**	kuwarenta'y siyete
6	**ánim**	seis			
7	**pitó**	siyete	50	**limampú**	sinkuwenta
8	**waló**	otso	55	**limampú't limá**	sinkuwenta'y sinko
9	**siyám**	nuwebe			
10	**sampû**	diyes	60	**animnapú**	sesenta
11	**labíng-isá**	onse	70	**pitumpú**	setenta
12	**labíndalawá**	dose	80	**walumpú**	otsenta
13	**labíntatló**	trese	90	**siyamnapú**	nobenta
14	**labíng-ápat**	katorse	100	**sandaán**	siyento
15	**labínlimá**	kinse	110	**sandaá't sampú**	siyento diyes
16	**labíng-ánim**	disiseis	200	**dalawáng daán**	dos siyentos
17	**labímpitó**	disisiyete	300	**tatlóng daán**	tres siyentos
18	**labíngwaló**	disiotso	400	**ápat na raán**	kwatro siyentos
19	**labínsiyám**	disinuwebe	500	**limáng daán**	kinyentos
20	**dalawampú**	beynte	1,000	**isáng líbo**	mil
21	**dalawampú't isá**	beynte uno			

Vocabulary List

limampú = fifty
labindalawá = twelve
úna = first

kalahatí = half
sandaán = one hundred
isáng líbo = one thousand

hulí = last
ikapú = tenth

Sample Sentences

Ang limá at ánim ay labíng-isá.	Five and six are eleven.
Ang dalawáng kapatíd ko ay marurúnong.	My two siblings are intelligent.
Sampúng tao ang umáwit sa palátuntúnan.	Ten people sang in the program.
May mga isáng daáng batà ang nag-áaral dito.	About a hundred children are studying here.
May labíndalawáng buwán sa isáng taón.	There are twelve months in a year.
Iláng taón ka na?	How old are you?
Akó ay dalawampú't limáng taón na.	I am 25 years old (already).

Approximate or estimated numbers may be expressed by using **mga** before a number such as **mga sampû**, which means *about ten*.

II. ORDINAL NUMBERS

An ordinal number indicates the place occupied by an item in an ordered sequence. Tagalog ordinals are easy to put together and remember. The prefix **ika-** is added to the cardinal numbers. There are a few irregularities, however—first and last are always **úna** and **hulí**, respectively, and the removal of the first two letters of **dalawá** and **tatló** before attaching the prefix **ika-**.

úna	first
ikalawá	second
ikatló	third
ikaápat	fourth
ikalimá	fifth
ikaánim (ikanim)	sixth
ikapitó	seventh
ikawaló	eighth
ikasiyám	ninth
ikasampû	tenth
ikalabing-isá	eleventh
ikadalawampú	twentieth
ikasandaán	one hundredth
hulí	last

Sample Sentences

Ikailán kang anák?	Which child are you?
Akó ay ikalimá.	I am the fifth.
Sino ba ang úna?	Who is the first?
Si Peter ang úna.	Peter is the first.
Ikáw ba ay pangánay?	Are you the first child?
Hindî, ako ay bunsô.	No, I am the youngest child.
Siyá ay nasa ikaánim na grado.	He/She is in the sixth grade.

III. FRACTIONS

One part of a whole is expressed by adding the prefix **ka-** (shortened form of **ika-**) to the denominator (the lower number in the fraction). The word **bahagi** (meaning *part*) is often added also for clarity. The term **kalahati**, however, is a set name for one half.

kalahatì (or **kalahatíng bahagi**)	for one half
katló (or **ikatlóng bahagi**)	for one third
kápat (or **ikápat na bahagi**)	for one fourth
kalimá (or **ikalimáng bahagi**)	for one fifth
kánim (or **ika-ánim na bahagi**)	for one sixth
kapíto (or **ikapitóng bahagi**)	for one seventh
kawaló (or **ikawalóng bahagi**)	for one eighth
kasiyám (or **ikasiyám na bahagi**)	for one ninth
kapulô (or **ikasampûng bahagi** or **ikapû**)	for one tenth

Bigger fractions are formed by adding a multiple in front:

dalawang-katlo	two-thirds
katlong-kapat	three-fourths

Note that the use of fractions today seems to be limited to schools and is not common in everyday speech. An exception is the word **kalahatì** which can be regularly heard in markets and even in homes.

Sample Sentences

Itó ay kalahatì ng mansánas.	This is half of an apple.
Ang dalawáng-katló ng aking salapî ay para sa iyó.	Two-thirds of my money is for you.
Maglagáy ng tatlóng-kápat ng kutsarítang asín sa pagkáin.	Put three-fourths teaspoon of salt in the food.
Ang ápat na kawaló ay parého ng dalawáng-kápat.	Four-eighths is equivalent to two-fourths.

IV. PRICES AND MONEY

Tagalog and Spanish numbers are used interchangeably in buying and selling, with sellers often giving preference to the Spanish numbers because these are faster to say to prospective buyers. This is logical as the local market scene is fast-paced. To understand market vendors better, you need to know both.

The unit of exchange in the Philippines is the *peso* or **piso** in Tagalog and coins are in *centavos* or **séntimó** or **pera**. One peso is **isang piso** or simply **piso** while the others are:

	TAGALOG	SPANISH
P 1.20	**isáng piso at dalawampúng séntimó**	**uno beinte**
	(or isáng piso't dalawampúng séntimó)	
P 2.30	**dalawáng piso't tatlumpúng séntimó**	**dos treinta**
P 3.40	**tatlóng piso't apatnapúng séntimó**	**tres kuwarenta**
P 4.50	**ápat na piso't limampúng séntimó**	**kuwatro sinkuwenta**
P 5.60	**limáng piso't animnapúng séntimó**	**sinko sesenta**
P 6.70	**ánim na piso't pitumpúng séntimó**	**seis setenta**
P 7.80	**pitóng piso't walumpúng séntimó**	**siyete otsenta**
P 8.90	**walóng piso't siyamnapúng séntimó**	**otso nobenta**
P 9.00	**siyám na piso**	**nuwebe pesos**
P 10.00	**sampûng piso't sampúng séntimó**	**diyes-diyes**

Sample Sentences

Ang áking sapátos ay nagkákahalagá ng pitóng daán at limampúng piso.

My pair of shoes costs seven hundred and fifty pesos.

Ang halagá ng kanyáng damít ay walóng daán siyámnapú't siyám na piso at pitúmpú't limáng pera.

The cost of her dress is eight hundred ninety-nine pesos and seventy-five centavos.

Dalawáng libong piso ang halagá ng silya.

The chair costs two thousand pesos.

In writing Tagalog cardinals above ten, bear the following in mind:

1. The prefix **labíng-** (might be a contracted form of **labis ng** or *excess of*, thus a prefix meaning excess of ten) is added to the cardinals **isá** (one) to **siyám** (nine) to create numbers above ten. The pefix, however, becomes **labín-** when attached to **dalawá** (two), **tatló** (three), **limá** (five) and **siyám** (nine). The prefix becomes **labím-** when attached to **pitó** (seven).

2. In writing tens, the particle **puó** (meaning *ten*) is added as suffix to numbers from one to nine but is written as **-pû**. For example, ten is basically **isáng puó**. The ligatures **-ng** and **-g** after the cardinals are then changed to **-m** to adjust phonetically to **-pu**. Thus, **isang puó** becomes **sampú**.

3. Basically, the numbers above **siyám** (nine) all have ligatures as these numbers are combinations of several words. For those above **siyám** (nine) but below one hundred, the numbers are written as one word such as **siyámnapú** (ninety). On the other hand, a number word higher than a hundred is written as separate words such as **siyám na raán** (nine hundred). In addition, **daán** (hundred) is used after numbers ending in consonants or after the suffix **-ng** while **raán** is used after numbers ending in consonants or the suffix **na**.

4. The connective **at** (shortened to **'t**) is only used between the last two numbers in a series of numbers and words such as **tatlóng líbo sandaá't siyám** (three thousand one hundred nine).

5. Other numbers and their equivalents are:

ten	**pûo**	hundred	**daán**
thousand	**líbo**	ten thousand	**laksâ**
hundred thousand	**yutà**	million	**ángaw**

Exercises

Write down all the numbers from 1 to 30. Make sure that the rules on this page are followed.

Tell something about yourself and focus on details that involve numbers (your age, your mother's age, the number of siblings you have, your place in the family, others), fractions (percentage of your life you have lived in a certain place, heritage, others) and prices (cost of sending you or yosur kids to school, others).

-Um- and **Mag-** Verb Forms

Sentences using **-um-** and **mag-** verbs are generally similar to sentences in the active voice in English, where the subject is the actor although many sentences in English using the active voice would be translated by Tagalog speakers into the equivalent of the passive voice. This is because Tagalogs prefer to construct sentences in the inverted word order where the predicate containing the verb is found at the beginning of the sentence, because to them, that is the more important part of the sentence.

The most commonly used verbs in subject-focused sentences have an **-um-** infix or **mag-** prefix (an infix is inserted in the midde of a root word to form a new word whereas a prefix is attached at the front of the root word). These verbs emphasize the doer of the action or the act itself. These verb forms may be used in sentences that do not require an object to complete the meaning or in sentences with an object when the emphasis is on the doer

Some verb roots occur only with an **-um-** (an example is **alís** which means *to go*) while others occur with **mag-** alone (an example is **labá** which means *to wash*). Some occur with both (such as **hingî** which means *to ask for*) although the derivatives (the new words formed from roots and affixes;) formed have different meanings. Usually, when a verb takes both forms, its **-um-** form expresses non-intensive or casual action (an example is **kumakáin** or *is/are eating*) while its **mag-** form expresses frequency and intensity of action (an example is **nagkákakáin** or *to always be eating* or *to continually be eating*). With regards to action, the **-um-** form expresses action toward the doer (such as **bumibilí** or *is/are buying*) while the **mag-** form expresses action away from the doer (such as **magbibilí** or *is/are selling*).

Forming -Um- and **Mag-** Derivatives

I. **-UM-** VERB FORMS

1. For verb roots beginning with vowels, attach **-um-** to the front of the root directly as a prefix.
   Example: **alís**   leave
   Infinitive: **umalís**   (**-um-** + root) to leave
   Imperative: **umalís**   (same)
   Past: **umalís**   (same) left
   Present: **umaalís**   (**-um-** + duplicate first syllable + root) is/are leaving
   Future: **aalís**   (duplicate first syllable + root) will leave

---

Vocabulary List

magtanóng = to ask a question	**magsayáw** = to dance
áral = study	**magbáyad** = to pay
uminóm = drank	**tumáwag** = called

2. For verb roots beginning with consonants, attach **-um-** as an infix to the root immediately following the initial consonant.

Example: **kain**   eat
Infinitive: **kumain**   (infix **-um-** after initial consonant) to eat
Imperative: **kumain**   (same)
Past: **kumain**   (same) ate
Present: **kumakain**   (duplicated first syllable, infix **-um-** between initial consonant and succeeding vowel + root) is/are eating
Future: **kakain**   (duplicated first syllable + root) will eat

II. **MAG-** VERB FORMS

1. For verb roots beginning with vowels, attach **mag-** followed by a hyphen before the verb root. The hyphen denotes a glottal stop after **mag-**.

Example: **áral**   study
Infinitive: **mag-áral**   (**mag-** + hyphen + root) to study
Imperative: **mag-áral**   (**mag-** + hyphen + root)
Past: **nag-áral**   (change **mag-** to **nag-** + hyphen + root) studied
Present: **nag-aáral**   (**nag-** + hyphen + duplicated first syllable + root) is/are studying
Future: **mag-aáral**   (**mag-** + hyphen + duplicated first syllable + root) will study

2. For verb roots beginning with consonants, attach **mag-** in front of the root.

Example: **lutò**   cook
Infinitive: **maglutò**   (**mag-** + root) to cook
Imperative: **maglutò**   (same)
Past: **naglutò**   (change **mag-** to **nag-**) cooked
Present: **naglulutò**   (**nag-** + duplicated first syllable + root) is/are cooking
Future: **maglulutò**   (**mag-** + duplicated first syllable + root) will cook

Note that the present tense denotes habitual and ongoing action. For verbs whose first syllables have three letters such as **sampáy** (*to hang something*), duplicate the first two letters only (thus, **magsasampáy**).

EXAMPLES OF **-UM-** AND **MAG-** VERBS

pumuntá	to go to a place	**bumilí**	to buy
umalís	to leave	**kumantá** }	to sing
dumatíng	to arrive	**umàwit**	
kumaín	to eat	**tumugtóg**	to play an instrument
umupô	to sit	**uminóm**	to drink
sumúlat	to write	**magsalitâ**	to speak
bumása	to read	**mag-usap**	to converse
humingî	to ask for	**magsulát**	to write
gumawâ	to do or make something	**maglutò**	to cook
lumangóy	to swim	**mag-áral**	to study
umiyàk	to cry	**maglaró**	to play

mag-áway	to quarrel with one another	**mag-isíp**	to think
maglakád	to walk	**maglínis**	to clean
magbáyad	to pay	**magpuntá**	to go
magtaním	to plant	**magtanóng**	to ask a question
magsayáw	to dance	**magbilí**	to sell

Exercises

Write the roots of the following **-um-** and **mag-** verbs.

magtanóng	to ask a question	_____
magpuntá	to go	_____
magbilí	to sell	_____
umalís	to leave	_____
dumatíng	to arrive	_____
kumaín	to eat	_____
mag-áway	to quarrel with one another	_____
maglakád	to walk	_____
magbáyad	to pay	_____
magtaním	to plant	_____
magsayáw	to dance	_____
mag-isíp	to think	_____
maglínis	to clean	_____
umupô	to sit	_____
sumúlat	to write	_____
bumása	to read	_____
humingî	to ask for	_____
gumawâ	to do or make something	_____

Affix **-um-** to the following roots.

pások	enter	_____	**ulán**	rain	_____
balík	go back	_____	**datíng**	arrive	_____
táwag	call	_____	**íbig**	love	_____
sakáy	ride	_____	**táwa**	laugh	_____
tayô	stand	_____	**kúha**	get	_____
úpa	rent	_____	**uwî**	go home	_____
ísip	think	_____	**sáma**	go with	_____

Sentence Patterns

There are two different sentence patterns for **-um-** and **mag-** verbs where the doer or subject occupies different positions within the sentences. In both of these patterns, the verb comes first. But in the first pattern the subject comes next whereas in the second pattern the object or modifier comes next.

I. FIRST SENTENCE PATTERN USING **-UM-** AND **MAG-** VERBS

VERB	DOER OR SUBJECT	OBJECT OR MODIFIER
1. **Kumáin**	si Peter	ng kánin.

Peter ate rice.

2. **Pumások**	ang batà	sa páaralán.

The child went to school.
(**pumások** means *entered* but translates to *went* when used with school or office)

3. **Sumúlat**	siyá	ng kuwénto.

He/She wrote a story.

4. **Naglakád**	si Mary	kahapon.

Mary walked yesterday.

5. **Naglutò**	silá	ng gúlay.

They cooked vegetables.

II. SECOND SENTENCE PATTERN USING **-UM-** AND **MAG-** VERBS

VERB	OBJECT OR MODIFIER	DOER OR SUBJECT
1. **Kumáin**	ng kánin	si Peter.

Peter ate rice.

2. **Pumások**	sa páaralán	ang batá.

The child went to school.

3. **Sumùlat**	ng kuwénto	siyá.

He/She wrote a story.

4. **Naglakád**	kahapon	si Mary.

Mary walked yesterday.

5. **Naglutò**	ng gúlay	silá.

They cooked vegetables.

Both sentence patterns are correct but in sentences with pronouns such as **siyá** and **silá** as the subject, the first structural pattern is preferred.

Sample Sentences

Dumatíng si Helen kahápon.	Helen arrived yesterday.
Sumúsulat si Gng. Smith.	Mrs. Smith is writing.
Nagsásalitâ ang batà.	The child is talking.
Naglálaro ang áking mga anák.	My children are playing.
Naglutò ba kayó ng kánin?	Did you cook rice?
Bumása táyo ng isáng kuwénto.	Let us read a story.
Uminóm kayó ng kapé.	You (plural) drink coffee.
Umíinom ng gátas ang batà.	The child is drinking milk.
	The child drinks milk.

Exercises

Write sentences using the **-um-** and **mag-** verbs in the imperative mood and in the three tenses (past, present, and future).

Read the following paragraphs aloud. Observe a slight pause at the end of every phrase as marked by the slanting line.

Siná G. at Gng. Smith / ay mga Amerikáno. / Dumating silá rito sa Pilipinas / noóng isang buwán. / Siná G. at Gng. Smith / ay nag-áaral ng Tagalog. / Nag-áaral siláng magsalitâ / ng wikà ng Pilipinas.

May dalawáng anák silá. / Ang mga pangálan / ng kaniláng mga anák / ay Peter at Mary. / Silá ay magagandá / at malulusóg. / Umíinom silá / ng maráming gátas / araw-araw. / Si Gng. Smith ang naglúlutò / ng kaniláng pagkáin. / Naglúluto siyá / ng gúlay / at karné. / Ang gúlay ay mabúti / para sa mga batà. / Ang gátas / ay mabúti rin. / Sina Peter at Mary / ay umíinom ng maráming gátas / áraw-áraw / kayâ silá'y malulusóg. / Sina G. at Gng. Smith / ay masasayáng magúlang. / Masasayá rin / ang mga anák nilá. /

Pick out all the action words from the two paragraphs above and give their tenses or forms.

Use the following phrases and words to make your own sentences:

1. **noong isáng buwan**	last month	5. **kayâ**	thus/so
2. **wikà**	language	6. **masasayá**	happy
3. **gátas**	milk	7. **magulang**	parents
4. **karne**	beef		

-In- Verb Forms

Unlike the active **-um-** and **mag-** verbs which emphasize the doer of the action or the action itself, the **-in-** verbs are passive in the sense that they emphasize the object or receiver of the action. The receiver of the action then becomes the subject of the passive sentence. **-In-** verbs indicate an action expressed by the root on the subject without necessarily naming the doer of the action.

A similar meaning can be conveyed by an active sentence with **-um-** and **mag-** verbs (for example, **Bumása ako ng libró** or *I read a book*) where an object is not necessary to complete the meaning (for example, **Bumása ako** or *I read*) and by a passive form of the verb with **-in-** or its alternant **-hin** (for example, **Binása ko ang libró** or *I read the book*).

The main difference is that in the latter, the object (**ang libró**) is necessary and cannot be omitted. And the emphasis is on the object (**ang libró**) rather than the subject (**ko**). You will find that Tagalogs generally prefer the second form using **-in-** verbs (see appendix on common verb forms).

Forming **-In-** Derivatives

-In- verbs are formed in the following ways:

I. FOR A VERB BEGINNING WITH A VOWEL

-In- is either added at the end or the front of the root form depending on the tense.

Example: **alís**	remove
Infinitive: **alisín**	(root + suffix **-in**) to remove
Imperative: **alisín**	(root + suffix **-in**)
Past: **inalís**	(prefix **-in** + root) was/were removed
Present: **ináalis**	(prefix **-in** + root and duplicated first syllable) is/are removing
Future: **áalisin**	(duplicated first syllable + root + suffix **-in**) will remove

II. FOR A VERB WITH AN END GLOTTAL CATCH BEGINNING WITH A CONSONANT

-In- is either added at the end or after the first consonant, depending on the tense. Refer to page 21 for the fourth type of stress with an end glottal catch.

Example: **basâ**	wet
Infinitive: **basaín**	(root + suffix **-in**) to wet
Imperative: **basaín**	(root + suffix **-in**)
Past: **binasâ**	(infix **-in-** after initial consonant) wetted

Vocabulary List

sabíhin = to tell	**pasúkin** = to enter
baguhin = to change	**gisíngin** = to awaken

Present: **binábasâ**	(duplicated first syllable, infix **-in-** between initial consonant and succeeding vowel + root) is/ are wetting	
Future: **bábasaín**	(duplicated first syllable + root + suffix **-in**) will wet	

III. FOR A VERB BEGINNING WITH A CONSONANT

-In- is added after the first consonant but becomes **-hin** when added at the end of the verb.

Example: **bása**	read	
Infinitive: **basáhin**	(root + alternant suffix **-hin**) to read	
Imperative: **basáhin**	(root + alternant suffix **-hin**)	
Past: **binása**	(infix **-in-** after initial consonant) read	
Present: **binábasa**	(duplicated first syllable, infix **-in-** between initial consonant and succeeding vowel + root) is/are reading	
Future: **babasahín**	(duplicated first syllable + root + suffix **-hin**) will read	

Conventions Used in Forming **-In-** Verbs

-In- is usually suffixed to verbs and its alternant (or variant form) **-hin** may take its place under certain circumstances. However, there are irregular cases where these conventions are ignored.

I. REGULAR VERB FORMATIONS USING **-IN-**

1. **-In-** is suffixed to
   a. a root word that ends in a consonant
   alís = **alisín** (to remove) **pások** = **pasúkin** (to enter)

   b. a root word with an end glottal catch and ends in a vowel
   sirâ = **sirain** (to break) **punô** = **punuin** (to fill)

2. **-Hin** is suffixed to a root word without a glottal catch that ends in a vowel.
   bása = **basáhin** (to read) **bilí** = **bilhín** (to buy)
   sábi = **sabíhin** (to tell)

II. IRREGULAR VERB FORMATIONS USING **-IN-**

1. After verb roots with an end syllable stress, the final vowel is omitted before adding the suffix **-hin**.
   bilí = **bilhín** (to buy) **dalá** = **dalhín** (to bring)

2. After verb roots whose last syllable is a VC or CVC syllable (see Lesson Two) containing the vowels **i** or **o**, the **i** or **o** of the last syllable is omitted before adding the suffix **-in-**.
   káin = **kánin** (to eat) **sunód** = **sundín** (to obey)
   dakíp = **dakpín** (to capture)

3. Before root verbs that begin with an **l**, **w** or **y**, the infix **-in-** becomes a prefix **ni-** to form the past and present tenses.

lutò (cook)	= **nilutò**	**walís** (sweep)	= **niwalis**
yarì (made of)	= **niyarì**		

Note that for the infinitive, imperative and future forms of a root verb whose last syllable is CVC containing **o**, the **o** changes to **u** and follows the regular pattern.

gamót (cure or treat)	= **gamutín, gágamutín**
inóm (drink)	= **inumín, iinumín**

EXAMPLES OF **-IN-** VERBS

áwit	= **awítin**	to sing	**káin**	= **kánin**	to eat (irregular)
lutò	= **lutúin**	to cook (irregular)	**dalá**	= **dalhín**	to bring or carry (irregular)
sábi	= **sabíhin**	to tell			
súlat	= **sulátin**	to write	**patáy**	= **patayín**	to kill
mahál	= **mahalín**	to love			to put out light or flame (colloquial)
bágo	= **bagúhin**	to change			
larô	= **laruín**	to play	**batì**	= **batíin**	to greet
gamót	= **gamutín**	to cure	**púri**	= **puríhin**	to praise
gísing	= **gisíngin**	to awaken	**linis**	= **linísin**	to clean
inóm	= **inumín**	to drink	**bílang**	= **bilángin**	to count
táwag	= **tawágin**	to call			

Sentence Patterns for **-In-** Verbs

In sentences with **-in-** verb forms, the doer is always expressed in the possessive form such as **ni Peter**, **ng batâ**, **ko**, **niyá**, **iyó**, **kanyà**, **ákin**, **átin**, and **kanilà**. The doer may also be **kita** (we), a pronoun equivalent to **ikaw** (you) and **ko** (I) exclusively. The verb always comes first, followed immediately by the doer or subject, then the object.

ACTION	DOER/SUBJECT (in possessive form)	OBJECT

1. **Pinilî**   **ng batà**   **ang aklát.**
   Was chosen   by the child   the book
   The child chose the book.

2. **Binása**   **ko**   **ang súlat.**
   Was read   by me   the letter.
   I read the letter.

3. **Kákanin**   **ni Peter**   **ang isdâ.**
   Will be eaten   by Peter   the fish
   Peter will eat the fish.

4. **Ibinilí**   **kitá**   **ng prútas.**
   Was bought   for you by me   the fruit
   I bought you a fruit.

Sample Sentences

Áawitin ng mga bata ang Báhay Kúbo.	Báhay Kúbo will be sung by the children.
Ginágamot ng doktór ang áking sakít.	My sickness is being treated by a doctor.
Nilínis ni Marta ang kanilàng báhay.	Their house is being cleaned by Marta.
Lúlutuin ng katúlong ang gúlay.	The vegetables will be cooked by the helper.
Bábasahin ko ang aklát ni Dr. Rizal.	The book by Dr. Rizal will be read by me.
Kákanin ba nila ang mga ságing?	Will the bananas be eaten by them?
Áalisin niya ang kanyang sapátos.	His/Her shoes will e removed by him/her.
Dinádala namin ang aklát ng Tagalog sa páaralán.	The Tagalog book is brought by us to school.

Sinirà ni Lucio ang papél.	The paper was torn by Lucio.
Bilángin natin ang pera.	Let the money be counted by us.

Exercises

Give the three tenses of each of the following verbs:

áwit   **awítin**   to sing

past   _____

present _____

future   _____

lutò   **lutúin**   to cook (irregular)

past   _____

present _____

future   _____

sábi   **sabíhin**   to tell or say

past   _____

present _____

future   _____

súlat   **sulátin**   to write

past   _____

present _____

future   _____

táwag   **tawágin**   to call

past   _____

present _____

future   _____

káin   **kánin**   to eat (irregular)

past   _____

present _____

future   _____

dalá   **dalhín**   to bring or carry (irregular)

past   _____

present _____

future   _____

Change the following active sentences using **-um-** and **mag-** forms of the verbs into passive sentences using the **-in-** forms. Then translate the sentences into English.

1. **Ang aming katúlong ay naglutò ng manók** (chicken).
2. **Umáawit ng kundiman** (a Tagalog love song) **ang mga batà.**
3. **Nagbágo silá ng barò.**
4. **Tayo ay umiinòm ng gátas áraw-áraw** (everyday).
5. **Bumábasa ako ng páhayagan** (newspaper) **sa umaga.**
6. **Naglarô ang mga batang lalaki ng patintero** (a native game).
7. **Nagpatáy na ng ilaw** (light) **ang aking inà.**
8. **Nagbasâ ng paá ang magsasaká** (farmer).
9. **Kumain ng masarap na gulay ang malusóg** (healthy) **na batà.**
10. **Bumílang** (count) **ka ng sampúng píso.**

Use the imperative forms of the seven **-in-** verbs from the first exercises to create sentences.

Change the following sentences from the passive into the active forms. Do not change the tense nor the person and number.

Áawitin ng mga bata ang Báhay Kúbo.
Báhay Kúbo will be sung by the children.

Lulutuin ng katúlong ang gulay.
The vegetables will be cooked by the helper.

Kákanin ba nilá ang mga ságing?
Will the bananas be eaten by them?

Aalisín niyá ang kanyang sapátos.
His/Her shoes will be removed by him/her.

Dinádala námin ang aklát ng Tagalog sa páaralán.
The Tagalog book is brought by us to school.

The Articles **Ang** and **Ng**

Two of the most commonly used words in the Tagalog language are the articles **ang** and **ng** (introduced in Lesson Eight along with **ni** as a word that shows possession). The word **ang** functions like the English definite article *the* and introduces the main character in a sentence, while **ng** introduces the other minor characters, among other things, and may be translated using the English preposition *of* or the indefinite articles *a* and *an*.

For many non-Tagalog speakers, when to use the articles **ang** and **ng** is a source of confusion. They use **ang** where **ng** should be used, and **ng** where **ang** should be used. The following rules should help to differentiate the usage of one from the other.

I. RULES FOR USING **ANG** AND **NG**

1. **Ang** is used:

a. To introduce a common noun as the subject of a sentence (**ang** is similar to the English definite article *the* in this case)

<u>Ang</u> <u>batà</u> **ay mabaít at masípag.** The child is good and diligent.

Kumakain ng manggà <u>ang</u> <u>dalaga</u>. The young woman is eating a mango.

b. Place **ay** to emphasize the identity of or mark the doer

<u>Akó</u> **ay sumúlat ng kuwénto.** I wrote a story.
<u>Akó</u> <u>ang</u> **sumúlat ng kuwénto.** I was the one who wrote the story.

Ang batà ay maysakít. The child is sick.
Ang <u>batà</u> <u>ang</u> maysakít. The child is the one who is sick.

2. **Ng** is used:

a. To introduce the receiver of an action
Bumili <u>ng</u> <u>pagkain</u> ang babáe. The woman bought food.
Si Elena ay nagluto <u>ng</u> <u>manók</u>. Elena cooked the chicken.

Vocabulary List

dalaga = young woman	**kápitbahay** = neighbor	**lóla** = grandmother
paléngke = market	**maysakít** = sick	**tinápay** = bread
magkákapatid = siblings	**kuwénto** = story	

b. To indicate association or possession

Ang <u>iná</u> <u>ng</u> <u>báta</u> ay nagpuntá sa paléngke.   The child's mother went to the market.

Ang <u>báhay</u> <u>ng</u> <u>laláki</u> ay bágo.   The man's house is new.

c. To introduce the doer of the passive action (observe the **-in-** verb forms)

Kináin <u>ng</u> <u>áso</u> ang tinápay.   The dog ate the bread.

Binilí <u>ng</u> <u>batáng</u> <u>babáe</u> ang aklàt. The girl bought the book.

II. THE PLURAL FORMS OF **ANG** AND **NG**

As Tagalog sentences follow the plurality rule initially mentioned in Lesson Four, plural words need to be introduced by the plural forms of **ang** and **ng**. Thus, **ang** becomes **ang mga** and **ng** becomes **ng mga**:

<u>Ang</u> <u>mga</u> <u>báhay</u> ng magkákapatid (denotes two or more siblings) **na babáe ay malalakì.**
The sisters' houses are big.

Bumilí <u>ng</u> <u>mga</u> <u>prutas</u> ang lóla.
The grandmother bought fruits.

Exercises

Fill in the blanks with **ang**, **ng**, **ang mga** or **ng mga** and then translate the sentences into English.

1. _____ báhay _____ áking kaibígan ay nasa Quezon City.

2. **Nasa Taft Avenue** _____ **páaralan** _____ **babáe.**

3. _____ pangálan _____ áking asáwa ay John.

4. _____ pangálan _____ kapatíd ko ay Peter at Mary.

5. **Kumákain** _____ **gúlay** _____ **malusóg na batà.**

6. **Umiinóm** _____ **gátas** _____ **anák** _____ **aking kápitbahay.**

7. **Si Peter** _____ **kúmain** _____ **prútas** _____ **punong-kahoy.**

8. **Magkáno ba** _____ **isáng kilo** _____ **asúkal?**

9. **Ilán** _____ **nag-áaral sa kláse** _____ **Tagálog?**

10. **Kináin** _____ **batà** _____ **isáng mansanas.**

Pseudo Verbs—**Dápat**, **Gustó** and Others

In the Tagalog language, there are pseudo verbs that accompany principal verbs and express the chief action in the sentence. These include **dápat**, **maaarí**, **puwéde**, **kailángan**, **íbig**, **gustó** and **áyaw**. Their individual meanings are:

dápat	must, should, would, has/have to
maáarì or **puwéde**	can, may, could
kailángan	needs to, is necessary to
ibig or **gustó**	likes, desires, wants
áyaw	does not like

These pseudo verbs shift the meaning of the main verb to indicate that an action should have been done or should not have been done, or can be carried out or cannot be carried out, etc.

<u>Dápat kumáin</u> ng gúlay ang mga batà.
The children <u>should eat</u> [their] vegetables.

<u>Puwédeng lutúin</u> ang báka.
(You) <u>may cook</u> the beef.

<u>Maáarì kayóng <u>lumákad</u> na.
You (plural) <u>may go</u> already.

<u>Áyaw</u> niláng <u>uminóm</u> ng gatas.
They <u>do not like to drink</u> milk.

<u>Kailángang maligò</u> tayo araw-araw.
We <u>need to take a bath</u> everyday.

<u>Ibig</u> kong <u>mag-áral</u> ng Tagálog.
<u>Gustó</u> kong <u>mag-áral</u> ng Tagálog.
I <u>like to learn</u> Tagalog.

Vocabulary List

mag-áral = to learn	**báka** = cow or beef	**magulang** = parent
estudyante = student	**balút** = steamed duck embryo	**dalandan** = orange fruit
tinápay = bread	**kaibígan** = friend	

Rules for Using Pseudo Verbs

1. Use only the infinitive form of the main verb with any of the following affixes: **-um-**, **mag-**, **-in-**, and **-hin**.

Correct:	**Dapat <u>kumáin</u> ng gulay ang mga batà.**
	The children must eat [their] vegetables.
Incorrect:	**Dapat kumákain ng gulay ang mga batà.**
Incorrect:	**Dapat kákain ng gulay ang mga batà.**
Correct:	**Kailángang <u>punuín</u> mo ng batò ang pasô.**
	You must fill up the claypot with stones.
Incorrect:	**Kailángang pupunuín mo ng batò ang pasô.**
Incorrect:	**Kailángang napunô mo ng batò ang pasô.**

Note the use of the ligature **-g** above to link **kailangan** with the main verb **punuin**. This applies to other pseudo verbs although with **ibig**, **áyaw** and **dápat** before a main verb, a ligature is not necessary. However, all pseudo verbs followed by a pronoun, such as **siyá** and **niyá**, requires ligatures after the pronoun.

2. For **ibig** and **gustó** pseudo verbs, use the form of possessive pronoun that comes after a subject (such as **ko** and **mo**, refer to Lesson Eight) and attach the appropriate ligature. Place the pronoun between the pseudo verb and the principal verb, whether the principal verb is active (with an **-um-** or **mag-** verb) or passive (with an **-in-** verb).

Correct:	**Ibig kong mag-áral ng Tagálog.**
	I want to learn Tagalog.
Incorrect:	**Ibig mag-áral ko ng Tagálog.**
Incorrect:	**Ibig mag-áral ng Tagalog ako.**
Correct:	**Gustó kong arálin ang Tagálog.**
	I want to learn Tagalog.
Incorrect:	**Gustó arálin ko ng Tagálog.**
Incorrect:	**Gustó arálin ng Tagálog ako.**

3. Except for **ibig** and **gustó**, all other pseudo verbs require a nominative pronoun (such as **akó** and **siyá**) with the appropriate ligature attached when used with an active **-um-** or **mag-** verb (see first example).

Correct:	**Dápat <u>siyáng</u> <u>uminóm</u> ng gátas.**
Incorrect:	**Dápat siyáng inumín ang gátas.**

Similarly, a pseudo verb requires a possessive pronoun (such as **niyá**) with the appropriate ligature attached when used with a passive **-in** verbs (see example below).

Correct: **Dápat <u>niyáng</u> <u>inumín</u> ang gátas.**

Incorrect: **Dápat <u>niyáng</u> <u>uminóm</u> ng gátas.**

4. A pseudo verb that ends in a consonant other than **n** does not need a suffix. Those ending in vowels need suffixes.

Correct: **<u>Ibig</u> <u>uminóm</u> ng gátas ang batà.**

Correct: **<u>Gustóng</u> <u>uminóm</u> ng gátas ang batà.**

Incorrect: **Gustó uminóm ng gátas ang batà.**

Sample Sentences

Dapat akóng sumúlat sa aking kaibígan sa Estados Unidos.

I must write to my friend in the United States.

Dapat sulatín ni Peter ang kanyang kuwénto ngayóng gabi.

Hi/Her story must be written by Peter tonight.

Maáarì bang linísin mo ang aking sapátos?

Could my shoes be cleaned by you?

Maáarì akong maglínis ng iyong sapátos.

I can clean your shoes.

Kailángang mag-áral ang mga estudyante áraw-áraw.

Students need to study every day.

Ibig niláng magsalitâ ng Tagálog.

They like to speak in Tagalog.

Áyaw niyáng kánin ang balút.

He/She does not like **balut** (steamed duck embryo) to be eaten.

Áyaw siyáng kumain ng balút.

He/She does not like to eat **balut**.

Exercises

Each of the exercise below has three words (a pseudo verb, an object, and a subject). Think of an appropriate main verb and use its proper form following the grammatical rules in this lesson to create a logical sentence. Translate the sentences into English.

1. **dápat**   **libró**   **estudyante**

   _____.

2. **lumipád**   **ibig**   **batà**

   _____.

3. **kailángan**   **lóla**   **gamot**

   _____.

4. **áyaw**   **pangáko**   **dalaga**

   _____.

5. **maáarì**   **pritong manók**   **kuya** (elder brother)

   _____.

Translate the following phrases into Tagalog.

1. We must eat vegetables every day.
2. Do you like to buy oranges (**dalandan**)?
3. The sick person needs to sleep.
4. It is necessary to take a bath every day.
5. He does not like to swim.
6. The child can eat now.
7. You need to clean the house.
8. I like to write stories.
9. We should love our parents.

Ma- and Maka- Verb Forms

Ma- is a prefix that is attached to the beginning of a verb root. In general, a verb with a **ma-** indicates capability to do something. A **ma-** verb has two types: active and passive. When **ma-** is used with an intransitive verb (verb does not take an object), it is in the active form and takes a noun or a nominative pronoun (such as **siyá** and **ikáw**) as the subject similar to **-um-** and **mag-** verb forms. If it is attached to a transitive verb (a verb which needs an object to complete its meaning), the **ma-** form is passive and requires a subject in the possessive form (such as **niyá** and **mo**) similar to the **-in-** verb.

 Maka- has the same meaning as **ma-** except that **maka-** is always active and takes a noun or a nominative pronoun (such as **siyá** and **ikáw**) as its subject. While a **ma-** verb can be formed from verb showing emotion or feeling, a **maka-** verb can only be formed from verb showing action. Thus, not all **ma-** verb forms have their equivalent in **maka-** verb forms.

Transitive and Intransitive Ma- and Maka- Verb Forms

I. INTRANSITIVE VERBS USING MA-

An intransitive verb with **ma-** does not need any other element besides the subject to form a sentence. Its derivatives are formed as follows:

Example: **túlog**	sleep	
Infinitive: **matúlog**	(**ma-** + root) to sleep	
Imperative: **matúlog**	(**ma-** + root)	
Past: **natúlog**	(**ma-** becomes **na-** + root) slept	
Present: **natútulog**	(**ma-** becomes **na-** + duplicated first syllable + root) sleeps/sleep	
Future: **matútulog**	(**ma-** + duplicated first syllable + root) will sleep	

EXAMPLES OF INTRANSITIVE VERBS USING MA-

matúlog	= to sleep	**maligò**	= to take a bath
magútom	= to be hungry	**magálit**	= to be angry
makiníg	= to listen to	**mahiyâ**	= to be ashamed
mahigâ	= to lie down	**maupô**	= to sit
matuwâ	= to be delighted	**matákot**	= to be afraid
mamatáy	= to die	**malungkót**	= to be sad

Vocabulary List

pag-ása = hope	**nakahigâ** = lying down	**áraw-áraw** = every day
mabásag = to be broken	**maysakít** = sick	**putók** = explosion

II. TRANSITIVE VERBS USING **MA-**

A transitive verb needs an object to complete its meaning. Its derivatives are formed similar to an intransitive verb except its imperative form.

Example: **kíta**	see	
Infinitive: **mákita**	(**ma-** + root) to be seen	
Imperative: none		
Past: **nákíta**	(**ma-** becomes **na-** + root) saw	
Present: **nákikita**	(**ma-** becomes **na-** + duplicated first syllable + root) sees/see	
Future: **mákikita**	(**ma-** + duplicated first syllable + root) will see	

EXAMPLES OF TRANSITIVE VERBS USING **MA-**

makita	to be seen
makáin	to be able to eat
maalála	to be remembered
makúha	to be able to get
marinig	to be heard
mabilí	to be able to buy
masúnog	to be burned
mabása	to be able to read
mabásag	to be broken

III. VERBS USING **MAKA-**

Generally, adding **maka-** to a verb expresses the capability to do something. It does not have an imperative form.

Example: **túlog**	sleep	
Infinitive: **makatúlog**	(**maka-** + root) to be able to sleep	
Imperative: none		
Past: **nakatúlog**	(**maka-** becomes **naka-** + root) was/were able to sleep	
Present: **nakatútulog**	(**maka-** becomes **naka-** + duplicated first syllable + root) is/are able to sleep	
Future: **makatútulog**	(**maka-** + duplicated first syllable + root) will be able to sleep	

EXAMPLES OF **MAKA-** VERBS

makatúlog	to be able to sleep	**makaalála**	to be able to remember
makaligò	to be able to bathe	**makakúha**	to be able to get
makahigâ	to be able to lie down	**makárinig**	to be able to hear
makaupô	to be able to sit	**makabilí**	to be able to buy
makabúhay	to be able to give life	**makasúnog**	to be able to burn
makakíta	to be able to see	**makabása**	to be able to read
makakáin	to be able to eat	**makabásag**	to be able to break

Sample Sentences

Ang mga batà ay dapat matúlog nang maága.

Children should sleep early.

Nagútom ako kagabí pagkatápos mag-áral.

I got hungry last night after studying.

Nagagálit ang aking iná sa mga bátang matigás ang úlo.

My mother gets angry with hard-headed (or stubborn) children.

Nákíta ko si Mary sa palengke kahapon.

I saw Mary in the market yesterday.

Makukúha mo na ang iyong suwéldo.

You can get your salary now.

Nakatúlog kagabi ang maysakít.

The sick person was able to sleep last night.

Hindi ako makaligò kung malamíg.

I cannot take a bath when it is cold.

Ang mga batà ay nakahigâ sa lupà.

The children are able to lie on the ground.

Ang pag-ása ay nakabúbuhay.

Hope is able to give life.

Náaalala ko ang aking anák sa gabí bago matúlog.

I think of my child at night before sleeping.

Exercises

Fill in the blanks with the appropriate tenses or forms of the verbs using **ma-** and **maka-** found in this lesson and underlined in the English translations below.

1. _____ **ang mga batà sa dadalhín mong regálo.**
   The children <u>will be delighted</u> with the gift you will bring.

2. _____ **kamí sa pagkawalà ng iyóng singsíng.**
   We <u>were saddened</u> by the loss of your ring.

3. **Sa kabiláng palengke** _____ **si Tess ng gulay.**
   Tess <u>was able to get</u> vegetables from the other market.

4. _____ **na mag-isá ang áking bunsô.**
   My youngest <u>can</u> now <u>take a bath</u> alone.

3. **Kung malakás ang tugtog mo, hindî ka** _____.
   If your music is loud, you <u>will</u> not <u>be heard</u>.

Stressed **Má-** and **Maká-** Verb Forms

To express unintentional or accidental actions, attach stressed **má-** and **maká-** to the beginning of verbs. The resulting verbs convey the performance of an act beyond the control of the doer or the receiver. These verbs do not have imperative forms and the accent marks on the **má-** and **maká-** verb forms are retained in all tense forms. Not all stressed **má-** verb forms have stressed **maká-** counterparts.

I. VERBS USING STRESSED **MÁ-**

Forming derivatives using the stressed **má-** prefixis similar to forming those using the unstresed **ma-**. However, because the stress remains on **má-** in all tenses, the pronunciation is different.

Example: **tulog**	sleep
Infinitive: **mátulog**	(**má** + root) to sleep unintentionally
Imperative: none	
Past: **nátulog**	(**má-** becomes **ná-** + root) slept unintentionally
Present: **nátutulog**	(**má-** becomes **ná-** + duplicated first syllable + root) sleeps unintentionallly
Future: **mátutulog**	(**má-** + duplicated first syllable + root) will sleep unintentionallly

EXAMPLES OF VERBS WITH STRESSED **MÁ-**

mátulog	to sleep unintentionally
mákita	to be seen accidentally
mákain	to be eaten accidentally
mábasa	to be read unintentionally
márinig	to be heard accidentally
máinom	to be drank accidentally
mábanggâ	to be bumped unintentionally
mábaril	to be shot accidentally
mápatay	to be killed unintentionally

II. VERBS USING STRESSED **MAKÁ-**

In forming a verb using stressed **maká-**, the second syllable of the prefix is duplicated in the present and future tenses.

Example: **tulog**	sleep
Infinitive: **makátulog**	(**maká-** + root) to sleep unintentionally
Imperative: none	
Past: **nakátulog**	(**maká-** becomes **naká-** + root) slept unintentionally
Present: **nakákatulog**	(**maká-** becomes **naká-** + duplicated **ka** + root) sleeps/sleep unintentionally
Future: **makákatulog**	(**maká-** + duplicated **ka-** + root) will sleep unintentionally

Example: **ligó**	bathe
Infinitive: **makáligó**	(**maká-** + root) bathe unintentionally
Imperative: none	
Past: **nakáligó**	(**maká-** becomes **naká-** + root) bathed unintentionally
Present: **nakákaligó**	(**maká-** becomes **naká-** + duplicate **ka** + root) bathe/bathes unintentionally
Future: **makákaligó**	(**maká-** + duplicate **ka-** + root) will bathe unintentionally

EXAMPLES OF VERBS WITH STRESSED **MAKÁ-**

makábili	to buy without previous intention
makábaril	to shoot accidentally
makákita	to see by chance, involuntarily
makákain	to eat accidentally
makáinom	to drink accidentally
makábangga	to bump against accidentally
makárinig	to hear unintentionally
makápulot	to pick up something accidentally
makápatay	to kill accidentally
makádalaw	to visit without previous intention

Sample Sentences

Nákita ko siyá sa palengke.	I saw her (by chance) at the market.
Nákain ko ang lúmang tinápay.	I (accidentally) ate the stale bread.
Nárinig námin ang kánilang áwit.	We heard (by chance) their song.
Nábanggâ ang kotse sa padér.	The car (accidentally) bumped against the wall.
Nakábaril ng pulís ang magnanakaw.	The robber (accidentally) shot the policeman.
Nakápulot ang batà ng sampûng píso.	The child (by chance) picked up ten pesos.
Nakárinig siyá ng putók.	He heard (by chance) an explosion.
Nakádalaw si Maria sa kaniyáng iná.	Maria visited her mother (without meaning to).
Nátulog ang laláki sa loób ng simbáhan.	The man fell asleep (without meaning to) inside the church.
Nakábili siya ng magandáng sapátos sa Marikina.	She bought (without previous intention) pretty shoes in Marikina.

Exercises

Look for the correct **ma-** and **maka-** verb forms needed to translate the following sentences and write them on the blanks.

1. _____ The sick man is now able to eat.

2. _____ I was seen by my teacher in the church.

3. _____ I can now read the Tagalog Bible.

4. _____ The old woman can take a bath now if (**kung**) the water is not cold (**malamìg**).

5. _____ I shall be able to leave tomorrow.

6. _____ The baby (**sanggól**) can now take the medicine.

7. _____ We were able to visit her (by chance) in the hospital.

8. _____ The man shot his companion accidentally in the hand.

9. _____ My father bought an expensive dress for me without planning to.

10. _____ I cannot sit.

Use the present tense forms of the following accented **má-** and **maká-** verb forms in sentences. Read the sentences aloud afterwards.

1. **makáinom**   to drink unintentionally
2. **makábangga**   to bump against accidentally
3. **makárinig**   to hear unintentionally
4. **makápatay**   to kill by accident
5. **makádalaw**   to visit without previous intention

Maging—*To Be* or *To Become*

When the word **maging** (means *to be* or *to become*) is placed before a noun or adjective, the phrase expresses the speaker's or the subject's desire to change from one state or condition to another. **Maging** is in fact a very common helping verb in Tagalog. Examples of **maging** phrases include the following:

maging mabaít	to become good (or to be good)
maging Pilipino	to become a Filipino (or to be a Filipino)
maging masamâ	to become bad (or to be bad)
maging gurò	to become a teacher (or to be a teacher)
maging abugádo	to become a lawyer (or to be a lawyer)
maging tahímik	to become quiet (or to be quiet)
maging mayáman	to become rich (or to be rich)
maging bulág	to become blind (or to be blind)

Forming Phrases with **Maging**

Example: **baít**	kindness
Infinitive: **maging mabaít**	(**maging** + **ma-** attached to root) to be kind
Imperative: **maging mabaít**	(**maging** + **ma-** attached to root) Be kind!
Past: **naging mabaít**	(**maging** becomes **naging** + **ma-** attached to root) became kind
Present: **nagíging mabaít**	(**maging** becomes **nagíging** + **ma-** attached to root) become kind
Future: **magíging mabaít**	(**maging** becomes **magíging** + **ma-**attached to root) will become kind

Sample Sentences

Ang anák niya ay nagíging mabaít na ngayón. Her/his child is becoming good now. (literal)
Her/his child is better behaved now.

Ang aking kaibígan ay magíging mayáman na. My friend will soon get rich.

Vocabulary List

kapitbáhay = neighbor	**malusóg** = healthy	**tahímik** = quiet/peaceful
panahón = weather	**maíngay** = noisy	**bulág** = blind

Kailángang magíng malusóg ang lahat ng mga batà.	All children need to be healthy.
Nagíging tahímik na ang aming báhay.	Our house is becoming quiet now.
Nagíng kápitbahay namin silá.	They were once our neighbors.
Gustó kong magíng gurò.	I want to become a teacher.
Áyaw mo bang maging doktór?	Don't you want to become a doctor?
Nagíging masamâ ang panahón.	The weather is going bad. (literal)
	The weather is getting worse.
Mahírap magíng bulág.	It is difficult to go blind.

Exercises

Translate the following phrases into Tagalog and use them in sentences.

1. becoming noisy   _____

2. will become poor   _____

3. became a hero   _____

4. becoming industrious _____

5. will be a lawyer   _____

6. became dirty   _____

7. becoming dark   _____

8. will be rainy   _____

9. was a teacher   _____

10. will be happy   _____

Select five names of friends and describe what they wanted to become when they were still young. Compare this to what they are now or what they want to be five years from now.

Magkaroón—To Have

The word **magkaroón** means *to have*. It is usually placed before a noun to indicate to have what the noun expresses. **Magkaroón** may be shortened to **magka-** and is similar in meaning to **may** and **mayroón** (see Lesson Twelve) which also express existence and/or actual possession. However, **magkaroón** has tense forms—past, present and future—while **may** and **mayroón** do not have any except when **may** is followed by a verb.

Forming Phrases and Words with **Magkaroón**

To create a **magkaroón** phrase or form a **magka-** word, follow the formulas below:
    magkaroón + article **ng** + noun
or **magka-** + noun

Example:	**magkaroón ng pera**	to have money
	or **magkapera**	
Past:	**nagkaroón ng pera**	(**magkaroón** becomes **nagkaroón**)
	or **nagkapera**	(**nagka** + noun) had money
Present:	**nagkakaroón ng pera**	(**magkaroón** becomes **nagkakaroón**)
	or **nagkákapera**	(**nagkaka** + noun) has money
Future:	**magkakaroón ng pera**	(**magkaroón** becomes **magkakaroón**)
	or **magkakapera**	(**magkaka** + noun) will have money

The subject of a sentence using **magkaroón** or a **magka-** word is introduced by **si** or **ang** or is indicated by a nominative pronoun such as **siyá**. A pronoun subject is always placed after **magkaroón** while a subject introduced by **si** or **ang** may be inserted after **magkaroón** or after the object. The meaning, however, does not change.

Nagkaroón <u>si Maria</u> ng asó.	Had Maria a dog. (literal)
	Maria had a dog.
Nagkaroón ng asó <u>si Maria</u>.	Maria had a dog.

Vocabulary List

anák na kambál = twins	**radyo** = radio	**taním** = plant (noun);
ubó = cough	**trabáho** = work	to plant (verb)
bisíta = visitor	**ánay** = termite	

To state the negative of **magkaroón**, the word **hindî** (meaning *not* within a sentence or *no* when used as a response) is placed before the word **magkaroón**. For example, **Hindi nagkaroón si Maria ng asó** (Maria did not have a dog).

Sample Sentences

Past:	**Nagkaroón siyá ng anák na kambál.**	She had twins.
	Nagkaanák siyá ng kambál.	

Present:	**Nagkákaroón ako ng ubó kapág malamíg.**	I have a cough when the weather is cold.
	Nagkákaubó ako kapág malamíg.	

Future:	**Magkákaroón kamí ng bisita.**	We will have visitors.
	Magkákabisita kamí.	

Past:	**Nagkaroón ng sakít ang batà.**	The child got sick.
	Nagkasakít ang batà.	

Present:	**Nagkákaroón ng ánay ang báhay.**	The house has termites.
	Nagkákaánay ang báhay.	

Future:	**Magkákaroón si Pedro ng trabáho.**	Pedro will have a job.
	Magkákatrabáho na si Pedro.	

Negative:	**Hindî nagkákaroón ng bulaklák ang taním.**	The plant does not bear flowers.
	Hindî nagkákabulaklák ang taním.	

Negative:	**Hindî silá nagkaroón ng báhay.**	They did not have a house.
	Hindî sila nagkabáhay.	

Negative:	**Hindî kamí magkákaroón ng rádyo.**	We will not have a radio.
	Hindî kamí magkakarádyo.	

Exercises

Write the correct tense forms of the **magkaroón** and **magka-** phrases and words in the blanks. Afterwards translate these sentences into Tagalog.

1. _____

   They will have a pretty house in Quezon City.

2. _____

   Did you get sick last year?

3. _____

   We are having a grand time (**kasiyá-siyáng panahón**) on the beach (**dalampasigan**).

4. _____

   He will have a car next month (**susunód na buwán**).

5. _____

   His business does not have plenty of money.

6. _____

   My child will have a friend.

7. _____

   We shall have a good teacher.

8. _____

   The rich man will have a new car.

9. _____

   I would like to have a good friend.

Form 10 other examples of **magkaroón** and **magka-** phrases and words not found in this lesson.

Expressing Thoughts and Actions

When expressing their thoughts and actions, Filipinos make use of the words **tila**, **akalá**, and **isip** (all of which simply mean *to think* in English) as well as **pumuntá** (means *to go*) and a multitude of other verbs to indicate what they did, are doing and will do.

I. TO THINK

1. **Tila**, **sa akalà** and **sa palagáy**

The English word *to think* may be translated in three ways in Tagalog but all three indicate opinions, ideas and assumptions. Basically, they all mean the same—*I think, He/She thinks, They/We think*—when used in sentences but individually, they have the following definitions:

tila	= an adverb that means *it seems*
sa akalà or **sa palagáy**	= to my thinking (literal), a preposition meaning *to assume* or *to have an opinion*

Tila, **sa akalà** and **sa palagáy** phrases are formed this way:

tila + verb or adjective or nominative pronoun such as **silá** or **ikáw**

particle **sa** + **akalà** or **palagáy** + possessive noun or pronoun (**ni Jay, ko, niyá, nilá, mo, ng lahat** or *of everybody*)

Tila is placed mostly at the beginning of a sentence in common conversations and always implies the speaker's own perception.

Tila úulan.	It seems it will rain.
Ang sagot niyá ay tila mali.	His/her answer seems wrong.
Tila siya'y lalong magandá ngayon.	She seems prettier now.

On the other hand, **sa akalà** or **sa palágay** is followed by a noun or a pronoun in the possessive form such as (**ni Coi, niyá** or **mo**).

Sa akalà ko ikaw ay matalíno.	To my thinking, you are an intelligent man. (literal) I think you are an intelligent man.
Sa palagáy ko ay mananálo tayo.	To my thinking, we will win. (literal) I think we will win.

Vocabulary List

paraán = way	**pupuntá** = will go	**mananálo** = will win
langóy = to swim	**tabíng-dágat** = beach	**palagáy** = opinion
dumálaw = visited	**maysakít** = sick	

Sa akalà nila, siyá'y may sakít.	To their thinking, he is sick. (literal)
	They think he is sick.
Sa palagáy ni Gem ay tama ako.	To Gem's thinking, I am right. (literal)
	Gem thinks I am right.

To a Tagalog speaker, a sentence with **sa akala** leaves room for validation or contradiction as the speaker's assumptions may be proven wrong. For example, **Sa akalà ko ikaw ay matalíno** (*I thought you were intelligent*) somehow negates the subject's intelligence as perceived by the speaker. On the other hand, the statement **Akalà ko Amerikáno siyá** (*I thought he is an American*) invalidates a previous assumption. Note that Tagalog speakers may sometimes omit **sa** before **akala**, replace sa with **ang** as well as omit the linking verb **ay**. Such practices result in the following sentences, which are brief and still correct:

Sa akalà ko ay Amerikáno siyá.	To my thinking, he is an American.
Akalà ko Amerikáno siyá.	To my thinking, he is an American.
Ang akalà ko Amerikáno siyá.	My assumption is that he is an American.

On the other hand, **sa palagáy** voices a personal opinion. An informal translation of *to think* similar to **sa palagáy [ko]** is **sa tingín [ko]** which roughly means *in [my] view*.

2. Isip

When used to mean *to do some real thinking* or *to ponder over something*, the equivalent of *to think* in Tagalog is **umisip** or **mag-isíp** (active form) or **isípin** (passive form).

Umiísip siyá ng lálong mabúting paraán.	He is thinking of a better way.
Iniísip niyá ang kanyáng mga sinásabi.	She thinks about what she says.
Mag-isíp ka ng magagawâ.	(You) Think of what can be done.

II. TO GO

1. Common usage of the word *to go*

To simply indicate direction or itinerary, the verb **pumuntá** is the exact translation of the English word to go although **pumuntá** can also mean to come (see first sample of an imperative sentence below). When used in this sense, **pumuntá** has an imperative form and all tenses of the **-um-** and **mag-** forms.

Imperative: **Pumuntá ka díto.**	Come here.
Imperative: **Pumuntá ka doón.**	Go there.
Future: **Pupuntá kamí sa simbáhan.**	We will go to church.
Past: **Pumuntá silá sa tabíng-dágat.**	They went to the beach.
Present: **Pumupuntá siyá sa Mayníla áraw-áraw.**	He/She goes to Manila everyday.

2. *To go* plus verb

The other use of the word *to go* beyond *to go to a place* has no exact translation in Tagalog but will depend on the verb immediately following *to go*. For example, the phrase *went swimming* translates into **lumangóy** only whereas the phrase *will go to sleep* translates into **matutulog**. The imperative form and various tenses of the second verb are used in this sense. These sentences are usual responses to the questions **Anó ang ginawâ mo? Anó ang ginágawâ mo? Anó ang gágawin mo?** (*What did you do? What are you doing? What will you do?*) and other similar questions. Note that the English sentences use the various tenses of the word *to go* plus the *-ing* form or various tenses of the verb but the Tagalog translations mention the tenses of the verb only. The Tagalog language does not really use **pumuntá** along with another verb in the same way that the English language uses *to go* as an auxiliary to another verb.

Imperative: **Maglákad ka.**   You go to walk (or You walk).
Future: **Lalangóy kamí.**   We will go swimming.
Past: **Dumálaw kamí sa isáng kaibígan.**   We went to visit a friend.
Present: **Natútúlog sila sa kabilâng kuwarto.**   They are sleeping in the next room.

Exercises

Fill in the blanks with **tíla**, **akalá**, or **palagáy** and the correct Tagalog forms of the English nouns or pronouns given at the end of each sentence. Afterwards, translate the sentences into English.

1. _____, nasa báhay _____. (everybody, I)

2. _____ ay umalís na _____. (*they, we* excluding person spoken to)

3. _____ malí ang _____ iniísip. (*our* including person spoken to)

4. **Téka,** _____nawawalâ _____. (*we* including person spoken to)

Fill in the blanks with the appropriate tenses or forms of *to go* in Tagalog based on the available list of verbs: **aral** (study)   **tanóng** (ask)   **súlat** (write)   **larô** (play)   **taním** (plant)

1. _____ kamí sa báhay ng gurô.

2. _____ tayó ng mga haláman sa hardín.

3. _____ silá kung hindí nilá alám ang lugár.

4. _____ ba ang mga basketbolísta?

5. _____ akó ng isáng kuwénto.

Expressing Emotions

I. TO LOVE

The English word *to love* has two rather different meanings in Tagalog, as expressed by **mahalín** or **ibigin**. The root words are **mahál** and **ibig**, respectively.

Mahál literally means *noble* and *expensive* (a derivative is **mahalága** or *important*). As a term of endearment, it means *dear* or *beloved*. **Mahál** implies that someone values something or someone.

On the other hand, **ibig** means *a fondness for someone or something*; it can also mean *affection, desire, purpose, whim,* and *love*. The emotions it captures range from the simple (caprice) to the complex (love).

> **Mahál kitá.**
> I love you.

> **Minámahál niya ang kanyang áso.**
> He/She loves his/her dog.

> **Minámahal nilá ang kaniláng gurô.**
> They love their teacher.

> **Dápat náting mahalín ang áting báyan.**
> We should love our country.

> **Minámahál ko ang áking mga magúlang.**
> I love my parents.

> **Minámahál niyá ang kanyáng bunsô nang higít sa lahát.**
> He/She loves his/her youngest child the most.

What is the difference between **mahalín** and **ibigin**?

When you are referring to a sensual love between a man and a woman, use **ibig**. Thus, the mutual feelings a man and a woman may share are called **pag-iíbígan** (*mutual love*) and they have **pag-ibig** (*love*) for each other. You may also use a weaker term—but nonetheless implying strong affection—**pagmamáhálan** (*bond of love*).

Vocabulary List

bunsô = youngest child	**bináta** = bachelor	**magkakapatíd** = siblings
báyan = country	**ulán** = rain	**bágo** = before

However, for the filial love that exists between a parent and a child, between siblings, between friends or in all other types of relationships, the various forms of the verb **mahál** are used instead. Thus, either **pagmamahál** or **pagmamáhálan** (both of which means *love*) is used.

Proper:	**Minámahál ko ang áking anák.** I love my child.
Improper:	**Iniibig ko ang áking anák.**

Proper:	**Minámahál nilá ang kaniláng amá.** They love their father.
Improper:	**Iniibig nilá ang kaniláng amá.**

An exception to this is the poetic and patriotic use of the noun **pag-íbig** when referring to the love for one's country (or **pag-ibig sa tinubúang lúpa**, as used by Filipino heroes Dr. Jose Rizal and Andres Bonifacio in their writings for their fellowmen in the late 19th century, refer to appendices).

II. TO LIKE

The English word *to like* indicates fondness for someone or for doing certain activities. Its Tagalog equivalent is either **gustó** or **ibig**, which may be used interchangeably.

The ligatures **-ng** or **-g** are attached to possessive pronouns such as **niyá**, **ko**, and **namín** in sentences containing **gustó** or **ibig**, and the possessive word **ni** (or **ng**, see Lesson Eight) and the ligature **na** are used to conform to the usual rules. Also take note of the usage of the articles **si** (which precedes a name such as Claudette), **siná** (if the noun is plural), **ng** (which should precede the name of a thing), and **sa** (which should precede the name of a place).

Gustó (or **ibig**) **niyáng lumangóy.**	He/She loves to swim.
Gustó kong maglúto.	I love to cook.
Gustó ko si Claudette.	I love Claudette.
Gustó nilá sa Tagaytay.	They like Tagaytay.
Gustó namíng lumákad sa ulán.	We love to walk in the rain.
Gustó kong magbasá bago matulog.	I love to read before going to bed.
Gustó ni Tom na basahin ang libró.	Tom likes to read the book.

Gustó may be duplicated—as in **gustóng-gusto**—to indicate an intense feeling or desire for something or someone.

Exercises

Compose a paragraph made up of not less than six sentences that detail the things you like and the activities you like to do.

Translate the following sentences into Tagalog.

1. I love to walk in the rain.
2. Peter's dog loves him very much.
3. God loves us all.
4. I love my brother more than my sister.
5. Are you in love with that man?
6. Do you like this?
7. I love to play the piano.
8. The rich bachelor loves the poor girl.

Who, *Which* and *That*

An English sentence may contain any of the following relative pronouns—such as *who*, *which* or *that*. This type of pronoun establishes a connection with a preceding noun. A similar relationship is found in Tagalog sentences. A ligature (**-ng**, **-g** and **na**) connects the noun or pronoun to a verb (or vice-versa) and results in a phrase that acts as a relative pronoun.

In the phrases below, the underlined ligatures stand for *who*, *which* and *that*. The rules in using these ligatures are laid out in Lesson Seven (Words that Link and Describe). Note that changing the sequence of the noun or pronoun and the verb does not change the meaning of the phrase (see Lesson Seven).

ang batà<u>ng</u> kumakain or **ang kumakaing batà**
the child <u>who</u> is eating

ang báhay <u>na</u> nasúnog or **ang nasúnog <u>na</u> báhay**
the house <u>which</u> was burned

ang pagkaing nilutò or **ang nilutò<u>ng</u> pagkain**
the food <u>that</u> was cooked

Sample Sentences

Ang súlat na tinanggáp ko ay kanyá.
The letter that I received was his/hers.

Maliít ang sapátos na binilí ko.
The shoes that I bought were small.

Kamíng nag-áaral ang ináabala mo.
We who are studying are being disturbed by you. (literal)

Magagandá ang mga babáeng umáawit.
The women who are singing are beautiful.

Vocabulary List

nasúnog = burned	**ginígising** = being awakened	**ináabala** = being disturbed
tinanggáp = received	**nilutò** = cooked	**tinátawag** = being called

Ang laláking natútulog ay ginígising ng batà.

The man who is sleeping is being awakened by the child.

Ang mga tinátawag mo ay iyóng mga umáalis.

The ones that you are calling are those who are leaving.

In case of names of persons as subjects, it is not wrong to say:

Si <u>Pedrong umáawit</u> ay kaibígan ko.

Pedro, the one who sings, is my friend.

Si <u>Juang sumulat</u> nitong kuwento ay may sakít.

Juan, the who wrote this story, is sick.

Note however, that the use of the ligature **na** after a name of a person is more common, as in:

Si <u>Pedro na umáawit</u> ay kaibígan ko.

Si <u>Juan na sumulat</u> nito ay may sakít.

Exercises

Translate the underlined words into Tagalog.

1. The <u>man who is talking</u> is my father.   _____

2. The <u>pair of shoes that I bought</u> was very large.   _____

3. The <u>boy who eats</u> vegetables is healthy.   _____

4. The <u>dog which we bought</u> is very pretty.   _____

5. The <u>book which I read</u> was written by Romulo.   _____

6. The <u>child who was sick</u> was taken to the hospital. _____

7. The <u>chicken that I ate</u> was delicious.   _____

8. <u>They, who are sleeping,</u> are lazy.   _____

9. The <u>dress which she will wear</u> (**isusuót**) is expensive. _____

10. The <u>chair that he broke</u> is old.   _____

Saying *Please*

Saying *please* in Tagalog requires the use of the prefixes **paki-** and **maki-**, which when added to action roots form derivative verbs that are used for requests.

A **paki-** verb is passive like an **-in-** verb and needs a doer of the action in the possessive form such as **niyá** and **mo**.

On the other hand, a **maki-** verb is active like an **-um-** verb and needs a doer in the nominative form such as **si Nestor**, **ako**, **siyá**, and **ikáw**.

These verbs have tenses but the imperative form is mostly used. And as Tagalogs prefer to speak in the passive, **paki-** verbs are more widely used in making requests.

Forming **Paki-** and **Maki-** Derivatives

Example: **kúha**	to get
Infinitive: **makikúha**	(**maki-** + root) to please get
Imperative: **makikúha**	(**maki-** + root)
Past: **nakikúha**	(**naki-** + root)
Present: **nakikikúha**	(**nakiki-** + root)
Future: **makikikúha**	(**makiki-** + root)
Example: **kúha**	to get
Infinitive: **pakikúha**	(**paki-** + root) to please get
Imperative: **pakikúha**	(**paki-** + root)
Past: **pinakikúha**	(**pinaki-** + root)
Present: **pinakikikúha**	(**pinakiki-** + root)
Future: **pakikikúha**	(**pakiki-** + root)

Sample Sentences

Pakikúha mo ang aking baró.
(You) Please get my dress.

Vocabulary List

kúnin = get

maáarì = possible

pakikúha = (please) get

pinakíkisakáy = (please) give a ride

pakibása = (please) read

pakidalá = (please) bring

Pakibása mo sa akin ang kuwénto.

(You) Please read to me the story.

Pakisulat mo ang iyóng pangálan.

(You) Please write your name.

Pakidalá mo ang áking sulat sa koreo.

(You) Please take my letter to the post ffice.

Makilutò ka ng adóbong manók.

(You) Please cook the chicken *adobo* (a Filipino dish).

Makitáwag ka ng doktór para sa ákin.

(You) Please call a doctor for me.

Pinakitáwag ko ang doktór sa kanyá.

I requested him/her to call the doctor for me.

Makíkidala ako ng balútan sa iyó.

I shall request you to carry a package for me.

Pakikikúha ko sa katúlong ang aking sapátos.

I shall request the housemaid to get the shoes for me.

Pinakíkisakáy niya ang batà sa aming kótse.

She requests us to give the child a ride in our car.

Using either **ngâ** or **namán** signals a request and softens an order even without the **paki-** or **maki-** verbs. **Ngâ** means *truly* or *indeed* and indicates affirmation (**Oô ngâ.** *Yes indeed/of course.*) or emphasis (see imperative sentences below).

Pakikúha mo <u>ngâ</u> ang aking barò.	(You) Please get my dress.
Kúnin mo <u>ngâ</u> ang aking barò.	

Namán means a lot of things, including *also*, *too* and *instead*. When used in imperative sentences, it does not specifically translate into any word but it softens requests and expresses emphasis—even without the **paki-** or **maki-** verbs.

Pakikúha mo namán ang aking barò.	(You) Please get my dress.
Kúnin mo namán ang aking baró.	

A way of expressing a request in question form is by using **maáarì** followed by **ba** with the ligature **-ng** properly attached.

Maáarì bang kúnin mo ang aking damít?

May you get my dress?

Maáarì bang basahin mo ang kuwento?

May you read the story?

Maáarì bang bumilí ka ng tsokoláte para sa ákin?

May you buy a chocolate for me?

A positive answer to these requests is **Opô**, **maáarì** (which is demanded in the polite Filipino society) or **Oô**, **maáarì**.

Take note, however, that using **ngâ** and **namán** when talking to elders and the authorities without the **paki-** and **maki-** verbs is considered impolite. Requests should always be made with all the necessary polite appendages mentioned in Lesson Three such as **pô** and the plural forms of pronouns like **silá** and **kayó**.

Saán and Násaán (Where)

Lesson Nine mentions **saán** and **násaán** as two of the 14 question words. Both Tagalog words mean *where* but each requires different and specific answers.

I. USING **SAÁN**

The question word **saán** is used when asking for the location of an action. It is followed by a verb (see underlined words in sample sentences) in any of the three tenses—past, present and future. A pronoun such as **táyo** or **silá** may be placed between **saán** and the verb. An answer to a question that starts with **saán** is answerable by the following phrase:

> **sa** + name of place

The answer indicates the place where an act was, is, or will be performed. A **saán** question may also be answered by:

> **díto** (or *here*, place is near the person speaking)
> **díyan** (or *there*, place is near the person spoken to)
> **doón** (or *there*, place is far from both)

QUESTIONS	ANSWERS
Saán <u>pumuntá</u> si Peter?	**Pumuntá si Peter <u>sa Baguio.</u>**
Where did Peter go?	Peter went to Baguio.
Saán <u>magsásalitâ</u> si Dr. Smith?	**Magsásalitâ si Dr. Smith <u>sa ospital</u>.**
Where will Dr. Smith speak?	Dr. Smith will speak in the hospital.
Saán táyo <u>kákain</u>?	**<u>Díto</u> táyo kákain.**
Where shall we eat?	We shall eat here.

Vocabulary List

saán = where	**nasaán** = where
magsásalita = will talk	**silíd** = room
díto = here, place is near the person speaking	
díyan = there, place is near the person spoken to	
doón = there, place is far from both speaker and listener	

Saán silá <u>magbábasá</u>?
Where will they read?

<u>Doón</u> silá magbábasá.
They will read there.

Saán kayó <u>nagpaskó</u>?
Where did you spend Christmas?

<u>Sa Tagaytay</u> kamí nagpaskó.
We spent Christmas in Tagaytay.

II. USING **NÁSAÁN**

The question word **násaán** is used when asking for the location of a person or thing. **Násaán** is always followed by either a noun or a pronoun that is introduced by either a **si** or **ang** article (**siná** or **ang mga** is used when the noun or pronoun is plural). A question that starts with **násaán** requires a response using the following phrase:

nása + name of place

The answer indicates the place where a person or a thing is. A **násaán** question may also be answered by the following single-word responses:

nárito (or *here*, place is near the person speaking)
náriyan (or *there*, place is near the person spoken to)
naroón (or *there*, place is far from both)

QUESTIONS
Násaán ang batà?
Where is the child?

ANSWERS
Nása páaralán ang batà.
The child is in school.

Násaán ang aking sapátos?
Where are my shoes?

Nása silid ang iyóng sapátos.
Your shoes are in the room.

Násaán ang báhay ninyó?
Where is your house?

Ang báhay namin ay nása Fairview.
Our house is in Fairview.

Násaán si Mary?
Where is Mary?

Nása báhay si Mary.
Mary is in the house.

Násaán sila?
Where are they?

Nása páaralán silá.
They are in school.

Exercises

Answer the following questions orally:

1. **Násaán ang iyóng lápis?**
2. **Saán nagpuntá ang kaibígan mo?**
3. **Saán nakatirá ang iyóng mga magúlang?**
4. **Saán siyá gáling?**
5. **Násaán ang batàng nag-áaral?**
6. **Saán kayó kumáin kanína?**
7. **Saán pumuntá ang mga báta?**
8. **Saán kayó nag-áaral ng Tagalog?**
9. **Násaán ang páaralán ninyó?**
10. **Násaán ang inyóng gurò?**

Write ten sentences about your city or hometown using **sa** and **nása**.

The Preposition **Sa**

Prepositions indicate a relationship between words in a sentence by linking a phrase to the rest of the sentence. While there are *in, to, from, into, on, for, through, at,* and still many others, there is only the versatile Tagalog word **sa** that does most of the jobs of these various English prepositions.

I. THE MAIN USES OF **SA**

1. As *in*

   Nag-áaral kamí sa silíd-aralán.   We are studying in the classroom.

   Aáwit siyá sa áming palátuntunan.   She will sing in our program.

2. As *to*

   Pupuntá kamí sa Tagaytay búkas.   We shall go to Tagaytay tomorrow.

   Ibíbigáy ko itó sa kanyá.   I shall give this to her.

3. As *from*

   Gáling kamí sa Baguio.   We came from Baguio.

   Sa nabása ko, iyán ay hindî totoó.   From what I read, that is not true.

4. As *for*

   Nagbigáy ako ng sálu-salo para sa áking kaibígan.   I gave a party for my friend.

   Ang damít na itó ay para sa kanyá.   This dress is for her.

5. As *on*

   Ang aklát sa mesa ay bago.   The book on the table is new.

   Nakatirá ako sa Taft Avenue.   I live on Taft Avenue.

6. As *into*

   Tumalón ang aso sa ilog.   The dog jumped into the river.

   Itinápon ko ang basúra sa lata.   I dumped the garbage into the can.

7. As *over*

   Aawit siya sa radyo.   She will sing over the radio.

Vocabulary List

silíd-aralán = classroom	**dyip** = jeepney (a mass transport)	**sálu-salo** = party
hindî totoó = not true		**bintana** = window
tumalón = jumped	**palátuntunan** = program	**umakyát** = climbed

8. As *through*

Siyá ang pangulo námin sa taóng itó.   She is our president through this year.
Nagdaán siyá sa bintanà.   He passed through the window.

9. As *at*

Nililinis niyá ang mga bintanà sa páaralán.   She cleans the windows at school.
Nagsúsulát ako sa gabí.   I usually write at night.

The universal use of **sa** in Tagalog and other Philippine languages could be the reason why Filipinos find it difficult to learn the different meanings and uses of the various English prepositions.

II. THER USES OF **SA**

1. To indicate location

a. In the following phrases and sample sentences, **sa** is followed by a noun that expresses position or location to indicate the direction or location of a person or a thing.

sa loób = *inside*
Ang iná ay pumások sa loób ng báhay.   The mother went inside the house.

sa labás = *outside*
Kamí ay kumáin sa labás ng báhay.   We ate outside the house.

sa haráp = *in front*
Silá ay nakatirá sa haráp ng áming páaralán.   They live in front of our school.

sa tabí = *beside*
Umupô ka sa tabí ko.   Sit beside me.

sa itaás = *above, up*
Umakyát (*climb* or *go up*) **siyá sa itaás.**   He/She went up.

sa gitnâ = *in the middle*
Ang batà ay umupô sa gitnâ.   The child sat in the middle.

sa pagítan = *between*
Táyo ay násá pagítan ng lángit at lupà.   We are between heaven and earth.

sa likurán = *behind*
Lumákad sa likurán ng dyip ang tao.   The person walked behind the jeepney.

sa ibabâ = *below / downstairs*
Nagpuntá sa ìbabâ ang laláki.   The man went downstairs.

The article **sa** may be changed to **nása** to indicate the location of a person or thing such as **nása loób** or **nása likurán** in response to a question that starts with **násaán** (see also Lesson Thirty-Three).

Similarly, **sa** + **may** is used to mean *near* or *about.* Use the phrase to express your doubt as to where the location of someone or something is.

Siyá ay nakatirá sa may Roxas Boulevard.	She lives near Roxas Boulevard.

b.   To indicate where a person has been, it is clearer to use any of the phrases **gáling sa**, **mulâ sa** or **búhat sa**—which are all equivalent to the English preposition *from* rather than **sa** alone. In fact, the combination of these words literally translates to *from from* as **gáling**, **mula** and **búhat** basically mean *from* also. To indicate location, the **sa** phrase is then followed by a name of a place (see Lesson Twenty-Five).

<u>**Gáling sa Baguio**</u> **ang mga bágong kasál.**	The newlyweds came from Baguio.
<u>**Mulâ sa Maynila**</u> **ang áking sapátos.**	My shoes are from Manila.
<u>**Búhat sa Tagaytay**</u>**, kamí ay nagbús.**	From Tagaytay, we rode on a bus.

If a speaker wishes to point out a subject's hometown, only **mulâ sa** and **búhat sa** may be used to mean *a native of* or *belonging to a place.*

Siyá ay <u>**mulâ sa áming náyon**</u>**.**	He/She is from our town.
Ang áking iná ay <u>**búhat sa Maynila**</u>**.** **Ang áking iná ay taga-Maynila.**	My mother is from Manila.

2.   To indicate periods of time

Similar to the previous subsection on the use of **gáling sa**, **mulâ sa** or **búhat sa**, the prolific word **sa** may also be used to indicate a period of time (see also related uses in Lesson Twenty-Eight).

However, only **mulâ** and **búhat** are applicable. A third word is **hanggáng** (or *until*). These three are partnered with **noón** (literally means *then*), **sa**, **ngayón** and hours or dates. Some combinations are as follows:

mulâ noón hanggáng sa ngayón (since then until now)
mulâ sa / búhat sa + time, date or period (from + time, date or period)
hanggáng sa ngayón (until now)
hanggáng sa + time, date or period (until + time, date or period)

Non-Tagalog speakers may notice that most of the times, native speakers omit **sa** from phrases that indicate time. The result though is still widely understood.

Mulâ sa Lunes, sa umaga na ang klase námin.
Mulâ Lunes, umaga na ang klase námin.
From Monday, our classes will be in the morning.

Búhat sa isang linggó, kamí ay magkasama na.
From next week, we will be together.

Mulâ sa Lunes hanggáng Biyernes, walâ kamíng klase.
Mulâ Lunes hanggáng Biyernes, walâ kamíng klase.
From Monday to Friday, we will not have classes.

Búhat sa Oktubre hanggáng Pebrero, magiging malamíg na.
From October to February, it will be cool.

Exercises

Translate the following account of a visitor to the cool and scenic Tagaytay City into Tagalog. Refer to the vocabulary list after the account for the meaning of words. Afterwards, underline all phrases in the translation with **sa**.

We went to Tagaytay for a picnic. Travel (**biyahe**) from Manila to Tagaytay was 45 minutes by car. There were many fruits that could be bought along the road. When we reached Tagaytay, we bought pineapples, bananas and oranges at a store. When we reached Tagaytay, we saw smoke on top of the Taal volcano. We then went down to Taal Lake through difficult passages along the side of the mountains. The scenery (**tánáwin**) was very beautiful. We walked near the lake and took many pictures.

We had some pictures with the children of the place. They were selling oranges. We wanted to swim but the water was dirty. We returned to the picnic place and ate our lunch. We were all hungry. Afterwards, some played ball while the others just sat on the grass (**damó**). From the picnic site, we could see the whole Taal Lake down below. We left the picnic site at three in the afternoon. We went to Taal Vista Lodge, a nice hotel in Tagaytay, and drank delicious juice (**tubig ng niyóg**) from young coconuts. We went home to Manila at four in the afternoon, tired but very happy.

Vocabulary List

minute = **minuto**	young coconut = **buko**	afternoon = **hapon**
pineapple = **pinyá**	pictures = **laráwan**	delicious = **masaráp**
banana = **ságing**	smoke = **úsok**	top = **tuktók; itaás**
orange = **dalandan**	fruit = **prutas**	road = **daán**
lake = **lawà**	mountain = **bundók**	

The Prepositions **Para Sa** and **Para Kay**

An indirect object is either a noun or pronoun. In an English sentence, an indirect object answers any of the questions *to whom*, *to what*, *for whom*, or *for what*. However, an indirect object in a Tagalog sentence is easy to spot as it is introduced by the prepositions **para kay**, **para sa**, **kay** and **sa**. The prepositions **para kay** and **para sa** both mean *for* while **sa** and **kay** both mean *to*. The use of **sa** and **kay** is not interchangeable as the following formulas show:

para sa / sa + possessive pronoun (+ ligature **-g** + noun, optional)

para kay / kay + proper name of a person

Sample Sentences

Bumilí siyá ng aklát <u>para sa ákin</u>.	He/She bought a book for me.
Bumilí siyá ng aklát <u>para sa áking iná</u>.	He/She bought a book for my mother.
Sumulat ako ng kuwento <u>para sa mga batà</u>.	I wrote a story for the children.
Bumilí siyá ng aklát <u>para kay Mary</u>.	He/She bought a book for Mary.
Magbayad kayó ng útang <u>sa kanyá</u>.	Pay your debt to him.
Bumasa siyá <u>sa ákin</u> ng isang kuwento.	He/She read to me a story.
Binasa niya ang páhayagan <u>sa kanyáng amá</u>.	He/She read the newspaper to his father.
Dinalá ko ang aklát <u>sa gurò</u>.	I brought the book to the teacher.
Sumulat siyá <u>kay Bob</u> kahapon.	He wrote to Bob yesterday.

In contrast to an English sentence, a Tagalog sentence with an indirect object need not have a verb. In many cases, the action is implied as in the sample sentences below with the demonstrative pronouns **ito** and **iyan**. In either word order, the meanings of the sentences below do not change and verbs are still absent.

Itó ay regalo ko <u>para sa iyó</u>. **Regalo ko itó para sa iyó.**	This is my gift for you.
Iyán ay <u>para sa kanilá</u>. **Para sa kanilá iyán.**	That is for them.
Itó ay regalo ko <u>kay Helen</u>. **Regalo ko itó kay Helen.**	This is my gift to Helen.

Vocabulary List

regalo = gift	**magbáyad** = to pay
kapatíd na babáe = sister	**páhayagan** = newspaper

When an indirect object introduced by the preposition is plural, some changes also take place (refer to the plurality rule introduced in Lesson Four). Instead of **para kay** or **kay**, **para kina** is used. On the other hand, there are no changes in sentences with **para sa** or **sa** as pronouns have plural forms (such as **para sa kanila** or **sa amin**).

Magbayad kayó <u>kina G. at Gng. Smith</u>.   You pay to Mr. and Mrs. Smith.

Bumasa siyá <u>kina Peter at Johnny</u>.   He read to Peter and Johnny.

In an informal situation, one may hear Filipinos use **sa kay**, **para sa kay**, **sa kina**, and **para sa kina**. However, it is acceptable to omit **sa** in the two sample sentences below.

Magbayad ka <u>sa kina G. at Gng. Smith</u>.   You pay to Mr. and Mrs. Smith.
Magbayad ka <u>kina G. at Gng. Smith</u>.

Bumasa siya <u>sa kina Peter at Johnny</u>.   He read to Peter and Johnny.
Bumasa siya <u>kina Peter at Johnny</u>.

Exercises

Identify the complete prepositional phrases in the following sentences Afterwards, translate the sentences into Tagalog.

1. _____ He wrote to me.

2. _____ She cooked for us.

3. _____ He sold the shoes of John.

4. _____ The mother cooks the food for her children.

5. _____ She went with Charles to the Post Office.

6. _____ The boy brought the book to his mother.

7. _____ These flowers are for Annie.

8. _____ You sing for us.

9. _____ I shall sing for Mr. and Mrs. Brown.

Write ten sentences with pronouns as indirect objects and change the pronouns to names of persons.

Telling Time

Tagalogs love to ask the time. **Anóng oras na?** *What time is it?*, they ask strangers. A learner may thus do well to know how to tell time in Tagalog so as to be able to respond properly in the language of the one who asks.

The following vocabulary words and phrases are fundamental in telling time; please memorize them.

umaga	morning	**tangháli**	noon (basically 11 a.m to 1 p.m.)
hápon	afternoon	**gabí**	night
hátinggabí	midnight	**oras**	hour
kalahatí	half	**minuto**	minute
beses	frequency	**ilang beses**	few times
hanggáng	until	**madalíng-áraw**	dawn
sandalî	second, moment (as a response, it means *for a while*)		

mulâ sa umaga hanggáng gabí
(use in sentences to indicate present or future activities)
from morning until evening

mulâ noóng Enero hanggáng ngayón (use in sentences to indicate past activities)
From last January until now

To express time in Tagalog, the prefix **ika-** is placed before cardinal numbers. The Spanish equivalent (in Tagalog orthography) of time is included in this lesson as it still has a wider use among Tagalogs and non-Tagalogs.

ENGLISH	TAGALOG	SPANISH
1:00 a.m.	**unang oras ng umaga**	**a la una ng umaga**
2:00 a.m.	**ikalawá ng umaga**	**a las dos ng umaga**
3:00 a.m.	**ikatló ng umaga**	**a las tres ng umaga**
4:00 a.m.	**ika-ápat ng umaga**	**a las kuwatro ng umaga**
5:00 a.m.	**ikalimá ng umaga**	**a las sinko ng umaga**
6:00 a.m.	**ikaánim ng umaga**	**a las seis ng umaga**

Vocabulary List

umaga = morning   **oras** = hour
madalíng-áraw = dawn   **noóng Martes** = last Tuesday
samakalawá = day after tomorrow   **sa isáng buwán** = next month

ENGLISH	TAGALOG	SPANISH
7:00 a.m.	ikapitó ng umaga	a las siyete ng umaga
8:00 a.m.	ikawaló ng umaga	a las otso ng umaga
9:00 a.m.	ikasiyám ng umaga	a las nuwebe ng umaga
10:00 a.m.	ikasampû ng umaga	a las diyes ng umaga
11:00 a.m.	ikalabing-isá ng umaga	a las onse ng umaga
12:00 nn	ikalabindalawá ng tánghali	a las dose ng tánghali
1:00 p.m.	únang oras ng hápon	a la una ng hápon
2:00 p.m.	ikalawá ng hápon	a las dos ng hápon
3:30 p.m.	ikatló at kalahatí ng hápon	a las tres y medya ng hápon
4:00 a.m.	ika-ápat ng hápon	a las kuwatro ng hápon
5:15 p.m.	ikalimá at labinlimang minuto ng hápon	a las sinko y kuwarto ng hápon
6:40 p.m.	ikaánim at apatnápung minuto ng gabí	a las seis kuwarenta ng gabí
7:00 p.m.	ikapitó ng gabí	a las siyete ng gabí
8:00 p.m.	ikawaló ng gabí	a las otso ng gabí
9:10 p.m.	ikasiyám at sampúng minuto ng gabí	a las nuwebe diyes ng gabí
10:00 p.m.	ikasampû ng gabí	a las diyes ng gabí
11:00 p.m.	ikalabíng-isá ng gabí	a las onse ng gabí
12:00 midnight	ikalabíndalawá ng hátinggabí	a las dose ng hátinggabí

The shortened forms of time, most common in writing, are :

n.u. = **ng umaga**, a.m.   **n.h.** = **ng hápon**, p.m.

n.t. = **ng tangháli**, noon   **n.g.** = **ng gabí**, evening

Lesson Nine mentions **kailán** (or *when*) as one of the question words. **Kailán** questions are used to ask what time an act happened, happens or will happen or what time someone did, does or will do something. Such questions starting with **kailán** may be answered by using any of the phrases below. Note that each grouping (past, present and future) uses specific words to express time. These words and phrases—**ngayón, noóng** (**noón** + ligature **-g**), **kaninang** (**kanina** + ligature **-ng**), **sa** or **sa isáng** (**isá** + ligature **-ng**), and **sa susunod na**—may be attached to dates to indicate a specific time.

Present:	**ngayón**	now
	ngayóng áraw	today
	ngayóng umaga	this morning (assume that it is still morning)
Past:	**kanína**	a moment ago
	kahápon	yesterday
	kagabí	last night
	kamakalawá	day before yesterday
	noóng áraw	in the olden times

noóng unang panahón	a long time ago
noóng Linggo	last Sunday
noóng Martes	last Tuesday
noóng isáng linggó	last week (as opposed to **Linggó** or *Sunday*)
noóng isáng buwán	last month
noóng isáng taón	last year
noóng Enero	last January
kanínang umága	this morning (assume that it is now afternoon)

Noón(g) cannot be paired with the more recent **kahapon** nor **kagabi**. However, **noóng isáng hapon** and **noóng isáng gabí** are acceptable.

Future:	**mámayâ**	later within the day
	mámayâng hapon	later this afternoon
	mámayâng gabí	later this evening
	bukas	tomorrow
	samakalawá	day after tomorrow
	sa Linggó	next Sunday
	sa Martes	next Tuesday
	sa isáng linggó	next week
	sa isáng buwán	next month
	sa isáng taón	next year
	sa Enero	next January
	sa susunód na Lunes	next Monday
	sa susunód na buwán	next month

Sa bukas is an exception as **bukas** is enough.

Sample Sentences

Anóng oras na?
What time is it?

Ngayón ay ika-ápat ng hapon.
It is four p.m.

Anóng áraw at oras ka ba áalis?
What day and time are you leaving?

Áalis ka ba mámayâ?
Will you leave later (within the day)?

Oo, mámayâng ikalima ng hapon.
Yes, later at five in the afternoon.

Púpunta kamí sa kapilya búkas sa ikapitó ng umaga.
We will go to the chapel tomorrow at seven in the morning.

Dádalaw kamí sa amíng kaibígan sa ikalimá ng hapon.
We shall visit our friend at five in the afternoon.

Ang mga batà ay áawit sa Luneta búkas ng hapon.
The children will sing at the Luneta tomorrow afternoon.

Tútugtóg ang bánda (musical band) **sa gabí.**
The band will play in the evening.

Sa isáng linggó, kamí ay púpuntá sa Tagaytay.
Next week, we shall go to Tagaytay.

Noóng isáng buwán, pumuntá kamí sa Baguio.
Last month, we went to Baguio.

Exercises

Tell the following times in Tagalog. Give the Spanish equivalents.

1. 8:00 pm _____

2. 10:00 am _____

3. 5:30 pm _____

4. 6:00 am _____

5. 1:00 pm _____

6. 6:15 am _____

7. 3:00 pm _____

8. 6:30 pm _____

9. 7:45 pm _____

10. 12:00 am _____

Answer the following questions in complete Tagalog sentences.
1. **Anóng oras ka ba áalis búkas?**
2. **Anó bang áraw ngayón?**
3. **Anóng áraw búkas?**
4. **Anóng oras ka ba pupuntá sa ospitál?**
5. **Anóng oras ka ba pupuntá sa kapílya?**
6. **Iláng oras ang inyóng pag-aáral sa Tagalog?**
7. **Anóng oras kayo nag-aáral?**
8. **Iláng beses** (*how many times*) **ang inyóng pag-aáral sa isáng linggó?**
9. **Iláng oras ang inyóng pag-aáral áraw-áraw?**
10. **Iláng oras ang inyóng pag-aáral sa isáng linggó?**

Read the following aloud:
1. **ika-6:00 n.h.**
2. **ika-2:30 n.u.**
3. **ika-12:00 n.t.**
4. **ika-8:15 n.u.**
5. **ika-7:00 n.g.**
6. **ika-6:45 n.g.**
7. **ika-2:15 n.g.**
8. **ika-10:00 n.u.**

The Word *When* in Tagalog

The word *when* can be translated in various ways in Tagalog. It can be a question using the word **kailán**; or the conjunctions **nang** or **noón** to express an action in the past; or the words **kung** or **kapag** to express a present or future action similar to the English word *if*.

I. KAILÁN

When is translated using **kailán** when used in a question (see Lesson Nine).

Kailán ka áalis?	When will you leave?
Kailán ka dumatíng?	When did you arrive?

II. NANG OR NOÓN

When is translated using either **nang** or **noóng** (**noón** + ligature **-g**) to indicate an action that occurred in the indefinite or vague past.

Nang / Noóng ako'y maliít, ako'y may aso.	When I was small, I had a dog.
Nakita ko siyá nang / noóng ako ay nasa Estados Unidos.	I saw him when I was in the United States.

III. KUNG OR KAPÁG

When is translated using **kung** or **kapág** (shortened form is **pag**) to indicate an action that is happening in the present or will still happen in the future. In this sense, the English word *if* shares a similar meaning.

Kung áalis ka, sásáma ako sa iyó.	When you leave, I shall go with you.
	If you leave, I shall go with you.
Naghihilík siya kapág natutulog.	He snores when he is sleeping.
Magtatampó ako pag aalís ka.	I will be displeased if you leave.

In addition to expressing action in a certain time frame, **kung** may also be paired with question words to create phrases that start with *as to*. When translated into English, *as to* may be omitted.

Vocabulary List

kailán = when	**sabihin** = say
naghihilík = snores	**kung síno** = as to who
magtatampó = will be displeased	**kung kailán** = as to when
bábalík = will return	**Hindî ko alám.** = I do not know.

1. **kung síno** = *as to who*
   Ewan ko kung síno siyá.   I do not know who he/she is.

2. **kung anó** = *as to what*
   Sabihin mo kung anó ang iyóng gustó.   Say what you like.

3. **kung saán** = *as to where*
   Pupuntá tayo kung saán mo gustó.   We shall go to where you like.

4. **kung alín** = *as to which*
   Hindî ko alám kung alín ang pipilíin ko.   I do not know which to choose.

5. **kung kailán** = *as to when*
   Alám mo ba kung kailán siyá bábalík?   Do you know when he will return?

6. **kung paáno** = *as to how*
   Hindî ko alám kung paáno magsayáw ng Tinikling (a Philippine folk dance).
   I do not know how to dance the **Tinikling**.

7. **kung k13níno** = *as to whom*
   Sasabihin ko kung kaníno iyón.   I shall tell to whom that belongs.

Exercises

Translate the following sentences into Tagalog.
1. We shall study Tagalog if you like.
2. We shall study Tagalog when you like to.
3. Are you coming with us if we go to Tagaytay?
4. I asked him (as to) who his father is.
5. We eat when we are hungry.
6. I know when he will speak.
7. She cries when she is angry.
8. If you eat much you will be sick.
9. We were friends when we were young.
10. I shall eat if she eats.

Create sentences using the following meanings of *when*:
1. *When* as **kailán**
2. *When* as **nang**
3. *When* as **noón**
4. *When* as **kung**
5. *When* as **pag** or **kapág**
6. **Kung** with all the interrogatives

Verb Roots

A verb root is the basic form of a verb such as **áral**. When an affix is added, the root takes on different tenses (**nag-aral** is in past tense while **mag-aarál** is in the future tense) or becomes an adjective (**arál na tao,** educated person; **kilaláng guró**, well-known teacher). Observe the examples of verb roots below, the derived verb forms and their meanings in English.

VERB ROOTS	DERIVATIVES	MEANING
aral	mag-áral	to study, to learn
sábi	sabihin	to say
alám	málaman	to know (things)
kilála	mákilala	to know (persons)
dalá	dalhín	to bring or carry
tanóng	tanungín	to ask
sagót	sagutín	to answer
lakí	lumakí	to grow
ibig	ibígin	to love or like
galíng	manggáling	to come from
ayaw	umayáw	to decline or dislike
	or **ayawán**	to be declined or disliked
lakád	lumákad	to walk

However, when preceded by the article **ang** or its plural form **ang mga**, the verb root becomes a noun (see underlined words below) and may be used as a subject in the sentence.

<u>Ang aral</u> niyá ay mabágal.   His/Her study is slow.
<u>Ang sagót</u> ko ay tamà.   My answer is right.

<u>Ang sabi niyá</u> ang mas matimbáng sa sinábi mo.
His/Her statement has more weight than yours.

<u>Ang alám</u> ko lamang ay ang pangalan niyá.
All I know is his name.

Vocabulary List

tanóng = question
mabágal = slow
mas matimbáng = has more weight

mahirap sagutin = difficult to answer
sagót = answer
katamtaman = average

Ang kilalá ko ay ang kanyáng amá.

I know his father.

Ang ayaw ng gurò ay tamád na estudyante.

What is disliked by the teacher is a lazy student. (literal)

Ang dalá ni Peter ay bóla ng kanyáng kuya.

Peter is carrying his brother's ball.

Ang tanóng ng batà ay mahírap sagutín.

The question of the child is difficult to answer.

Ang lakí ng báhay ko ay katamtaman lamang.

The size of my house is average only.

Ibig ng lalaki na makuha ang pagmámáhal ng babáe.

The desire of the man is to get the love of the woman.

Exercises

Write down the verb root in each sentence. Afterwards, translate the sentences into Tagalog.

1. _____ I know that he is good.

2. _____ What was said by you?

3. _____ Is he liked by the woman?

4. _____ He does not like the life in the province (**lalawigan**).

5. _____ Our walk last Saturday was fun.

6. _____ This gift came from my sister.

7. _____ Let us listen to his complaint.

8. _____ The judgement (**hatol**) has been handed down.

9. _____ The guard has left.

10. _____ The hold of the child to his/her mother is tight.

When the roots are preceded by the article **ang** or its plural form **ang mga**, they are used as subjects in the sentence. Write five sentences using verb roots as subjects.

Ex.: **Ang aral sa unibersidád ay mahírap.**
A university education (or study) is difficult.

Forming Nouns

In the Tagalog language, a verb or an adjective is turned into a noun simply by placing the articles **ang** or **ng** or the preposition **sa** before the verb or adjective. If the noun is plural, this should be reflected in **ang**, **ng** and **sa** as well, which become **ang mga**, **ng mga** and **sa mga** (see Lesson Four). The verb may be in any of its tenses—past, present or future.

With **ang**, **ng** and **sa**, the new noun expresses any of the following:
— the one who
— the thing that
— the one which
— what is

The person or thing being talked about in the resulting sentence may either be stated or implied. Observe the two sentences below:

<u>Ang kumain</u> ng manggá ay si Jose.
The one who ate the mango is Jose.

<u>Ang batàng kumain</u> ng manggá ay si Jose.
The child who ate the mango is Jose.

Both sentences are correct but the first one is more widely used for its brevity. The first sentence is shorter and thus easy to articulate whereas the second one is redundant with the mention of **batà**, which is understood to be **Jose**.

Sample Sentences

Binabása mo ba <u>ang sinulat</u> ko?
Are you reading what was written by me? (literal)

<u>Ang nagsásalitâ</u> ay ang pangulo.
The one who is speaking is the president.

<u>Ang natútulog</u> ay parang anghél.
The one sleeping is like an angel.

Vocabulary List

pangulo = president	**igálang** = to respect	**nagagálit** = is angry
sipág = diligence	**naaáwà** = to pity	**masípag** = hardworking

Masaráp <u>ang mga lúlutuin</u> ko para sa iyó.
Delicious, what I shall cook for you. (literal)
I shall cook a delicious meal for you.

<u>Ang mga sinásabi</u> niyá ay hindî totoó.
What are said by him/her are not true. (literal)
What he is saying is not true.

Nákita ko <u>ang binabása</u> niyá.
I saw what she was reading.

<u>Ang mabaít</u> ay maraming kaíbígan.
The one who is good has many friends.

<u>Ang mga mahihírap</u> ay walang maraming kagamitán.
The poor people do not have many possessions.

Dápat náting igálang <u>ang matatandâ</u>.
We should respect the elders.

Hindî magugútom <u>ang masípag</u>.
Will not go hungry, the hardworking. (literal)
The hardworking will not go hungry.

Humíhingî siyá <u>ng kinakáin</u> ko.
He is asking for what I am eating.

Naaáwà ako <u>sa mga humíhingî</u> ng pera.
I pity those who are asking for money.

Nagagálit ang gurò <u>sa mga tamád</u>.
The teacher is angry with the lazy ones.

<u>Sa nag-áaral</u>, <u>ang sípag</u> ay kailangan.
To one who is studying, diligence is necessary.

Note that there are two nouns in the last sentence, the noun **sa nag-áaral** (one who is studying) formed from a verb and a true noun **sípag** (diligence).

Exercises

Look for the nouns in the following sentences, Afterwards, translate the sentences into Tagalog.

1. _____ What he writes is good.

2. _____ The one who arrived was my father.

3. _____ This will be for the poor.

4. _____ The one she loves is an intelligent man.

5. _____ I shall give this to the one who is leaving.

6. _____ The one which he read was Rizal.

7. _____ The thing she ate was not good.

8. _____ The one which is good is the thing I bought.

9. _____ The expensive one should not be bought.

10. _____ The fat are happy.

Construct sentences using the following phrases as subjects, predicates, or objects.

1. **ang mayáman**
2. **ang nag-áaral**
3. **sa naglulútò**
4. **sa mga magagandá**
5. **ang naglilínis**
6. **ang umalís**
7. **sa dumatíng**
8. **ang natutúlog**
9. **ang mga masaráp**
10. **ang magágalit**

I- Verb Forms

The prefix **i-** is added to words to form passive verbs indicating that something is used to do something. For example, it may be added to the noun **sulat** (letter) to form the verb **isulat** (*to write down something*). When the prefix **i-** is added to a verb, it also indicates that something is done for someone else (**isulat mo ako**, *you write for me*) as well as performing the act expressed by the root word on or for the subject (**ihulog ang sulat**, *post the mail for someone*). Generally, the meaning of the **i-** verb is *to do something for another person.*

The **i-** form of a verb is used only when an active **-um-** or **mag-** verb has a direct object (the noun or pronoun that receives the action of the verb). To find out if there is a direct object in an **-um-** or **mag-** sentence, do the following steps: isolate the verb; place *whom* (or **sino**) or *what* (or **ano**) after the verb; and make it into a question. For example, **Bumilí ng isdâ ang babáe para sa kanyáng iná**. **Bumilí** *what?* The answer (**isdâ**) is the direct object (**ang babáe** is the subject and **para sa kanyáng iná** is the indirect object).

Usually, the **i-** verb is the passive form of a **mag-** verb and seldom of an **-um-** verb. Sometimes, instead of the **i-** verb, a **mag-** verb takes the variant form of **ipag-** that expresses doing something for another (see formation of derivatives in following page) and normally follows the first sentence pattern.

Forming I- Verb Forms

I. For verb roots beginning with consonants, the prefix **i-** (or its variant **ipag-**) is attached to all forms and tenses while the infix **-in-** is attached to past and present tenses

Example: **sulat**	letter
Infinitive: **isulat**	(**i-** + root word) to write for another
Imperative: **isulat**	(**i-** + root word) write for another
Past: **isinúlat**	(**i-** + infix **-in-** after first letter of root word) wrote for another
Present: **isinusúlat**	(**i-** + infix **-in-** between first syllable + root word) writes for another
Future: **isusúlat**	(**i-** + duplicated first syllable + root word) will write for another

Example: **sama**	accompany
Infinitive: **isáma**	(**i-** + root word) to take someone along
Imperative: **isáma**	(**i-** + root word) take someone along

Vocabulary List

ihánap (ng) = to have someone look for something
ihúlog (ang) = to let something fall
idagdág (ang) = to add
ihirám (ng) = to borrow for someone else
ilagáy (ang) = to place in or on

Past: **isináma**	(**i-** + infix **-in-** after first letter of root word) took someone along
Present: **isinasáma**	(**i-** + infix **-in-** between first syllable + root word) takes someone along
Future: **isasáma**	(**i-** + duplicated first syllable + root word) will take someone along

Example: **sulat**	write
Infinitive: **ipagsulát**	(**ipag-** + root word) to write for another
Imperative: **ipagsulát**	(**ipag-** + root word) write for another
Past: **ipinagsulát**	(infix **-in-** after first two letters of prefix **ipag-** + root word) wrote for another
Present: **ipinagsusulát**	(infix **-in-** after first two letters of prefix **ipag-** + duplicate first syllable + root word) writes for another
Future: **ipagsusulát**	(**ipag-** + duplicate first syllable + root word) will write for another

II. For verb roots beginning with vowels and the consonants **h**, **l**, **y** and **w**, the prefix **i-** is attached to all forms and tenses, and the infix **-in-** becomes infix **-ni-** that is attached to the past and present tenses

Example: **hanap**	search
Infinitive: **ihánap**	(**i-** + root word) to have someone look for something
Imperative: **ihánap**	(**i-** + root word) have someone look for something
Past: **inihánap**	(**i-** + infix **-ni-** + root word) had someone look for something
Present: **inihahánap**	(**i-** + infix **-ni-** + duplicate first syllable + root word) having someone look for something
Future: **ihahánap**	(**i-** + duplicate first syllable + root word) will have someone look for something

Example: **lutò**	cook
Infinitive: **ilutò**	(**i-** + root word) to cook something
Imperative: **ilutò**	(**i-** + root word) cook something
Past: **inilutò**	(**i-** + infix **-ni-** + root word) cooked something
Present: **inilúlutò**	(**i-** + infix **-ni-** + duplicate first syllable + root word) is cooking something
Future: **iluluto**	(**i-** + duplicate first syllable + root word) will cook something

Sentence Patterns for **I-** Verbs

An **i-** verb is used only when an active **-um-** or **mag-** verb has a direct object in a sentence. This rule in turn dictates which of the direct or indirect object in the **-um-** or **mag-** sentence becomes the subject in the **i-** sentence. Refer to the following sentence patterns of **i-** verbs.

I. FIRST SENTENCE PATTERN

When the **i-** verb has its active form in **-um-**, the indirect object (underlined in the following examples and introduced by the prepositions **sa**, **para sa**, **kay** and **para kay**) becomes the subject (see Lesson Twenty-Seven on these prepositions and indirect objects).

Note that the article **ang** shifted its place from **ang anák** in the first sentence to **ang iná** in the second sentence and made **ang iná** the subject in the passive **i-** sentence. Remember that the article **ang**—along with **si**—introduces the noun that is used as the subject in a sentence (see Lesson Four on these articles).

1. **Bumilí ng isdâ ang babáe <u>para sa kanyáng iná.</u>**   The woman bought fish for her mother.
   Ibinilí ng babáe ng isdâ <u>ang kanyáng iná</u>.

2. **Bumása ng aklát ang gurò <u>para kay Joe.</u>**   The woman bought fish for her mother.
   Ibinása ng gurò ng aklát <u>si Joe</u>.

Because Joe is a name of a person, **si** is used instead of **ang** since **ang** introduces names of places and things.

II. SECOND SENTENCE PATTERN

When the **i-** verb has its active form in **mag-** (or in its variant form **nag-** in the past tense), the direct object (underlined in the following examples) becomes the subject, appropriately introduced by either **si** or **ang**, in the passive **i-** sentence.

1. **Naglutò siyá <u>ng pagkain</u> para sa anák.**   She/He cooked the food for her/his child.
   Inilutò niyá <u>ang pagkain</u> para sa anák.

2. **Nag-áyos <u>ng silíd</u> si Benjamin.**   Benjamin arranged the room.
   Iniáyos ni Benjamin <u>ang silíd</u>.

Note that when a personal pronoun (such as **siyá**) or a name of a person (**si Benjamin**) is used in the **mag-** sentence, the article before the pronoun changes into a possessive pronoun (such as **niyá**) or a possessive pronoun (such as **ni Benjamin**) in the **i-** sentence.

III. THIRD SENTENCE PATTERN

When the **-um-** and **mag-** verbs have similar meanings (refer to Lesson Fourteen on the **-um-** and **mag-** verbs), the **i-** verb follows the first sentence pattern.

Bumása ng aklát ang gurò <u>para sa batà.</u>   The teacher read the book to the child.
Nagbasá ng aklát ang gurò <u>para sa batà</u>.
Ibinása ng aklát ng gurò <u>ang batà</u>.

EXAMPLES OF i- VERBS

In the list of i- verbs below, the articles in the parentheses should be used to introduce the receiver of the action in the i- sentence. The first four i- verbs require a subject introduced by **si** or **ang** whereas the remaining i- verbs require a subject introduced by **ni** or **ng**.

ihánap	**(ng)**	to have someone look for something
ibilí	**(ng)**	to have someone buy something
ibása	**(ng)**	to read for another
ihirám	**(ng)**	to borrow for someone else
isúlat	**(ng)**	to write for another
ilutò	**(ang)**	to cook
iturò	**(ang)**	to teach
ihúlog	**(ang)**	to let something fall
itápon	**(ang)**	to throw away
ibigáy	**(ang)**	to give something to someone
iwalâ	**(ang)**	to lose
idagdág	**(ang)**	to add
ibalità	**(ang)**	to give information
ilagáy	**(ang)**	to place
ibilád	**(ang)**	to place under the sun

Sample Sentences

Ihahánap ko siyá ng bagong aklát.	I shall look for a new book for him/her.
Ilutò mo ang isdâ ngayong gabí.	You cook the fish tonight.
Ibigáy mo sa ákin ang páhayagan.	Give me the newspaper.
Iniwalâ ni Peter ang áking bóla.	Was lost by Peter my ball. (literal)
	Peter lost my ball.
Ihuhúlog ko ang sulat sa koreo.	I will drop the letter at the Post Office.
Itinuturò niyá sa ámin ang wíkang Tagálog.	She/He is teaching us the Tagalog language.
Ibinilí ako ng baró ng áking iná.	Bought for me a dress by my mother. (literal)
	My mother bought a dress for me.
Ibíbilád ko ang sapátos.	Will put under the sun by me the shoes. (literal)
	I shall put the shoes under the sun.
Itátaním ng áming katúlong ang ságing.	Will be planted by our helper the banana tree. (literal)
	Our helper will plant the banana.
Itinápon niyá ang lúmang tinápay.	Thrown away by him/her the stale bread. (literal)
	He threw away the stale bread.

COMMON ERRORS WITH **I**- VERBS

Note the following non-existent words in the Tagalog vocabulary and their correct derivatives:

balitain   from **balità**   but there is **ibalità**   = to relay or give out news
hulugin   from **húlog**   but there is **ihúlog**   = to let something fall or drop
tanimin   from **taním**   but there is **itaním**   = to plant
punasin   from **púnas**   but there is **ipúnas**   = to use something to wipe with
turuin   from **turò**   but there is **iturò**   = to teach
tapunin   from **tápon**   but there is **itápon**   = to throw away
walain   from **walâ**   but there is **iwalâ**   = to lose
balikin   from **balík**   but there is **ibalík**   = to return
bukasin   from **búkas**   but there is **ibukás**   = to cause to open
sarahin   from **sará**   but there is **isará**   = to shut

Thus, the past forms of the verbs above

are: and not:
ibinalità   **binalita**
inihúlog   **hinulog**
itinaním   **tinanim**
ipinúnas   **pinunas**
iturò   **tinuro**
itinápon   **tinapon**
iniwalâ   **niwala**
ibinalík   **binalik**
ibinukás   **binukas**
isinará   **sinara**

Exercises

Pick out the **i**- verb forms from the following sentences and translate the sentences into Tagalog.

1. _____   Peter lost his ball.

2. _____   Cook the meat for us.

3. _____   He returned the book to the library.

4. _____   Open the door.

5. _____   He closed the windows.

6. _____   She taught me Tagalog at the Philippine Women's University.

7. _____   I shall buy a dress for my child.

8. _____   He gave me a pretty flower.

9. _____   Get some food for the old man.

10. _____   The woman planted the tree in the garden.

Create your own sentences using the other **i-** verbs in the previous page.

Change the **i-** sentences above into their active forms using **mag-** or **-um-** verbs based on the three sentence patterns. The subjects of the **i-** sentences will now become the direct or indirect objects of the **mag-** or **-um-** sentences.

Try to repeat orally the different tense forms of as many **i-** verbs as possible.

-An Verb Forms

When the suffix **-an** is attached to a word, the **-an** word that is created then represents a place associated with the root word such as **aklátan** (root word is **aklát** or *book*, thus **aklátan** is a *library*) or **gúpítan** (**gupít** is *to cut*, **gúpítan** is *a place where they cut* or a *barber shop* or *beauty salon*).

The **-an** word forms may also express action in the passive form similar to the **-in** verb (**sulatan** is *to write* or the *act of writing* from the root **sulat** or *writing*). It is also used to indicate a description of size (**damihan** is *to increase the number* from the root **dami** or *many*) and quality (**putikan** is *muddy* from the root **putik** or *mud*).

Note that this lesson will focus on the formation of **-an** words rather than on the context of the words in the **-an** sentences.

Forming **-An** Words

The suffix **-an** is attached to roots ending in consonants as well as roots that end in vowels and pronounced with a glottal catch (such as **hingî** or *to request*). On the other hand, its variant form **-han** is attached as a suffix to roots that end in vowels and pronounced without a glottal catch (such as **sama** or *to accompany*). Derivatives of **-an** verbs are formed in the following manner:

I. FOR VERB ROOTS ENDING IN CONSONANTS
   Example: **alís**   remove
   Infinitive: **alisán**   (root word + **-an**) to remove something from someone
   Imperative: **alisán**   (root word + **-an**) remove something from someone
   Past: **inalisán**   (prefix **in-** + root word + **-an**) was/were removed
   Present: **ináalisán**   (prefix **in-** + duplicate first syllable + root word + **-an**) is/are being removed
   Future: **áalisán**   (duplicate first syllable + root word + **-an**) will be removed

II. FOR VERB ROOTS ENDING IN VOWELS
   Example: **basa**   read
   Infinitive: **basáhan**   (root word + **-han**) to read to someone
   Imperative: **basáhan**   (root word + **-han**) Read to someone
   Past: **bínasáhan**   (infix **-in-** after first letter of first syllable + **-han**) was/were read to someone
   Present: **binábasahan**   (infix **-in-** after first letter of first syllable + root word + **-han**) is/are being read to someone
   Future: **bábasahan**   (duplicate first syllable + root word + **-han**) will be read to someone

Vocabulary List

kuwento = story	**pakinggán** = to listen	**tawánan** - to laugh at
anyayáhan = to invite	**halikán** = to kiss	**mukhâ** = face
hingán = to ask	**hugásan** = to wash	

III. FOR IRREGULAR VERB ROOTS

Example: **lagay**   put

Infinitive: **lagyán**   (root word without the last vowel + **-an**) to put in something

Imperative: **lagyán**   (root word without the last vowel + **-an**) put in something

Past: **nilagyán**   (**ni-** + root word without the last vowel + **-an**) (Note that with the consonants **l**, **w** and **y**, the infix **-in-** becomes the prefix **ni-**, see irregular verb formations using **in-** in Lesson Fifteen) was/were put in

Present: **nilálagyán**   (**ni-** + duplicate first syllable + root word without the last vowel + **-an**) is/are being put in

Future: **lálagyán**   (duplicate first syllable + root word without the last vowel + **-an**) will be put in

EXAMPLES OF REGULAR -AN VERBS

bawásan	to diminish or reduce	**anyayáhan**	to invite someone
butásan	to bore a hole	**ayawán**	to be refused
bantayán	to watch	**upáhan**	to rent
halikán	to kiss	**sulátan**	to write to
damitán	to dress up someone	**upuán**	to seat on
bayáran	to pay	**bihísan**	to change someone's dress
sabúgan	to scatter	**samáhan**	to accompany
abután	to hand someone something	**hugásan**	to wash (not referring to clothes)
alagáan	to care for		

EXAMPLES OF IRREGULAR -AN VERBS

In forming the derivatives of irregular **an-** verbs, the second vowel of the root word is dropped. What should have been the regular derivatives of the verbs are enclosed in parentheses below. There are also other changes in forming the derivatives of irregular verbs as seen in the last example (**hipan**) where the second syllable (**hi**) is deleted altogether.

labhán	(**labahan**)	to wash (clothes)
lagyán	(**lagayan**)	to put in something
sundán	(**sunuran**)	to follow someone
lakhán	(**lakihan**)	to enlarge something
bigyán	(**bigayan**)	to give someone something
tamnán	(**taniman**)	to have a place planted with
takpán	(**takipan**)	to cover
hingán	(**hingian**)	to ask someone for something
asnán	(**asinan**)	to mix with salt
tirhán	(**tirahan**)	to leave remains for someone
tingnán	(**tinginan**)	to look at
higán	(**higaan**)	to lie down on something
sakyán	(**sakayan**)	to go aboard
saktán	(**sakitan**)	to hurt
buksán	(**bukasan**)	to open
tawánan	(**tawahan**)	to laugh at

kúnan	(**kuhanan**)	to take from
dalhán	(**dalahan**)	to bring someone something
bilhán	(**bilihan**)	to buy from
hipan	(**hihipan**)	to blow into or on something (from the root **hihip**, which means blow)

Sentence Patterns for **-An** Verbs

To change **-um-** or **mag-** sentences into **-an** sentences, take note of the following guidelines:

I. WITHOUT A DIRECT OBJECT

For an **-um-** or **mag-** sentence without a direct object, the indirect object introduced by the any of the prepositions **para kay**, **kay**, **para sa** and **sa** or the place introduced by **sa** becomes the subject in the **-an** sentence. The doer of the act, on the other hand, is then preceded by a possessive article (either **ni** or **ng**) in the **-an** sentence.

1. **Su<u>múlat</u>**   **ang batà**   <u>**sa aklát.**</u>
                (doer)   (place)

   Sinulá<u>tan</u>   **ng batà**   <u>**ang aklát.**</u>
                (doer)   (subject)

   The child wrote on the book.

2. **Magbasá**   **ka**   **sa ákin.**
                (doer)   (indirect object)

   Basáhan   **mo**   **akó.**
               (doer)   (subject)

   You read to me.

Note that the indirect object **sa ákin** in the **mag-** sentence above becomes the subject **ako** in the **-an** sentence (see Lesson Six on personal and demonstrative pronouns).

II. WITH A DIRECT OBJECT

In an **-um-** or **mag-** sentence with a direct object (the noun or pronoun that receives the action of the **-um-** or **mag-** verb), the object shall be preceded by the possessive article **ng** in the **-an** sentence.

As to the indirect object and the doer of the act in the **-um-** or **mag-** sentence, apply the preceding rule.

1. **Sumúlat**   **ang batà**   <u>**ng pangalan** niyá</u>   **sa aklát.**
               (doer)   (direct object)   (place)

   Sinulá<u>tan</u>   **ng batà**   **ng pangalan niyá**   **ang aklát.**
              (doer)   (direct object)   (subject)

   The child wrote his name on the book.

2. **Magbasá**   ka   **ng kuwento**   sa ákin.
                    (doer)   (direct object)   (indirect object)

   Basá<u>han</u>   mo   ako   **ng kuwento**.
                    (doer)   (subject)   (direct object)

   You read to me a story.

III. WITHOUT **-IN-** VERBS

When an **-um-** or **mag-** verb has no **-in-** form, the direct object becomes the subject in the **-an** sentence.

Magbukás   ka   ng pintô.
                  (doer)   (direct object)

Buksán   mo   ang pintô.
                  (doer)   (subject)

Open the door.

Sample Sentences

Lagyán mo ng álak ang báso.   Fill the glass with wine.

Sundán ninyó ang itinuturò ko.   Follow what I am teaching.

Pakinggán ninyó ako. (a **pa-** + **-an** verb)   Listen to me.

Buksán mo ang bintanà.   Open the window.

Súsulatan ko ang áking iná.   I will write to my mother.

Bayáran mo ang iyóng útang sa ákin. Pay your debt to me.

Inalisán ng babáe ng pagkain ang anák.
Removed by the woman the food from her child. (literal)
The woman removed the food from her child.

Hinalikán ng batà ang kamáy ng kanyáng lóla.
Was kissed by the child the hand of her grandmother. (literal)
The child kissed the hand of her grandmother.

Bábasahán ko ng magandáng kuwento ang áking amá.
Will be read by me a nice story for my father. (literal)
I will read a nice story to my father.

Nilabhán ng katúlong ko ang áming damít.
Were washed by my helper our clothes. (literal)
My helper washed our clothes.

Exercises

Identify the subjects in the ten passive sample sentences in the previous page: is the subject an indirect object or a place? Then change the sentences into their active forms.

Example:
Passive	**Inalisán ng babáe ng pagkain ang anák.**
Subject	**anak** (indirect object)
Active	**Nag-alís ang babáe ng pagkain sa anák.**

Form the derivatives of all regular and irregular **-an** verbs in this lesson.

Change the following active sentences into passive sentences using both **i-** and **-an** verbs.

1. **Bumása ang batà ng páhayagan sa kanyáng lóla.**
   The child read the newspaper to her grandmother.

2. **Naglutò ang babáe ng isdâ sa kawalí.**
   The woman cooked the fish in the pan.

3. **Nagbáyad siyá ng dalawáng libong piso sa ákin para sa sapatos.**
   He paid me two thousand pesos for the shoes.

4. **Maglálagay siyá ng tubig sa mga baso.**
   She/He will put water into the glasses.

5. **Magtakíp ka ng panyô sa mukhâ.**
   Cover your face with a handkerchief.

Adverbs

Some words depict actions: **tumalón, gumulong, lumuhá** (*jump, roll, cry*). Other words describe how the action was done: **tumalón nang mataás, gumulong nang pababâ, lumuhá nang malakás** (*jumps high, rolled down, cried loudly*). In this lesson, one will learn about adverbs, which modify action words by describing how, where and when an action has happened, happens or will happen.

I. ADVERBS OF MANNER

An adverb modifies how an action occurred, occurs or will occur. Generally, the article **nang** introduces this kind of adverb that is formed by attaching the prefix **pa-** to a verb root.

When translated into English, the combination of "**nang** + **pa-** + verb root" produces *-ing* verbs that resemble a participle such as the words *sitting* and *standing*. However, a **pa**-prefixed Tagalog word modifies verbs whereas a participle modifies nouns or pronouns.

Examples of adverbs of manner are the following:

1. **paupô** = *sitting down*
   patayô = *standing*
   pahigâ = *lying down*

   Ang batà ay nagbasá nang paupô.   The child read sitting down.
   Ang batà ay nagbasá nang patayô.   The child read standing.
   Ang batà ay nagbasá nang pahigâ.   The child read lying down.

2. **ganitó** = *like this* (near the speaker)
   ganyán = *like that* (near the one spoken to)
   ganoón = *like that* (far from both)

   Ganitó siyá kung lumákad.
   She is like this when she walks. (literal)
   She walks like this.

3. **mabilís** = *fast*
   Si Peter ay kumakáin nang mabilís.   Peter is eating fast.

Vocabulary List

paupô = sitting down	**sandalî** = for a while	**sa labás** = outside
biglâ, agâd = suddenly	**dáhan-dáhan** = slowly	**marami** = many, much

4. **dáhan-dáhan** = *slowly; softly*
   Lumálákad siya nang dáhan-dáhan.   She walks slowly.
   Dáhan-dáhan siyang lumálákad.   She walks slowly.
   Dáhan-dáhan si Dulce na lumálákad.   Dulce walks slowly.

Adverbs of manner may be placed before or after verbs as shown in the examples above. But when the adverb comes before the verb and the subject is a name of a person (see last example), use the ligature **na** (similar examples can be found in Lesson Twenty-Three) after the subject **Dulce**. As for the second example, use the ligature **-ng** after the subject **siya**. However, **nang** is lost in the second structure where the adverb is placed before the verb.

5. **biglâ**, **agâd** = *suddenly; at once*

   Siyá ay tumayó nang biglâ.
   Siyá ay tumayóng biglâ. (or **biglâng tumayó**)

   Siyá ay agâd na tumayó. (or **agad tumayó**)   He/She stood up suddenly.
   Siyá ay tumayó agâd.

The sequence "verb + **nang** + adverb" (**tumayó nang biglâ**) may be appropriately replaced with the sequence "verb + ligature **-ng**, **-g** or **na** + adverb" (**tumayóng biglâ**) or the sequence "adverb + ligature **-ng**, **-g** or **na** + verb" (**biglâng tumayó**) as the arrangement will not affect the meaning of the sentence. Similarly, in the case of the second set of sentences above where the ligature **na** is deleted, the meaning of the statement does not change.

II. ADVERBS OF PLACE

Similarly, adverbs describe where an action took place, is taking place or will take place. Note that all phrases with the preposition **sa** before a name of a place, either specific or general, are adverbs of place. Examples are **sa baryo** (in the barrio or village), **sa kusinà** (in the kitchen), and **sa eskuwelahán** (in school).
   Other adverbs of place include the following:

1. **díto** = *here* (near the speaker)
   díyan = *there* (near the listener)
   doón = *there* (far from both speaker and listener)

   Naglalaro ang aking kapatid na lalaki dito.   My brother plays here.

2. **saanmán** = *wherever*
   Saanmán siyá pumuntá, sásama ako.   Wherever she goes, I shall go with her.
   Saán ka man pumuntá, sásama ako.   Wherever you go, I shall go with you.

The adverb **saanmán** is only broken up when the shortened pronoun **ka** (the singular *you*) is the subject in the sentence. All other pronouns in the Tagalog language come after **saanmán**.

3. **sa loób** = *inside*
   sa labás = *outside*

   Naglalaro ang mga bata sa loób.
   The children are playing inside (the home).

4. **búhat** = *from*
   magbúhat = *from*
   mulâ = *from*
   búhat sa ... hanggáng = *from ... to*

Kamí ay lumakad búhat (mulâ) sa baryo.
We walked from the barrio.

Kamí ay lumakad búhat sa baryo hanggáng sa lungsód.
We walked from the barrio to the city.

III. ADVERBS OF TIME

There is a considerable number of adverbs of time which Tagalogs use. Some are monosyllabic words (introduced in Lesson Ten) while others are phrases.

Because the preposition **sa** is such a versatile word (see Lesson Twenty-Six), it is also used to indicate adverbs of time when it is placed before hours, days, months and years such as **sa Lunés** (*on Monday*), **sa hapon** (*in the afternoon*) and **sa Márso** (*in March*).

Other adverbs of time include the following:

1. **na** = *already*
   Siyá ay umalís na.   He left already.

2. **pa** = *yet, more*
   Hindî pa ako kumákain.   I have not eaten yet.
   Gustó ko pa ng matamís.   I like more sweets.

3. **nang**, **noóng** = *when*
   Nagálit siyá nang umalís ako.   He/She got angry when I left.

Noóng followed by date (hours, days, months or years) also means *last*. Thus, **noóng Lunés** means last Monday.

   Natapos niyá ang kolehiyó noóng Márso.   He/She finished college last March.

4. **sandalî** = *for a while*
   Halika sandalî.   Come here for a while.

5. **pagkatapos** (+ infinitive verb) = *after*
   Tayo ay matulog pagkatapos kumáin.   Let us sleep after eating.

6. **bágo** (+ infinitive verb) = *before*
   Kumain siyá bágo umalís.   He/She ate before he/she left.

7. **pirmí**, **paráti**, **lagí** = *always*
   Paráting nag-aáral si Peter.   Peter always studies.

8. **tuwî** (+ ligature **-ng** + date) = *every*
   Tuwíng Lúnes, siyá ay tinátamad.   Every Monday, she feels lazy.

9. **saká na** = *later*
   Saká na tayó mag-úsap.   Let us talk later.

10. **búhat noón...hanggáng** = *from...until; since*
    Búhat noóng Lúnes hanggáng ngayón ay walâ pa siyá.
    From Monday until now he has not been here.
    Since Monday, he has not been here.

11. **kung mínsan** = *sometimes* (use with the present tense of verbs)
    Kung mínsan, nagagálit siyá.   Sometimes she gets angry.

12. **bihirá** = *seldom*
    Bihiráng maglarô si Mary.   Mary seldom plays.

13. **samantála, habang** = *meanwhile, while* (use with the present tense of verbs)
Samantála, tamà na ang isang libong piso para sa iyo.

Meanwhile, a thousand pesos is enough for you.

Samantálang / habang nagsasalitâ siyá, ako'y nakikinig.

While he is talking, I am listening.

14. **hábang-panahón** = *forever*
Silá ay magigíng magkaíbígan hábang-panahón.

They will be friends forever.

15. **sa tanáng búhay ko** = *in my whole life*
Hindî pa ako naglálakbáy sa tanáng búhay ko.

I have never travelled in my whole life.

16. **sa ibáng áraw**; **sa ibáng oras** = *some other day, some other time*
Sa ibáng áraw na kamí dádalaw sa iyó.

We shall visit you some other day.

IV. ADVERBS OF QUANTITY

Adverbs can also describe the scale of an action. Some examples of these adverbs are:

1. **marámi** = *many; much*
   Maráming kinain si Tom.   Tom eats much.
   Malakás kumain si Tom. (colloquial)

2. **kauntî** (shortened to **kontî**) = *little*
   Kauntî lamang ang sinabi niyá.   He just said a little.

   Nagbigáy ng kontíng pagkain ang batàng maramot.
   The stingy child gave a little amount of food.

3. **walâ** = *none; nothing*
   Waláng kinákain ang sanggól na may sakít.   The sick infant eats nothing.
   Walâ akóng gustó.   I like nothing.

Exercises

Complete the sentences below by adding five possible adverbs of manner then translate the sentences into English.

1. **Ang batà ay kumakáin nang** _____.

   _____.

   _____.

   _____.

   _____.

2. **Ang matandáng laláki ay lumalákad nang** _____.

   _____.

   _____.

   _____.

   _____.

3. **Si Mary ay umáwit nang** _____.

   _____.

   _____.

   _____.

   _____.

Write sentences using these words and others of their kind.

Write a composition describing a party, a picnic or a trip you had in the past. Put a modifier to all the action words you use. Underline the modifiers.

Conjunctions and Interjections

Conjunctions and interjections are very important. Conjunctions join together two clauses, phrases or words to show a relationship between them whereas interjections are added to a sentence to express a particular emotion.

I. CONJUNCTIONS

Conjunctions join individual words, phrases and clauses, and show the relationship between them by pointing out that a thought—expressed in the word, phrase or clause—is less important than or as important as the other one. The most common example of a Tagalog conjunction is the word **at** which means *and* in English. Following are the meanings and examples of **at** and other Tagalog conjunctions:

1. **at** = *and* (may be shortened to **'t** when the first word ends in a vowel)
   Nagsúsulat siyá, gabí at áraw.   He writes night and day.
   Nagsúsulat siyá, gabi't áraw.

2. **o** = *or*
   Akó ba o siyá ang ibig mo?   Do you like me or him/her?

3. **péro, nguni't, datapuwa't, subali't** (last two conjunctions are not to be used in ordinary conversation) = *but*
   Ibig kong umalís péro umúulan.   I like to leave but it is raining.
   Akó'y matabâ nguni't siyá'y payát.   I am fat but he/she is thin.

4. **kung** = *if* (synonymous to **pag**)
   Aalís áko kung sásama ka.   I will leave, if you are coming along.
   Kung umulán, hindî áko lálakad.   If it rains, I shall not go.
   Pag umulán, hindî áko lálakad.

5. **samantalá, habang** = *meanwhile, while* (use with the present tense of verbs)
   Táyo ay umáwit samantaláng naghihintáy sa kanilá.
   Let us sing while waiting for them.

Vocabulary List

naghihintáy = waiting   **pagdiríwang** = celebration
sáyang = what a pity   **búnga** = fruit

Samantaláng natútúlog ang sanggól, akó'y maglalabá.
While the baby sleeps, I shall do the laundry.

6. **nang** = *in order that, so that, so*
   Huwág kang maingay nang áko'y makatúlog. Do not be noisy so I can sleep.
   Kumáin ka nang hindî ka magútom.   You eat so that you'll not go hungry.

7. **kung hindî** (shortened to **kundî**) = *except, but (*literally, *if not)*
   Waláng naparíto kundî si Mary.   Nobody came except Mary.
   Síno ang tútulong sa ákin kundí ikáw?   Who will help me but you?

8. **dáhil sa** = *because of*
   Dáhil sa iyó, áko ay dádalo sa pagdiríwang.   Because of you, I shall attend the celebration.
   Umiyák siyá dáhil sa ákin.   He cried because of me.

9. **sapagká't, mangyári** = *because* (used to answer the question **bakit** or *why*)
   Bakit ka ba malungkót?   Why are you sad?
   Mangyári áko'y may sakít.   Because I am sick.
   Sapagká't áko'y may sakít.

10. **samakatuwíd / samakatwíd** = *therefore*
    Hindî ka mabaít, samakatuwíd, ayoko sa iyó.   You are not nice, therefore, I do not like you.
    Samakatwíd, áyaw mong mag-áral?   Therefore, you do not like to study?

11. **kung anó ... siyá rin** = *as ... so is ...; like ... like ...*
    Kung anó ang amá ay siyá ring anák.   Like father, like son.
    Kung anó ang punò ay siyá ring búnga. As the tree is, so is the fruit.

12. **at sa wakás** = *finally, at last*
    At sa wakás, pagpaláin kayó ng Diyós.   Finally, may God bless you.

II. INTERJECTIONS

Emotions are expressed in Tagalog sentences by using an interjection such as **nakú** followed by an exclamation mark. A shortened term for **Ináy ko pô!** (*Oh my mother!*), **nakú** expresses surprise, amazement ot disbelief. There are other Tagalog interjections of this type, two of which reflect the Tagalog's Spanish heritage of faith such as **Susmaryosep!** (shortened form of the names Jesus, Maria y Jose or *Jesus*, *Mary* and *Joseph*) and **Sus!** (shortened form of *Jesus*).

An interjection is not related to or dependent on any other part of the sentence. It can stand alone or may be added to a sentence. It is common in conversations but not in formal writing.

Some common examples of Tagalog interjections, including **nakú**, are the following. Note where they are usually placed:

1. **Ay!**   = expresses despair   **Ay! Ang hírap ng búhay.**
What a hard life!

2. **Abá!**   = expresses surprise   **Abá! Kailán ka dumatíng?**
When did you arrive?

3. **Aráy!**   = expresses pain   **Aráy! Masakít ang ulo ko.**
My head is aching!

4. **Nakú!**   = expresses surprise   **Nakú! Ang gandá ng báhay mo!**
Your house is beautiful!

    = expresses disbelief   **Nakú! Totoó ba?**
Is it true?

5. **Sáyang!**   = expresses pity   **Nawalâ ang pera ko. Sáyang!**
Sáyang! Nawalâ ang pera ko.
My money was lost. What a pity!

6. **Mabúhay!**   = expresses welcome   **Mabúhay!**
(a welcome greeting to foreign visitors)

    = expresses adoration   **Mabúhay si Pacquiao** (a Filipino boxing champion)!
Long live Pacquiao!

Magpa- and Pa- + -In Verb Forms

The affixes **magpa-** and **pa-** + **-in** are used to fom verbs that express an order to be done to the subject of the verb (such as **magpápakáin sa mga bisita**, which means *will feed (food to) visitors* or **pinakain ang mga bisita** which means *visitors were fed*). While **magpa-** verbs are active, **pa-** + **-in** and its variant **pa-** + **-an** verbs are passive. Both of these verbs differ from the passive **i-** verbs which express actions done for someone. **Magpa-** and **pa-** + **-in** verbs suggest that someone is giving orders to have something done to another.

Forming Magpa- and Pa- + -In Derivatives

The derivatives of **magpa-** and **pa-** + **-in** verbs are formed differently. In addition, **pa-** + **-in** verbs make use of the **-hin** suffix when the roots end in vowels.

I. FOR VERB ROOTS ENDING IN CONSONANTS

1. Active **magpa-** verbs

Example: **kain**	eat
Infinitive: **magpakáin**	(**magpa-** + root word) to feed someone
Imperative: **magpakáin**	(**magpa-** + root word) Feed someone.
Past: **nagpakáin**	(**magpa-** becomes **nagpa-** + root word) fed someone
Present: **nagpápakáin**	(**magpa-** becomes **nagpa-** + duplicated second syllable of prefix + root word) feeds someone
Future: **magpápakáin**	(**magpa-** + duplicated second syllable of prefix + root word) will feed someone
Verbal Noun: **pagpapakáin**	(**magpa-** becomes **pagpa-** + duplicated second syllable of prefix + root word) feeding someone

Lesson Thirty-One discusses the forming of nouns by adding appropriate articles before the verbs and adjectives. The same may be done on both **magpa-** and **pa-** + **-in** derivatives whose verbal nouns become quite similar to the English gerund phrase wherein the verb ends in an *-ing* (for example, *Feeding someone makes him happy*).

Vocabulary List

magpakáin = to feed someone
magpabása = to order someone to read

mahihírap na táo = poor people
buhók = hair

2. Passive **pa-** + **-in** verbs

Example: **kain**		eat
Infinitive: **pakaínin**	(prefix **pa-** + root word + suffix **-in**) to feed someone	
Imperative: **pakaínin**	(prefix **pa-** + root word + suffix **-in**) Feed someone.	
Past: **pinakáin**	(infix **-in-** between first and second letters of prefix **pa-** + root word) was/were fed	
Present: **pinakákain**	(infix **-in-** between first and second letters of prefix **pa-** + duplicated first syllable of root word + root word) is/are fed	
Future: **pakákainin**	(prefix **pa-** + duplicated first syllable of root word + root word + suffix **-in**) will be fed	
Verbal Noun: **pagpapakáin**	(prefix **pa-** becomes **pagpa-** + duplicated second syllable of prefix + root word) feeding someone	

II. FOR VERB ROOTS ENDING IN VOWELS

1. Active **magpa-** verbs

Example: **basa**	read
Infinitive: **magpabása**	(**magpa-** + root word) to have someone read
Imperative: **magpabása**	(**magpa-** + root word) have someone read
Past: **nagpabása**	(**magpa-** becomes **nagpa-** + root word) had someone read
Present: **nagpápabasa**	(**magpa-** becomes **nagpa-** + duplicated second syllable of prefix + root word) have someone read
Future: **magpápabasa**	(**magpa-** + duplicated second syllable of prefix + root word) will have someone read
Verbal Noun: **pagpápabása**	(**magpa-** becomes **pagpa-** + duplicated second syllable of prefix + root word) having someone read

2. Passive **pa-** + **-in** verbs

Example: **basa**	read
Infinitive: **pabasáhin**	(prefix **pa-** + root word + suffix **-hin**) to order someone to read
Imperative: **pabasáhin**	(prefix **pa-** + root word + suffix **-hin**) order someone to read
Past: **pinabása**	(infix **-in-** between first and second letters of prefix **pa-** + root word) made someone read
Present: **pinabábasa**	(infix **-in-** between first and second letters of prefix **pa-** + duplicated first syllable of root word + root word) making someone read
Future: **pabábasahin**	(prefix **pa-** + duplicated first syllable of root word + root word + suffix **-hin**) will make someone read
Verbal Noun: **pagpápabása**	(prefix **pagpa-** + duplicated second syllable of prefix + root word) having someone read

Sample Sentences

Nagpápabasa silá sa mga páaralán ng mga aklát ni Rizal.
They order to be read in schools the books of Rizal. (literal)
They order the books of Rizal read in schools.

Pinabábasa sa mga páaralán ang mga aklát ni Rizal.
Are ordered read in schools the books of Rizal. (literal)
The books of Rizal are ordered read in schools.

Nagpakáin kamí ng mahihírap na táo.
Were fed by us the poor people. (literal)
We fed the poor.

Pinakáin namín ang mahihírap na táo.
Gave food by us the poor people. (literal)
The poor people were fed by us.

Although the translation of the above sentences are similar, the first sentence emphasizes the giving of food by the subject (**namín**) while the second sentence emphasizes the receiver (**mahihírap na táo**) of the action.

Nagpagupít siyá ng (kanyáng) buhók.
He/She ordered his/her hair cut. (literal)
He/She had a haircut.

Pinagupit niyá ang kanyáng buhók.
Had cut his/her hair. (literal)
He/She had a haircut.

Exercises

Change the following into passive sentences then translate into English.

1. **Ang áking katúlong ay nagpakáin ng batà.**
2. **Nagpápabasa ang aming gurò ng páhayagan áraw-áraw.**
3. **Nagpalínis ako ng silíd sa páaralán sa mga batà.**
4. **Nagpápagamót ng sakít ang matandáng babáe sa doktór.**
5. **Nagpaalís ng mga batà sa kanyáng hardín ang matandáng laláki.**

Change the following into active sentences then translate into English.

1. **Pinakuha ko ang aklát sa batà sa aklátan.**
2. **Pasusulatin ng iná ang kanyáng anák.**
3. **Pinaaayos ko ang áking silíd sa áming katúlong.**
4. **Pakukunin ko ng pera sa bangko ang áking asawa.**
5. **Pinakáin ko ang batà.**

Give ten other **magpa-** and **pa-** + **-in** verbs and use them in sentences.

Expressing Disagreement, Agreement or Doubt

As one person differs from another in terms of his or her beliefs and orientation, expressing disagreement and agreement on the convictions or statements of one another—as well as casting doubt on another's abilities or statements—is an important part of his human nature. To convey such differences or similarity in opinions using the Tagalog language, one must learn how to use the following words. Observe that most of these words can stand alone as a response or expression.

I. EXPRESSING DISAGREEMENT

1. **Hindî** (shortened to **'dî**) = *no*

The word **hindî** is the most common negative answer to a question except one that starts with **may** or **mayroón**. The negative answer to questions like **May aklát ba kayó?** (Do you have a book?) or **Mayroón ba siyáng asawa?** (Does he have a wife?) is **walâ** (or *none*) and not **hindî** (see Lesson Twelve). The following questions though may be answered by **hindî**:

Aalís ba tayó?	Are we leaving?
Hindî tayó aalís. (or **Hindî.**)	No, we are not leaving. (No.)
Ikáw ba si Jane?	Are you Jane?
Hindî, ako si Barbara. (or **Hindî.**)	No, I am Barbara. (No.)

The word **hindî** may be paired with monosyllabic words such as **pa** or **na** (for emphasis) or may be included in a sentence.

On the other hand, a word may be expressed in the negative or may take on a meaning contrary to its original definition in two ways. One is to simply place **hindî** before the word, which may be a verb, an adverb, a pronoun, a noun or a substantive (the technical term for a word or group of words that acts as a noun). The other is to affix the shortened form of **dî** or **di-** as a prefix. Observe the following sentences:

Ang batà ay hindî mabaít.	The child is not good.
Ang batà ay dî mabaít.	(with an end glottal catch on **dî** and an end stress on **mabaít**)
Ang batà ay di-mabaít.	(hyphen between **dî** and **mabaít,** and with an end stress on **mabaít** only)

Vocabulary List

madalás = often	**dilím** = dark
magpasyál = to take a walk	**totoó** = true

2. **Huwág** = *do not, not to, not*

The word **huwág** simply means *Don't!* In other cases, it may mean *Stop!* It can be said at anytime when one wants to put a stop to something one dislikes or to warn others not to do something.

Gustó mong paluin kitá?	Do you want me to beat you?
Huwág!	Don't!

Huwág may either stand alone as a negative response or be a part of a sentence. When a sentence containing **huwág** uses an active verb (such as an **-um-**, **mag-**, **ma-** and **magpa-** derivative), a personal pronoun like **ka**, **kayó** or **táyo** is required. On the other hand, when the sentence uses a passive verb (such as an **-in**, **i-** or **-an** derivative), it needs a possessive pronoun like **mo** or **nátin**.

ACTIVE

Huwág kang <u>um</u>alís.	Don't leave.
Huwág kayóng <u>bum</u>ása sa dilím.	Don't read in the dark.
Huwág tayóng <u>ma</u>tulog.	Let us not sleep.
Huwág kang <u>magpa</u>ulán.	Don't get caught in the rain.

PASSIVE

Huwág mong kan<u>in</u> iyán.	Don't eat that.
Huwág mong basa<u>han</u> ng sulat si Ate.	Don't read my letter to Ate.
Huwág nátin <u>i</u>bilí ng kendi si Jun.	Let us not buy candy for Jun.

Huwág also goes with the infinitive form or the future tense of a verb in a sentence that expresses a command or request.

Huwág kang <u>ma</u>ligò ngayón. (command, infinitive)
Do not take a bath now.

Huwág mong baba<u>sa</u>han ang batà bukas. (command, future)
Do not read to the child tomorrow

Huwág kayóng makikain nang madalás. (request, infinitive)
Don't eat often.

Huwág táyong makikigaya sa kanilá. (request, future)
Let us not imitate them.

3. **Ayaw** = *to dislike, do not like*

The opposite of the pseudo-verb **gustó** (*to like*) or **ibig** (*to like*) is **ayaw**, which is a verb root and expresses dislike of someone or something.

It may either be active as in **umayáw** or passive as in **ayawán**. Thus, similar to **huwag**, **ayaw** in its active form needs a personal pronoun and, in its passive form, needs a possessive pronoun. **Ayaw** also goes with the infinitive form of a verb.

ACTIVE

Ayókong (ayaw ako) kumain.	I don't like to eat.
Ayaw siyáng magsalitâ.	He does not like to talk.
Ayaw siláng lumakad.	They do not like to go.
Ayaw ba kayóng magpasyál?	Don't you like to take a walk?

PASSIVE

Ayaw kong kumain.	I don't like to eat.
Ayaw niyáng magsalitâ.	He does not like to talk.
Ayaw niláng lumakad.	They do not like to go.
Ayaw ba ninyóng magpasyál?	Don't you like to take a walk?

II. EXPRESSING AGREEMENT

1. **Oô** = yes (**opô/ohô** is a polite *yes*, equivalent to *yes, sir/ma'am*)

As discussed in Lesson Three, **opô** and **ohô** (*yes, sir/ma'am*) should pepper the sentences and questions of younger people to express respect for older people or persons with honorific titles or authority (regardless of age). The words reflect the speaker's good manners and his respect to the one spoken to.

Reserve **oô** as a response to people within one's age and status.

2. **Siyangâ** = *that is right, that is true*

Siyangâ is an idiomatic expression. Do not confuse with **siyangâ** nor with the personal pronoun **siyá** (*he/she*). Otherwise, this would give an altogether different meaning of *It is him/her indeed*.

Use **siyangâ** when you are in total agreement with another person's statement or when you want someone to confirm an information you heard from another source.

Siyangâ, mabait siyá.	That's right, he/she is good.
Siyangâ ba? Aalís kayó?	Is it true? Are you leaving?

3. **Totoó** = *true, indeed, truly*

The word **totoó**, as a one-word affirmative response, confirms an information. It may be the answer to either a **totoó** or **siyangâ** question (**Totoó? Siyangâ?**) and may even take the place of **oô** in some instances.

Totoó, hindî na siyá babalík.	Truly, he/she is not coming back anymore.
Totoóng-totoó.	It is very true.
Totoó ba ang balità? Totoó.	Is the news true? True.

4. **Talagá** = *yes, indeed; really*

Use **talagá** to emphasize the nature of the subject, as expressed by an adjective, or to affirm the truth in a sentence. Like other affirmative words, it can be a stand-alone response. It should be placed at the start of the sentence or near the adjective or adverb.

Mabuting táo talagá si G. Santos.	Mr. Santos is a really good man.
Talágang mabuting táo si G. Santos.	

Talagá, papuntá kamí sa Estados Unidos.	Yes, indeed, we are going to the United States.

A colloquial and negative definition of this expression is *Really?* that is spoken with raised eyebrows and raised intonation that connotes disbelief.

III. EXPRESSING DOUBT

1. **Maráhil** = *maybe*

Maráhil, which is also a one-word response, is placed either at the beginning of the sentence or near the subject, even at the end of the sentence.

Maráhil siyá ay daráting bukas.	Maybe he is arriving tomorrow.

Si Pépe na maráhil ang pinakamasuwerteng táo sa buong mundó.
Ang pinakamasuwerteng táo sa buong mundó ay si Pépe na maráhil.
Pepe maybe the luckiest person in the whole world.

2. **Tíla** = *it seems*

A **tíla** sentence expresses a speaker's view of things. The word **tíla** is placed at the start of a sentence or whenever another person's statement or view is included in the speaker's sentence (see Lesson Twenty-One).

Tíla úulan ngayón.	It seems it will rain today.

3. **Sigúro** = *maybe* or *definitely*

As discussed in Lesson Three, the meaning of **sigúro** depends on the response to the question being asked. For example, there may be three responses to the question **Sigúro ka?** or *Are you sure?*:

Oô, sigúro akó.	Yes, I am sure (or *Yes, definitely*).
Hindî akó sigúro (or sigurado).	I am not sure.
Sigúro.	Maybe.
Sigúro darating siyá bukas.	Maybe he is arriving tomorrow.
Daratíng siyá bukas sigúro.	

Observe that **sigúro** may be a one-word response and may be placed anywhere in the sentence.

4. **Bakâ** = *might be*

There is not much difference in the use of **maráhil**, **sigúro** (as *maybe*) and **bakâ** when expressing doubt. However, **bakâ** is the most widely used term because it is the shortest, most contemporary and the most pleasant among the three (see first example) although a speaker's delivery of the sentence or his choice of words may give exactly the opposite.

Bakâ ka magkasakít.	You might get sick.
Bakâ ikáw ang máuná.	You might be first.

Be careful in pronouncing the word **bakâ** and note the glottal catch on the last syllable as the Tagalog word for cow is the stressless **baka**.

5. **Maáarì** = *it can be* or *possible*

Maáaring totoó means *it can be true*. **Maáaring malî** means *it can be wrong*. Thus, **maáarì** functions similarly as **hindi**, which gives the opposite of a word. **Maáarì** gives a blanket of doubt over a word. However, **maáarì** on its own as a stand-alone response (although **posible** or **puwede** are more popular) means *It is possible*. Note also that **maáarì** is used in requests (see Lesson Twenty-Four).

Maáarìng totoó na siyá ay mag-áasawa na.
It could be true that he/she is getting married.

Maáarìng malî ang hinàla nátin.	Our suspicions could be wrong.

Exercises

What would be the response to each question or situation below? Is it **totoó** or **maráhil**? Give all three possible responses.

1. **Kayó na raw ang magkasáma sa eskuweláhan ngayón?**
   Is it true you are now a pair in school?

   sang-ayon/agree   _____

   dî sang-ayon/disagree   _____

   álinlangan/doubt   _____

2. **Tunay bang mahál ni Nilda si Andrew?**
   Does Nilda truly love Andrew?

   sang-ayon/agree   _____

   di sang-ayon/disagree   _____

   álinlangan/doubt   _____

3. **Gustó mo bang makilarô sa ámin?**
   Do you want to play with us?

   sang-ayon/agree   _____

   di sang-ayon/disagree   _____

   álinlangan/doubt   _____

LESSON THIRTY-EIGHT
Forming Nouns from Verbs

The English gerund is a verbal noun and is exactly what its name implies: a noun derived from a verb. A gerund or a verbal noun in English usually ends in *-ing*, or may also be a phrase with an *-ing* verb, and functions as a noun in a sentence. For example, in the sentence *Writing calms my mind*, the word *writing* is a gerund or a verbal noun. A pronoun may replace *writing* in a succeeding sentence (*It calms my mind*) and confirms that *writing*, as used in the sentence, is indeed a gerund.

In Tagalog, gerunds are formed in several ways as described below. Note that the article **ang** (along with **ng** and **sa**) helps in forming nouns from verbs or adjectives (see Lesson Thirty-One). In this lesson, however, **ang** (or **ang mga** if the verbal noun is plural) alone is needed to form gerunds along with six affixes.

I. FORMING NOUNS FROM **-UM-** VERB FORMS

formula: prefix **pag-** + root

Examples:
umalís	= **pag-alís**	= leaving
lumakad	= **paglakad**	= walking
umibig	= **pag-ibig**	= love

Siyá ay umalís patungong Estados Unidos. (verb)
He left for the United States.

Ang kanyáng pag-alís ay ikinalungkót ko. (gerund)
His departure made me sad.

II. FORMING NOUNS FROM **MAG-** VERB FORMS

prefix **pag-** + duplicated first syllable + root

Examples:
maglarô	= **paglalarô**	= playing
magtaním	= **pagtataním**	= planting

Gustó kong magtaním ng hasmín sa áming bakuran. (verb)
I like to plant jasmine in our yard.

Vocabulary List

pag-alís = departure   **bakuran** = yard   **madalás** = often
takdáng-aralín = homework   **buhay** = life   **trabaho** = job

Ang pagtataním ng hasmín ay mahirap. (gerund)
Planting jasmine is difficult.

III. FORMING NOUNS FROM **-IN** VERB FORMS

pag- + root

Examples: **basáhin**   = **pagbása**   = reading
             tawágin   = **pagtáwag**   = [act of] calling

Basáhin mo ang buhay ni Rizal. (verb)
I read the life of Rizal.

Ang pagbása ko ng buhay ni Rizal ay hindî nilá gustó. (gerund)
They did not approve of my reading of Rizal's life.

IV. FORMING NOUNS FROM **PAKI-** VERB FORMS

paki- + duplicated last syllable of **paki-** + root

Examples: **pakihirám**   = **pakíkihirám**   = borrowing
             pakisúlat   = **pakíkisúlat**   = writing

Pinakisúlat ko ang áking takdáng-aralín sa kanyá. (verb)
I requested her to write my homework for me.

Ang pakíkisúlat ko ng takdáng-aralín sa kanya ay dî-mabuti. (gerund)
My request that she write my homework is not good.

V. FORMING NOUNS FROM **MA-** VERB FORMS

pag- + root (for actions)
pagka- + root (for feelings)

Examples: **maligò**   = **pagligò**   = bathing
             magálit   = **pagkagálit**   = being angry; anger

Madalás ang kanyáng pagligò. (verb)
His bathing is frequent.

Natákot akó sa kanyáng pagkagálit. (gerund)
I was afraid of his being angry.

VI. FORMING NOUNS FROM **-AN** VERB FORMS

pag- + duplicated first syllable + root

Examples: **tawanan**   = **pagtatawa**   = laughing
                hugasan   = **paghuhugas**   = washing

Hugásan mo ang mga pinggán. (verb)
Wash the dishes.

Ang paghuhúgas ng pinggán ay mahirap na trabaho. (gerund)
Washing dishes is a tough job.

Exercises

Give the verbal nouns of the following verbs.

1. _____   **mag-isíp**   = to think

2. _____   **umiyák**   = to cry

3. _____   **buksán**   = to open

4. _____   **maglakbáy**   = to travel

5. _____   **umíbig**   = to love

6. _____ **tugtugín**   = to play an instrument

7. _____ **umáwit**   = to sing

8. _____ **magsalitâ**   = to speak

9. _____ **mag-alís**   = to remove

10. _____ **sakyán**   = to ride

Create sentences from the verbal nouns formed above.

Translate the following sentences into Tagalog.

1. His frequent eating will make him fat.
2. I will be sad on the departure of my friend.
3. Traveling is a good education.
4. She is thin because of playing much.
5. Bathing everyday is necessary.
6. He likes writing very much.
7. Selling a house in Manila is difficult.
8. I like his reading of Rizal's "My Last Farewell."
9. Planting during the rainy season is good.
10. His coming is sudden.

Forming Participles Using **Naka-**

The English verbal gerund and participle are both formed from verbs but they function differently. While the gerund functions like a noun, the participle functions like an adjective and modifies a noun or pronoun. An English participle can be either in the present form (ending in *-ing*) or past form (ending in *-ed*, *-n* or *-t*).

In Tagalog, participles are formed by affixing the prefix **naka-** to a root word (**naka-** + root word) that is either a noun or a verb. The **naka-** participle then expresses the state, condition or appearance of a person or thing based on the root. A **naka-** word has no tense forms as it is descriptive just like an adjective.

This prefix should not be confused with the past tense of a **maka-** verb, which indicates capability to do something and are purely action words (Lesson Eighteen).

Sample Sentences

Ang batà ay <u>nakaupô</u> sa mataás na sílya.
The child <u>is seated</u> on a high chair.

<u>Nakatayô</u> sa tabí ng pintô ang áking iná.
My mother <u>is standing</u> by the door.

Ang laláking <u>nakahigâ</u> ay tamád.
The man <u>lying down</u> is lazy.

Bulág ang táong <u>nakasalamíng</u> iyón.
That man with eyeglasses <u>is blind</u>.

Kailángang <u>nakasapatos</u> ang batà sa paglalarô.
Children need <u>to be in shoes</u> on when playing.

Silá ay <u>nakakotse</u> nang dumatíng.
They were <u>in a car</u> when they arrived.

Vocabulary List

mataás na sílya = high chair	**kagabí** = last night	**sinehan** = movie house
tamád = lazy	**pintô** = door	**maingay** = noisy

<u>Nakatulalâ</u> si Miriam nang dumatíng akó.

Miriam is <u>in shock</u> when I arrived.

Puwéde ka sumama pero dápat <u>nakamaóng</u> ka.

You may come along but you should be <u>in jeans</u>.

Exercises

Can you tell if the following are **naka-** participles or **naka-** verb formss (past tense of **maka-** verb forms)? Translate the sentences into English and find out.

1. **Nakapások kamí sa sinehán kagabí.**
2. **Nakalákad na ang matandáng maysakít.**
3. **Nakabása na siyá ng mga aklát ni Romulo.**
4. **Nakatúlog din akó kahit na maingay.**

Use the following **naka-** participles in sentences.

1. **nakasumbréro**
2. **nakaunipórme**
3. **nakaputî**
4. **nakakotse**
5. **nakakabáyo**
6. **nakasigarílyo**
7. **nakaitím**
8. **nakabús**
9. **nakasingsíng**
10. **nakapáyong**

Noun Affixes

In Lesson Thirty-One, you are introduced to the formation of nouns by placing the articles **ang** or **ng** or the preposition **sa** before a verb or adjective.

In this lesson, you will become acquainted with other affixes that turn a verb or an adjective into a noun, or even change the meaning of one noun into another.

The following are the various affixes that help to create new nouns and the formulas tat are used to create these nouns, which are then categorized according to their new meanings.

I. -AN OR -HAN SUFFIXES

1. (root + **-an**) Refers to a place where things are stored or placed

   aklát = book   **aklátan** = library
   káhoy = wood   **kahuyán** = woodpile
   báhay = house   **bahayán** = group of houses
   báboy = pig   **babúyan** = piggery

2. (root + **-an**) Refers to a season

   áni = harvest   **anihán** = harvest time
   pások = enter   **pasukán** = school day
   taním = plant   **tániman** = planting season

3. (root + **-an**) Refers to an article or instrument

   inóm = to drink   **inúman** = something to drink from
   sulat = to write, letter   **sulatán** = somethng to write on
   lutò = to cook, cooked   **lutuán** = cooking utensils, place for cooking
   sakáy = to ride   **sasakyán** = something to ride in

4. (root duplicated and hyphenated + **-an**) Refers to a miniature version

   báhay = house   **baháy-baháyan** = playhouse
   barò = damit   **barú-barúan** = doll clothes

Vocabulary List

kabutíhan = goodness   **sangkapuluán** = archipelago   **kartéro** = postman
kabatáan = youth   **kaligayáhan** = happiness   **panaúhin** = visitors
pagtatat ním = planting   **magsasaká** = farmer

5. (root duplicated and hyphenated + **-an**) Refers to an imitator or copycat

iná = mother	**iná-ináhan** = pretending to be like a mother
harí = king	**harí-harían** = acting like a king
pári = priest	**parí-parían** = not a real priest

II. KA- + -AN OR KA_HAN

1. (**ka-** + root + **-an**) Refers to an idea or concept

buti = good	**kabutíhan** = goodness
buhay = life	**kabuháyan** = livelihood
ligaya = happy	**kaligayáhan** = happiness

2. (**ka-** + root + **-an**) Refers to a group

bahay = house	**kabahayán** = place of many houses
bukid = farm	**kabukirán** = farmlands
Tagálog = refers to a language or people	**Katagalúgan** = place of the Tagalogs
batà = child	**kabatáan** = youth
tandâ = age	**katandaán** = elders

Note that for roots ending in **o** such as **lutò** and **barò** or with **o** in the last syllable such as **inóm** and **pások**, the vowel **o** is changed to **u** when a suffix is attached. In roots ending in **d** such as **bukid**, **d** becomes **r** when a suffix is attached.

III. MAG-

1. (**mag-** + hyphen for roots that start with a vowel + root) Refers to a relationship

iná = mother	**mag-iná** = mother and child
amá = father	**mag-amá** = father and child
asawa = spouse	**mag-asawa** = husband and wife
kapatíd = sibling	**magkapatíd** = brothers or sisters

2. (**mag-** + duplicated first syllable of root + root) Refers to a work or profession

bigás = rice	**magbibigás** = rice merchant
saka = farming	**magsasaká** = farmer

IV. MANG- OR MAN-

1. (**mang-** + duplicated first syllable of root + root) Refers to a work or profession

As with other roots that begin with the consonants **d**, **l**, **r**, **s** and **t**, the variant of most prefixes are used, for example, **man-** instead of **mang-** (see Lesson Eleven).

gamót = to cure   **manggagamot** = doctor
langóy = to swim   **manlalangoy** = swimmer
dagat = sea   **mandaragát** = seaman
digmâ = war   **mandirigmâ** = warrior
larô = to play, game   **manlalarò** = player

V. PAG-

1. (**pag-** + hyphen if root starts with a vowel + root) Creates gerunds or verbal nouns when affix replaces **-um-**
   umalís = left   **pag-alís** = departure
   lumakad = walked   **paglakad** = walk
   umibig = loved   **pag-ibig** = love

2. (**pag-** + duplicated first syllable + root) Creates gerunds or verbal nouns when affix replaces **mag-**
   maglarô = to play   **paglalarô** = act of playing
   magsulát = to write   **pagsusulát** = writing
   magtaním = to plant   **pagtataním** = planting

3. (**pag-** + root) Creates gerunds or verbal nouns when affix replaces **-in** or **-hin**
   basáhin = read   **pagbása** = reading
   tawágin = call   **pagtáwag** = calling

VI. SANG-, SAN-, SAM-

1. (**sang-** + **ka-** + root + **-an**) Means *the whole of*
The prefix **sang-** changes to **san-** when attached to roots starting with the consonants **d**, **l**, **r**, **s** and **t**. The prefix changes to **sam-** when the roots start with the consonant **p** (see Lesson Thirteen on Numbers).
   pulô = island   **sangkapuluán** = archipelago
   langit = heaven   **sangkalangitan** = heaven

2. (**sang-** + root) Means *one*
   gabí = night   **sanggabí** = one night
   buwan = month   **sambuwán** = one month
   taon = year   **santaón** = one year

VII. TAG-

1. (**tag-** + root) Refers to *season* or *time of*
   araw = sun, day   **tag-aráw** = dry season
   ulán = rain   **tag-ulán** = wet season
   lamíg = cold   **taglamíg** = cold season
   gutom = hunger   **taggutóm** = famine
   ani = harvest   **tag-ani** = harvest time

VIII. TAGA-

1. (taga- + name of place) Means *a native* or *resident of*

   Si Laurel ay taga-Batangas.   Laurel is from Batangas.
   Ang mga Muslim ay taga-Mindanao.   Muslims are from Mindanao.

   Ang mga taga-baryo ay marúnong magtaním.
   Those from the barrio know how to plant.

2. (taga- + root) Refers to one who frequently acts out the root

   dalá = bring   **tagadalá** = one who brings
   Ang kartéro (postman) **ay tagadalá ng sulat.**

   turò = teach   **tagaturò** = one who teaches
   Akó ay tagaturò ng Tagalog.

   bilí = buy   **tagabilí** = one who buys
   Si Julia ay tagabilí ng pagkain sa palengke.

   lutò = cook   **tagalutò** = one who cooks
   Ang áking maybahay ang tagalutò námin.

IX. TALA- + -AN

1. (taga- + root + -an) Refers to a list of things associated with the root word

   tinig = voice   **talátinígan** = dictionary
   aklát = books   **taláaklatan** = catalogue of books
   araw = day   **taláarawán** = diary or journal
   upa = rent   **taláupahán** = payroll

The Plurality Rule

The Tagalog language has a plurality rule (introduced in Lesson Four). Nouns, verbs, articles, prepositions and question words are made plural when the subjects are also plural.

As this discussion focuses on the affixes that turn a verb into a noun or the meaning of a noun into another, it becomes appropriate to further discuss how nouns can be made plural. Following are the means:

1. Use the plural forms of articles: **siná** with proper nouns and **ang mga** with common nouns.

2. Use numbers as well as adjectives such as **ilán** (*a few*) and **marami** (*many*) before a noun.

   Sampûng táo ang umalís.   Ten men left.
   Iláng táo ang umalís.   A few men left.
   Maraming táo ang umalís.   Many men left.

3. Use the formula for creating plural adjectives: **ma** + duplicated first syllable + root.

Magagandáng dalaga ang áming panaúhin. (visitors)
Our visitors are pretty ladies.

Mababaít na batà ang inyóng mga anák.
Your children are good.

Báhay na malalakí ang nákíta námin.
We saw big houses.

4. Duplicate the root word.

Pumaroón kamí sa mga baháy-baháy sa Lingayen.
We went from house to house in Lingayen.

Bumilí kamí ng mga bágay-bágay para sa kusína.
We bought several things for the kitchen.

Formation of Adjectives

There are five affixes which may be used to turn a root word into an adjective. The following are the various affixes that help to create adjectives and the formulas used to create these adjectives. These are then categorized according to their new meanings.

I. MA-

1. (**ma-** + root) Means having the quality expressed by the root; use with abstract nouns (refer to page 65, Lesson Twelve)

gandá = beauty	**magandá** = beautiful (**may ganda**)
baít = goodness	**mabaít** = good (**may bait**)
tamís = sweetness	**matamís** = sweet (**may tamis**)
dúnong = knowledge	**marúnong** = learned (**may dunong**)

Observe that with a **ma-** prefix, the initial letter and consonant **d** in a root word change to **r** as in **ma-** + **dúnong** becomes **marúnong**.

2. (**ma-** + root) Means having many or much of the feature expressed by the root; use with concrete nouns

bulaklák = flower	**mabulaklák** = many flowers
táo = person	**matáo** = many people
bigás = rice	**mabigás** = plenty of rice
búnga = fruit	**mabúnga** = plenty of fruits or fruitful

II. KA-

1. (**ka-** + root) Refers to a reciprocal relationship

balát = skin	**kabalát** = of the same skin
sama = to go along	**kasama** = accompanied

Vocabulary List

matamís = sweet	**pang-umága** = for morning	**matáo** = many people
mabúnga = with plenty of fruits	(literal)	**Kaybúti!** = How good!
	makabágo = modern	

III. KAY-

1. (**kay-** + root) An exclamation referring to the trait of the root word, **kay-** literally translates to *how*

gandá = beauty	**kaygandá** = how beautiful!
ága = early	**kay-ága** = how early!
buti = goodness	**kaybúti** = how good!

IV. MAKA-

1. (**maka-** + root, may be a proper name) Means *in favor of someone over another* or *inclined to believe in someone or something*

Rizal = Philippines' national hero	**maka-Rizal** = in favor of Rizal
bago = new	**makabágo** = (in favor of new); modern
lumà = old	**makalumà** = (in favor of old); old fashioned

V. PANG-, PAN- OR PAM-

1. (**pang-** + root) Refers to specific use as expressed by the root

The prefix **pang-** is used with words that start with the vowels (**a, e, i, o** and **u**) and the consonants **k, g, h, m, n, ng, w, y**. A hyphen separates **pang-** from roots that start with vowels. On the other hand, the alternant prefix **pam-** is used with words that start with **b** and **p** whereas the other alternant prefix **pan-** is used with roots that start with **d, l, r, s** and **t**.

umága = morning	**pang-umága** = of the morning
báyad = pay	**pambáyad** = for payment
salà = filter	**pansála** = for straining
kayod = scrape	**pangkáyod** = for scraping
walís = sweep	**pangwalís** = for sweeping
hila = pull	**panghila** = for pulling
tulog = sleep	**pantúlog** = for sleeping
lakad = walk	**panlakad** = for walking
pasok = enter	**pampások** = uniform (used for going to office or school)

Ang sapatos na <u>pambáhay</u> ay sirâ na.
The shoes <u>for [use in] the house</u> are already worn out.

Ang kláse ko ay <u>pang-umága</u>.
My class is <u>in the morning</u>. (literal)
I have a morning class.

Ang pérang itó ay <u>pambáyad</u> sa útang.
This money is <u>for payment</u> of debts.

Ang plúmang <u>pansúlat</u> ay nawalâ.   The pen <u>for writing</u> was lost.
Ang <u>pang-ospital</u> na uniporme ay puti. The <u>hospital uniform</u> is white.

IV. **MAPAG-** AND **PALA-**

The prefixes **mapag-** and **pala-**, when attached to a root, describe the habitual and frequent action of the doer as expressed by the root word. The prefixes are interchangeable except when attached to adjectives. The prefix **pala-** only goes with action roots while the prefix **mapag-** may go with both action and describing words. The resulting words are always accented on the last syllables.

1. **tawa** = laugh   **palatawá** or **mapagtawá** = laughs frequently
   Ayaw ang binatà sa dalagang palatawá / mapagtawá.
   The young man does not like a girl who laughs frequently.

2. **aral** = study   **palaarál** or **mapag-arál** = studies fequently
   Ang batáng palaarál / mapag-arál ay magíging marúnong.
   A child who studies habitually becomes learned.

3. **inóm** = drink   **palainóm** or **mapag-inóm** = drinks frequently
   Si Edwin ay palainóm / mapag-inóm ng tubig.
   Edwin is fond of drinking water.

4. **isip** = think   **palaisíp** or **mapag-isíp** = deep in thought
   Madalíng tumandâ ang mga táong palaisíp / mapag-isíp.
   Deep thinkers get old faster.

5. **mahál** = beloved   **mapagmahál** = loving or affectionate
   Gustó ni Claudette ang mapagmahál na si Pepeng.
   Claudette likes the affectionate Pepeng.

Exercises

Write five adjectives to describe the following subjects. Use a variety of affixes with the descriptive words.

New York

1. _____   4. _____

2. _____   5. _____

3. _____

gurò

1. _____   4. _____

2. _____   5. _____

3. _____

babáe

1. _____   4. _____

2. _____   5. _____

3. _____

Use **pang-**, **pam-** or **pan-** with the following roots to form adjectives.

1. _____ **bansâ**   6. _____ **langóy**

2. _____ **gámit**   7. _____ **batà**

3. _____ **aral**   8. _____ **kain**

4. _____ **bása**   9. _____ **barò**

5. _____ **lahát**   10. _____ **ilaw**

Plural Forms of Verbs

The grammar book (**Balarila ng Wikang Pambansa**) prepared by Lope K. Santos in 1939 as head of the Institute of National Language states that the use of plural forms of verbs with plural subjects is "not compulsory" and the use of a plural subject with a singular verb "does not make the sentence or the sense wrong." The plurality rule was introduced in this book in Lesson Four then discussed in detail in various pages and finally in Lesson Forty. This far, a student should have been familiar with the rule already.

While it is easy for native Tagalog speakers to say **mangagsikáin**, **mangagkaín**, **magsipagkaín**, **mangágsipagkáinan** and **mangagkaínan**, foreigners and non-Tagalog speakers will find these words very difficult to pronounce. Thus, the discussion on forming the plural derivatives of Tagalog words in this lesson shall be extended to the more simple plural affixes with two each in the active (**magsi-** and **magsipag-**) and passive voices (**pag-** + **-in** and **pag-** + **-an**). These will be enough to arm non-Tagalog speakers with necessary plural verbs to pass an advanced Tagalog conversation.

For Active Forms (**Magsi-** and **Magsipag-**)

Both **magsi-** and **magsipag-** verb forms are the plural forms of **-um-** and **mag-** (see Lesson Fourteen), which emphasize the doer of the action or the act itself.

I. **MAGSI-** VERB FORMS

The prefix **magsi-** is used to form the plural derivatives of **-um-** verb forms. Following are the formulas for the infinitive and imperative forms as well as the three tenses—past, present and future.

Example: **kain**	eat
Infinitive: **magsikáin**	(**magsi-** + root) to eat
Imperative: **magsikáin**	(**magsi-** + root) eat
Past: **nagsikáin**	(**magsi-** becomes **nagsi-** + root) ate
Present: **nagsísikáin**	(**magsi-** becomes **nagsi-** + duplicated second syllable of **magsi-** + root) are eating
Future: **magsísikáin**	(**magsi-** + duplicated second syllable of **magsi-** + root) will eat

Vocabulary List

magsikáin = to eat (plural)
hapúnan = supper
nagsísipagdasal = are praying

magsialís = to leave (plural)
pagsulatín = to write (plural)
bintanà = window

Example: **alís**	leave
Infinitive: **magsialís**	(**magsi-** + root) to leave
Imperative: **magsialís**	(**magsi-** + root) leave
Past: **nagsialís**	(**magsi-** becomes **nagsi-** + root) left
Present: **nagsísialís**	(**magsi-** becomes **nagsi-** + duplicated second syllable of **magsi-** + root) are leaving
Future: **magsísialís**	(**magsi-** + duplicated second syllable of **magsi-** + root) will leave

EXAMPLES OF **MAGSI-** VERBS

magsilákad	to go	**magsisúlat**	to write
magsibása	to read		

II. **MAGSIPAG-** VERB FORMS

The prefix **magsipag-** is used to form the plural derivatives of **mag-** verb forms. **Magsipag-** is followed by a hyphen when the verb root after it starts with a vowel such as **aral** (*study*) and **akyat** (*climb*).

Example: **lakad**	walk
Infinitive: **magsipaglakád**	(**magsipag-** + root) to walk
Imperative: **magsipaglakád**	(**magsipag-** + root) walk
Past: **nagsipaglakád**	(**magsipag-** becomes **nagsipag-** + root) walked
Present: **nagsísipaglakád**	(**magsipag-** becomes **nagsipag-** + duplicated second syllable of **magsipag-** + root) are walking
Future: **magsísipaglakád**	(**magsipag-** + duplicated second syllable of **magsipag-** + root) will walk

Example: **dasál**	prayer
Infinitive: **magsipagdasál**	(**magsipag-** + root) to pray
Imperative: **magsipagdasál**	(**magsipag-** + root) pray
Past: **nagsipagdasál**	(**magsipag-** becomes **nagsipag-** + root) prayed
Present: **nagsísipagdasál**	(**magsipag-** becomes **nagsipag-** + duplicated second syllable of **magsipag-** + root) are praying
Future: **magsísipagdasál**	(**magsipag-** + duplicated second syllable of **magsipag-** + root) will pray

EXAMPLES OF **MAGSIPAG-** VERBS

magsipagbaít	to be good	**magsipagpasyál**	to take a walk
magsipag-áral	to study	**magsipag-akyát**	to go up

Sample Sentences

Nagsísibása ba kayó ng Bibliya?	Do you read the Bible?
Magsilakád na kayó sa páaralán.	You all go now to school.
Nagsísikáin na ang mga batà ng hapúnan.	The children are eating their supper already.
Nagsísipag-áral nang mabuti ang áking mga anák.	My children study well.
Nagsísipagdasál ang mga babáe sa simbáhan.	The women pray in church.

For Passive Forms (**Pag-** + **-in** and **Pag-** + **-an**)

Both **pag-** + **-in** and **pag-** + **-an** verb forms are the plural forms of **-in** and **-an** verb forms (see Lessons Fifteen and Thirty-Three), which emphasize the receiver of the action.

I. **PAG-** + **-IN** VERB FORMS

The prefix **pag-** + **-in** or its variant **pag-** + **-hin** is used to form the plural derivatives of a passive **-in** verb.

Example: **lutò**	cooking
Infinitive: **paglutuín**	(**pag-** + root + **-in**) to cook
Imperative: **paglutuín**	(**pag-** + root + **-in**) cook
Past: **pinaglutò**	(infix **-in-** after first letter of prefix **pag-** + root) were cooked
Present: **pinaglulutò**	(infix **-in-** after first letter of prefix **pag-** + duplicated first syllable of root + root) are being cooked
Future: **paglúlutuín**	(**pag-** + duplicated second syllable of root + root + **-in**) will be cooked

Example: **sulat**	writing
Infinitive: **pagsulatín**	(**pag-** + root + **-in**) to write
Imperative: **pagsulatín**	(**pag-** + root + **-in**) write
Past: **pinagsulát**	(infix **-in-** after first letter of prefix **pag-** + root) were made to write
Present: **pinagsusulát**	(infix **-in-** after first letter of prefix **pag-** + duplicated first syllable of root + root) are being made to write
Future: **pagsúsulatín**	(**pag-** + duplicated second syllable of root + root + **-in**) will be made to write

Observe that the **o** in **luto** is changed to **u** before the second half of the affix **pag-** + **-in** is attached to the imperative form and the future tense. This change in vowels will be required for similar verbs ending in the vowel **o**.

Refer to Lesson Fifteen for the peculiarities in forming an **-in** verb form that ends in a vowel and with or without an end glottal catch, as well as when to use the variant **-hin**.

EXAMPLES OF **PAG-** + **-IN** VERBS

pag-alisín	to remove	**paglinisín**	to clean
pagbasahín	to read		

Note that in conversational language, the repetition of the first syllable in all forms and tenses of **pag-** + **-in** or **pag-** + **-an** verbs are allowed. See examples below.

	Conversational
Infinitive and imperative: **paglutuín**	**paglúlutuín**
Past: **pinaglutò**	**pinaglulutò**
Present: **pinaglulutò**	**pinaglúlulutò**
Future: **paglúlutuín**	**paglúlulutuín**

II. **PAG-** + **-AN** VERB FORMS

The prefix **pag-** + **-an** or its variant **pag-** + **-han** is used to form the plural derivatives of a passive **-an** verb form.

Example: **hugas**	washing
Infinitive: **paghuhugasán**	(**pag-** + duplicated first syllable of root + root + **-an**) to wash
Imperative: **paghuhugasán**	(**pag-** + duplicated first syllable of root + root + **-an**) wash
Past: **pinaghúhugasán**	(infix **-in-** after first letter of prefix **pag-** + duplicated first syllable of root + root + **-an**) were washed
Present: **pinaghúhuhugasán**	(infix **-in-** after first letter of prefix **pag-** + triplicated first syllable of root + root + **-an**) are being washed
Future: **paghúhuhugasán**	(**pag-** + triplicated first syllable of root + root + **-an**) will be washed

Example: **bukás** (irregular)	open
Infinitive: **pagbubuksán**	(**pag-** + duplicated first syllable of root + root without the last vowel + **-an**) to open
Imperative: **pagbubuksán**	(**pag-** + duplicated first syllable of root + root without the last vowel + **-an**) open
Past: **pinagbúbuksán**	(infix **-in-** after first letter of prefix **pag-** + duplicated first syllable of root + root without the last vowel + **-an**) were opened
Present: **pinagbububuksan**	(infix **-in-** after first letter of prefix **pag-** + triplicate first syllable of root + root without the last vowel + **-an**) are being opened
Future: **pagbububuksan**	(**pag-** + triplicate first syllable of root + root + **-an**) will be opened

EXAMPLES OF **PAG-** + **-AN** VERBS

pag-aayusán	to arrange	**pagpipintahán**	to paint
pagbibihisán	to change clothes		

Many **-an** verb forms are derived from irregular verb roots (see list of some of these roots on page 183). Usually, the second vowel of the root is dropped. In others, the second syllable is deleted. A student should try to memorize these irregular roots.

bukás	**pagbubuksán**	= to open
labá	**paglalabhán**	= to wash clothes
lagáy	**paglalagyáan**	= to put something

Sample Sentences

Paghuhugasán na ninyó ang mga pinggán.   You (plural) have the plates washed.
Pinagbúbuksán niyá ang lahat ng mga bintana.   The windows are being opened by her/him.
Pag-áaayusán námin ng buhók ang mga batà.   We will fix the children's hair.
Pinagpípintahán ng laláki ang mga pasô.   The pots are being painted by the man.

Exercises

Change the verbs in the following sentences into their plural forms. Afterwards, transform the sentences into English.

1. **Bumasa ang batà ng páhayagán sa kanyáng lola.**
2. **Naglutò ang babáe ng isdâ sa kawalì.**
3. **Nagbayad siyá ng dalawáng libong piso sa ákin para sa sapatos.**
4. **Maglalágay siyá ng tubig sa mga baso.**
5. **Magtakíp ka ng panyô sa mukhâ.**

Contractions

When we talk or write to a person with whom we are very familiar, we usually skip over some words or syllables or press them together rather than pronouncing them completely. The economical use of words in speech or writing—or brevity—matters. Contractions allow much to be said or written in a shorter time. It is done by shortening a word, syllable or word group or by omitting some letters to create a new, shorter word.

Contracted English words like *don't* and *let's* follow certain rules. So do *isn't, don't, we're* and *he's*. However, in Tagalog words, many different letters and syllables might be omitted or changed depending on the speaker. For example, in **hintáy ka** (or *wait*), the syllable **hin** is omitted and the syllable **tay** is changed to **te** and attached to **ka**. A simple rule to follow in spotting Tagalog contractions is that these are not regular words with noticeable affixes or root words.

Below is a list of common contractions used in everyday conversation. Once these are memorized, look out for new contractions used by the younger generation that may creep and be accepted into the language.

1. **téka** (from **hintáy ka**) = *Wait!*
   Téka sandalî, kakain muna akó. Wait a moment, I will just eat.

2. **dalíka** (from **magmadalî ka**) = *Be quick!*
   Dalíka, mahúhulí táyo. Be quick, we will be late.

3. **téna** (from **táyo na**) = *Let's go!*
   Téna, hulí na táyo. Let's go, we are already late.

4. **tamó** (from **nákita mo**) = *You see?* or *See?*
   Tamó, bágay sa iyó iyán! You see? That suits you!

5. **hámo** *(from **hayaán mo**) = *Let her/him/it be.*
   Hámo siyá, ayaw siyáng makiníg. Let him be, he does not like to listen.
   Hámo, makakalimútan mo rin iyán. Let it be, you will soon forget it.

6. **ayóko** (from **ayaw ko**) = *I don't like.*
   Ayóko ng biruán. I do not like jokes.

Vocabulary List

téka = wait	**pénge** = give me
ikámo = you said	**hámo** = let it be

7. **'lika** (from **hali ka**) = *Come* or *Come here.*
   'Lika, alis na tayo.   Come, we're leaving now.

8. **méron** (from **mayroón**) = *has* or *have*
   Méron akong anak.   I have a child.

9. **'lâ** (from **walâ**) = *nothing* or *None.*
   'Lâ ákong pera.   I don't have money.

10. **pénge** (from **pahingî**) = *Give me.*
    Pénge ng tinapay, gutóm ako.   Give me bread, I am hungry.

The first ten contracted words may stand alone as responses to questions or as single-word command sentences (such as **dalika** and **'lika**). Note also that contracted words with missing initial syllables or letters, such as the following words, are very common in the Tagalog language.

11. **'dî** (from **hindî**) = *not* or *Right?* (use as a tag question)
    'Dî siyá sásáma.   He/She is not coming along.
    Ákin 'yán, 'dî ba?   That is mine, isn't it (right)?

12. **'nó** (from **anó**) = *Right?* (use as a tag question)
    Tamà itó, 'nó?   This is correct, right?

13. **ikámo** (from **wiká mo**) = *you said*
    Ikámo [ay] mánonoód tayó ng pelíkulá.   You said we are going to see a movie.

14. **ikáko** (from **wiká ko**) = *I said*
    Ikáko ay bukas na táyo aalís.   I said we are going tomorrow.

The contractions **ikámo** and **ikáko** (or **kámo** and **káko** in some areas) are more commonly used by older people in the rural areas while **sabi ko** (*I said*) or **sabi nilá** (*they said*) is more commonly used by younger people.

15. **éka** (from **pahingî ka**) = give me
    Eka ng mais.   Give me a cob of corn.

16. **tangkó** (from **tingnán ko**) = *let me see* or *let me have a look*
    Tangkó nga, ngayón ko lang nákítà iyán.   Let me have a look, I have not seen that yet.

17. **kaná** (from **ákin na**) = *give me* (used as a command)
    Kaná ang aklát ko.   Give me my book.

Colors

The English names for colors in the Tagalog language are quite incomplete. The language, for instance, has no equivalent for brown and its different shades such as golden brown. What is commonly used for golden brown is **pulá** (*red*) as in the following direction for cooking:

Prituhin mo ang isdâ hanggáng pumulá.
Fry the fish until it turns golden brown.

However, the Tagalogs use **kayumanggí** when referring to the color of the Filipino race and their skin color (sometimes called **morena**, which is Spanish in origin). This word is specific to the race and skin color, and does not apply to anything that is brown. Descriptive words are used instead to indicate the brownness of a thing or object like **kulay kapé** (*coffee-colored*) or **kulay tsokoláte** (*chocolate-colored*).

I. BASIC COLORS

The Tagalog term for black is **itím** and that for white is **putî** while the terms for the primary and secondary colors are:

red	**pulá**	green	**bérde** or **luntían**
blue	**asúl** or **bugháw**	violet	**ube**
yellow	**diláw**	orange	**kulay kahél**

II. DARK COLORS

When expressing the darker, solid or brilliant shades of colors, duplicate the names of colors by using the ligatures **na** and **-ng**. Refer to the following examples of dark colors.

navy blue	**asúl na asúl**	dark green	**bérdeng-bérde**
bright yellow	**diláw na diláw**	very black	**itím na itím**

III. LIGHT COLORS

Lighter colors, unless those that have specific Tagalog names, such as pale blue, light green, pale yellow, require the word **murá** (which means *pale* or *light* although **murá** also refers to an *unripe fruit* as well as *something that is cheap or not expensive*) attached either before or after the Tagalog names.

Vocabulary List

kayumanggí = brown (referring to race or color of skin)

bérde/luntían = green

kulay kahél = orange
itím = black
asul/bughaw = blue

ube = violet
lila = purple

pale blue	**asúl na murá**	purple	**lila**
light green	**muráng bérde**	pink	**rósas**
pale yellow	**diláw na murá**	gray	**abó** (literally *ash*)

IV. SHADES

To express shades of primary and secondary colors, make use of the prefix **ma-** (following this formula: **ma-** + duplicated root word separated by a hyphen) or the suffix **-an** or **-han** (following this formula: root word + **-an**). Note that **asul** and **itim** use the prefix **mang-** instead of **ma-**.

blue   **mangasúl-ngasúl** or **asúlan** (note that the **-ng** in **mang-** in the first half of the word is repeated in the second half after the hyphen)

green   **mabérde-bérde** or **luntían**

red   **mapúla-púla / mamúla-múla** or **pulahán**

white   **maputî-putî / mamutî-mutî** or **putián**

yellow   **maniláw-niláw** or **dilawán**

Note that with a prefix such as **ma-**, the initial **d** in **diláw** is changed to **n** and the **p** in **pula** and **puti** is changed to **m**. These changes are highlighted in previous lessons.

V. OTHER COLORS

Other color names are more specific and use common materials as a points of reference whose mere mention of their names connote a specific color, such as those listed below:

apple green   **bérdeng mansánas**

moss green   **bérdeng lúmot**

gold/golden   **gintô/ginintuán**

silver   **pilak/pinilakan**

Sample Sentences

Puláng-pulá ang kanyáng sapatos.
His/her shoes are bright red.

Ang mga luntíang dáhon ay malamíg sa matá.
Green leaves are refreshing to the eyes.

Ang diláw na murá ay bagay sa maputíng balát.
Pale yellow is suited to those who are fair skinned.

Marami ákong baróng tagalog na kulay-abó.
I have many ash-colored barong tagalog (formal wear for men).

Appendices

FOODS

Foreigners in the Philippines who look for certain items in the vegetable, fruit, fish or meat sections in wet markets may find difficulty in communicating with local vendors who do not know the local names of some, if not most, of the products they need. Although most supermarkets may have these products as well as the English names of the products on the packages, wet markets still offer cheaper prices and wider variety of these food items. This is on top of the experience of having to haggle prices with local vendors. Take note though that a number of food items are known by their English names such as carrot, cauliflower, greenshells and yellow fin tuna.

To help you look for what you exactly need, here is a comprehensive list of food items in their English names and their Tagalog equivalents.

Vegetables

Bamboo shoots = **labóng**
Banana heart = **pusó ng ságing**
Bean sprouts = **tóge**
Beets = **remolátsa**
Bitter melon = **ampalayá**
Bottle gourd = **úpo**
Cabbage = **repolyo**
Cashew nut = **kasúy**
Cassava = **kamóteng káhoy**
Chayote = **sayóte**
Chili = **síli**
Chinese bok choi = **petsáy**
Chinese celery = **kintsáy**
Coconut heart = **úbod**
Coriander leaves = **wansóy**
Corn = **maís**
Cucumber = **pipíno**
Daikon radish = **labanós**
Eggplant = **talóng**
Garbanzo beans = **garbánzos**
Garlic = **bawang**
Horseradish = **malunggáy**
Hyacinth beans = **bátaw**
Leeks or chives = **kutsáy**
Lettuce = **letsúgas**
Lime = **dáyap**
Long beans = **sítaw**
Malabar nightshade or Malabar spinach = **alugbáti**
Mung bean = **mongó**
Mushroom = **kabutè**
Mustard = **mustása**
Native onions = **sibúyas Tagalog**
Onion = **sibúyas**
Peanuts = **maní**
Potato = **patátas**
Red yam = **úbe**
Snowpeas = **sítsaro**
Soybeans = **útaw**
Spinach = **kulítis**
Sponge gourd = **patóla**

Spring onions/shallots = **sibúyas na múra; sibúyas dáhon**
String beans = **abitswélas**
Sweet potato = **kamóte**
Tomato = **kamátis**
Turnip or jicama = **síngkamas**
Water chestnut = **apúlid**
Water spinach = **kangkóng**
Wax gourd = **kundól**
Winged beans = **sigarílyas**
Yellow squash = **kalabása**

Fish and Shellfish

Anchovy = **dílis**
Blue sturgeon = **labahíta**
Catfish (freshwater) = **hitò**
Catfish (saltwater) = **kandulì**
Cavalla = **talakítok**
Clam = **haláan**
Crab = **alimasag**
Dried shrimp = **híbi**
Goby = **biyá**
Golden caesio (or yellow tail fusilier) = **dalagang búkid**
Grouper = **lápu-lápu**
Herring = **tambán**
Lobster = **banagán**
Mackerel = **hása-hása**
Milkfish = **bangús**
Mud crab = **alimángo**
Mud fish = **dalág**
Mullet = **bának**
Mussel = **tahóng**
Oyster = **talabá**
Pompano = **pompáno; maratíni**
Prawn = **sugpô**
Red snapper = **máya-máya**
River shrimps = **uláng**
Salt cod (dried) = **bacaláo**
Seabass = **apáhap**

Small shrimps = **alamáng**
Snail = **kuhól**
Sole = **dapâ**
Spanish mackerel = **tanigue**
Squid = **pusít**
Striped mackerel = **alumáhan**
Tilapia = **tilápia**

Noodles

Fine wheat noodles = **míswa**
Glass or cellophane noodles = **sotánghon**
Rice vermicelli = **bíhon**
Wheat noodles with egg = **míki**
Yellow egg noodles = **cantón**

Meats

Beef = **karné ng baka**
Beef shank = **biyás ng baka**
Brisket = **punta y pecho**
Deer = **usá**
Gizzard = **balún-balúnan**
Goat or lamb = **kambíng**
Ground beef = **giníling na karné ng baka**
Ground pork = **giníling na karné ng baboy**
Ham = **hamón; pigî**
Liver = **atáy**
Meat = **karné**
Ox tongue = **díla; lengua**
Pork = **karné ng baboy**
Pork belly = **liyémpo**
Rabbit = **kuného**
Sheep = **túpa**
Spare ribs = **tadyáng**
Water buffalo or carabao = **kalabáw**
Wild boar = **báboyramó**

Poultry

Chicken = **manók**
Duck = **pato**
Egg = **itlóg**
Eggwhite = **putî ng itlóg**
Egg yolk = **púla ng itlóg**
Quail = **pugò**
Quail egg = **itlóg ng pugò**
Turkey = **pábo**

Spices and Condiments

Anise wine = **anisádo**; **anís**
Annatto seeds = **atswéte**
Bay leaf = **laurél**
Black wood ear mushrooms = **ténga ng dagâ**
Cinnamon = **kanéla**
Clove = **clavio de comer**
Dry mustard = **pulbós ng mustasa**
Fermented soybeans = **taúsi**
Fish paste = **bagoong isdâ**
Fish sauce = **patís**
Garlic = **báwang**
Green or red pepper = **síling bérde**; **síling pulá**

Lemongrass = **tánglad**
Lye = **líhiya**
Monosodium glutamate = **vétsin**
Nutmeg = **anís maskádo**
Oregano = **orégano**
Paprika = **pamintón**
Pepper = **pamintá**
Peppercorn = **pamintáng buô**
Saffron = **kasubhâ**
Saltpeter = **salítre**
Sesame seeds = **lingá**
Soybean paste = **misó**
Soy sauce = **toyò**
Turmeric = **lúyang diláw**
Vinegar = **sukà**

COOKING TERMS

Filipino cuisine has been influenced and inspired by various eastern and western cuisines from which it has adopted various culinary procedures, imported ingredients and foreign dishes that were assimilated to fit local culture. Filipinos adopted culinary influences from China, Spain, Mexico and the United States and each of the various regions in the Philippines then provided their own local taste to these foods.

According to the late teacher and food critic Doreen Fernandez, what makes up the Filipino kitchen are the "history and society that introduced and adapted them; the people who turned them to their tastes and accepted them into their homes and restaurants, and especially the harmonizing culture that combined them into contemporary Filipino fare." Thus, Filipino food today is a gastronomic presentation of Philippine history.

The previous lesson introduced you to the Tagalog names of food items. In the following two lessons, you will be treated to cooking terms and culinary dishes that reflect this fusion of foreign inputs and local taste. For the meantime, reflect on these terms before moving on to the next lesson.

1. Bake = **ihurnó; lutúin sa hurnó** (oven)
    Naglutò akó ng pasta sa hurnó.
    I baked a pasta (dish) in the oven.

2. Baste = **pahíran ng mantikà** (cooking oil) **o ng sársa** (sauce)
    Pahíran mo ng mantikà ang balát ng baboy para hindî matuyô.
    Baste the pork skin to prevent drying.

3. Beat = **batihín**
    Batihín mo ang ánim na itlóg para sa tórta.
    Beat six eggs for the omelet.

4. Blanch = **banlián**
    Binanlián ko ang mga pili para maalís ang balát.
    I blanched the pili nuts to remove the skin.

5. Blend = **halúin**
    Halúin mo ang mga sangkáp nang mabuti.
    Blend the ingredients very well.

6. Boil = **pakuluín**
    Pakuluín mo ang túbig sa kaldéro.
    Boil the water in the kettle.

7. Broil = **iháwin**
   Iníhaw ko ang dáing sa bága.
   I broiled the dried fish on live coals.

8. Cut = **hiwáin** (with knife); **gupitín** (with scissors)
   Hiwáin ninyó ang tinápay sa gitná.
   Cut the bread in the middle.
   Gupitín ninyó ang talì ng súpot.
   Cut the string of the bag.

9. Chop = **tadtarín**
   Tadtarín mo ang baboy para sa tórta.
   Chop the pork for the omelet.

10. Drain = **patuluin**
    Pinatulò niyá muna ang langís mulâ sa baboy bago niyá itó hinango sa kawáli.
    She drained the oil from the pork before he/she removed it from the pan.

11. Fry = **pritúhin**
    Pinirito ng áming katúlong ang bangús.
    Our helper fried the milkfish.

12. Marinate = **ibábad sa sukâ** (vinegar), **toyò** (soy sauce) **at kalamansî** (native lemon)
    Ibabábad ko ang liémpo sa sukâ, toyò at kalamansî.
    I will marinate the pork belly in vinegar, soy sauce and kalamansi.

13. Melt = **tunawin**
    Tinúnaw ni Ana ang mantikílya sa kawáli.
    Ana melted the butter in the pan.

14. Mince = **dikdikín sa maliliít na piráso** (small pieces)
    Dikdikín mo ang bawang para sa adóbo.
    Mince the garlic for the **adobo** (see next page for description).

15. Peel = **talúpan**
    Talúpan mo ang mga mansánas para sa sálad.
    Peel the apples for the salad.

16. Pit = **alisán ng butó** (seeds)
    Alisán ninyó ng butó ang mga bayabas bago matamisín.
    Pit the guavas before preserving them.

17. Sauté = **igisá**
    Igisá mo ang giníling na karné sa bawang, sibúyas at kamátis.
    Saute the ground beef in garlic, onions and tomatoes.

18. Soak = **ibabad**
    Ibinabad ni Ana ang mongó sa túbig.
    Ana soaked the mung beans in water.

19. Steam = **pasingawan**
    Pinasingawan niya ang puto.
    She steamed the rice cake.

20. Toast = **tustahín**
    Masarap tustahín ang tinápay para sa agahan.
    It is nice to toast some bread for breakfast.

POPULAR FILIPINO DISHES AND DELICACIES

Filipinos love food. It plays an important role in the culture and contributes to myriad anecdotes regarding Filipino hospitality. Generally, foreign guests complain of overeating and being overfed when visiting Filipino homes. This is apparent because Filipinos eat three full meals, one morning snack and one afternoon snack each day. Cooked rice is essential in these meals plus a dish of meat and/or vegetables. Snacks are called **merienda** where, more often than not, rice in its sweet and glutinous form is also served.

Filipino dishes seem to retain that unique local touch whether prepared in simple roadside eateries called **karinde-ria** or **turo-turò** (so called because customers point to, or **turò**, the food they want to order) or in restaurants or homes. Basically, some dishes transcend regional or social border and grace every Filipino table. These dishes are enumerated below.

Adóbo is regarded by many Filipinos as the official national dish. It uses either pork or poultry, or both. It is cooked in vinegar with garlic, peppercorns, soy sauce and bayleaf.

Arroz cáldo is a rice-based gruel with bits of chicken and ginger. It is a favorite merienda dish and is best taken while steaming hot.

Balút, a street food delicacy, is actually a steamed fertilized 17-day old duck embryo. Inside the egg is the hardened yellow yolk, the harder egg white, some tasty broth and the embryo. It is eaten with either salt or vinegar.

Bibíngka is a glutinous rice cake with toppings such as cheese, salted egg or grated coconut and sugar. A small plain rice cake with just cheese or no topping at all is called **puto**. Similar preparations from cassava (**kamóteng káhoy**) and glutinous rice with coconut milk (**gatâ**) are called kakanín.

Dinuguán is pig's blood stew with cut-ups of pork and pig organs. The dark broth is made up of vinegar and pig's blood. **Dinuguán** is paired with **puto**.

Ginataán is a traditional merienda fare consisting of sweet potato, **nangkâ**, **sabá**, glutinous rice balls and tapioca pearls (**sagó**) cooked in a slightly thick coconut milk.

Hálo-halò literally means *mix-mix*. It is a cool salad-like preparation consisting of sweetened root tubers and fruits like sweet potato, **sabá** (a variety of banana used for cooking), **nangkâ** (jackfruit), garbanzos, ube, yam, red beans, and topped with shaved ice and evaporated milk.

Karé-karé or oxtail stew uses pork or calf leg and oxtail, vegetables like egg plant, banana heart, string beans and **pechay** (or bok choi) cooked in peanut sauce with a dash of **bagoóng** (shrimp paste).

Lechón (from Spanish **leche** or milk) or **litsón** is basically roasted suckling pig cooked over low charcoal fire for a day. The slow roasting produces crisp red skin and succulent meat. A **lechón** from the Luzon island is usually served with liver sauce while that from the Visayas and Mindanao islands is prepared with stuffings made of spices, wines and even **paélla** (a Spanish dish of meat and seafood) and needs no sauce.

Lumpiá has two varieties. One is the fried spring roll made of sauteed vegetables and ground meat rolled up in a thin egg or flour wrapper. It is topped with peanut sauce and crisp ginger bits. The other spring roll is **saríwang lumpiá** (fresh **lumpiá**) without the wrapper.

Menúdo is a dish made of diced pork and liver cooked with potato, garbanzos and tomato sauce or fresh tomatoes.

Paksíw is a fish or meat dish cooked with enough vinegar, ginger and other spices, usually bayleaf and pepper.

Pinakbét is a combination of sauteed native vegetables with **bagoóng** or strips of dried fish.

Sinigáng is a sour broth of shrimp, fish or pork, and vegetables (**okra**, **kangkong** and string beans). The broth is made sour by tamarind or **kamiás** (green sour fruit).

TAGALOG IDIOMS

An idiom is made up of words that, when taken together, means something other than the meaning of the individual words. Idioms carry a regional story or a logic behind them as well as lend color, grace and precision to speech and writing.

Every language has its own set of idioms, nonnative speakers of the language are challenged and experience difficulty in learning the cultural meaning of such phrases. They are sometimes hesitant to use idioms in conversation for fear of being misunderstood; but they just need confidence and practice to be able to use these expressions correctly.

Filipinos have thousands of idioms. The best way to get acquainted with them is by listening to Filipinos conversing in their own language, reading Filipino comic strips in leading newspapers (some have been made into comic books like Pol Medina Jr.'s depiction of Filipino life and society in his **Pugad Baboy**, literally *Pig's Nest*), watching Filipino TV variety shows and Tagalog dramas, listening to radio talk shows and listing down unfamiliar words or phrases. Below are some Filipino idiomatic expressions that make conversations in Filipino alive.

Anak-páwis (literally, child of perspiration) = poor people, laboring class
 Ang mga anak-páwis ay mahál ng Diyos.
 Poor people are loved by God.

Basâ ang papél (literally, the paper is wet) = cannot be trusted, no longer credible
 Basâ na ang papél niyá sa ákin.   He/She cannot be trusted.
                                                He/She is no longer credible.

Bukás ang palád (literally, with open palm of hand) = generous with money
 Ang áking áma ay bukás ang palád sa mahihírap.   My father is generous with the poor.

Butó't balát (literally, skin and bones) = very thin, emaciated
 Butó't balát na si Pedro nang lumabás sa óspital.   Pedro was very thin when he checked out of the hospital.

Dî-mahulúgang karáyom (literally, no needle may be dropped) = too crowded
   Dî-mahulúgang karáyom sa dami ng táo ang Rizal Park.
   Rizal Park is too crowded.

Hatíng-kapatíd (literally, divide among siblings) = divide or allocate equally, equal share
   Dápat hatíng-kapatíd ang pagbíbigay ng kendi sa mga batà.
   The candies should be divided equally among the children.

Hulog ng langit (literally, dropped from Heaven) = blessing from God, good fortune
   Ang batàng iyán ay hulog ng langit sa áming pamílya.
   That child is a blessing from God to our family.

Kánang-kamáy (literally, right hand) = efficient helper, assistant
   Siyá ang kánang kamáy ko sa tanggapán.
   He/She is my efficient helper in the office.

Kumukulô ang dugô (literally, the blood is boiling) = very angry
   Kumukulô ang dugô ko sa táong iyón.
   I am very angry with that person.

Mababà ang luhà (literally, shallow tears) = cries easily
   Ang áking iná ay mababà ang luhà.
   My mother cries easily.

Mabigát ang bibíg (literally, heavy mouth) = rude, uncouth, insulting, uncivil
   Waláng maraming kaibígan ang táong mabigát ang bibíg.
   Rude people do not have many friends.

Mabilís pa sa alas kuwatro (literally, faster than four o'clock) = acts swiftly, very fast
   Mabilís pa sa alas kuwatro kung siyá'y malígo.
   He/She takes a bath very fast.

Magbanat ng butó (literally, stretch the bone) = to work very hard
   Kailangang magbanat ng butó upang mabuhay.
   We must work hard to survive.

Magsúnog ng kílay (literally, to burn eyebrows) = to study hard
   Magsúnog ka ng kílay para sa iyóng kinábukasan.
   Study hard for your future.

Mahabá ang dilá (literally, long tongue) = gossiper, gossip monger
  Maraming babáe ang mahabá ang dilá.
  Many women are gossipers.

Mahabà ang buntót (literally, long tailed) = spoiled
  Huwág mong pagbigyán ang lahát ng gustó ng batà, bakâ humabà ang buntót niyá.
  Don't give in to everything the child wants lest he/she gets spoiled.

Mahábang dúlang (literally, long low table) = wedding, get married
  Kailán ka ba magmámahábang-dúlang?
  When are you getting married?

Mahangin (literally, windy) = boastful
  Umiwas ka sa táong mahangin.
  Avoid boastful people.

Mahírap pa sa dagâ (literally, poorer than a rat) = extremely poor
  Ang mag-anak na iyón ay mahírap pa sa dagâ.
  That family is extremely poor.

Maitím ang butó (literally, black bones) = evil
  Huwág kang makisáma sa táong iyán. Maitím ang kanyáng butó.
  Don't get involved with that person. He/She is evil.

Makítid ang noó (literally, narrow forehead) = dumb
  Makítid ang noó ng kanyáng kaklase.
  His/Her classmate is dumb.

Malikót ang kamáy (literally, restless hands) = pickpocket, a person who steals from pockets or bags
  Ang táong malikót ang kamáy ay náhuli.
  The pickpocket was arrested.

Matigás ang mukhâ (literally, hard face) = stern-faced
  Ayóko sa babáeng matigás ang mukhâ.
  I don't like a stern-faced woman.

Mukháng Biyernes Santo (literally, a Holy Friday face) = sad or gloomy face
  Siyá ay mukháng Biyernes Santo.
  She looks very sad.

Pagputî ng uwák (literally, when the raven turns white) = never, infinitely
  Makababáyad siya ng útang pagputî ng uwák.
  He/She can never pay his/her debts.

Parang palengke (literally, like a market) = noisy
  Parang palengke ang silíd ng mga batà.
  The children's room is noisy.

Saling-pusà (literally, join-cat) = not really part of the group
  Saling-pusà lamang si Raissa sa larô.
  Raissa is not part of the game.

Sirâ-úlo (literally, broken head) = crazy
  Huwág mong pansinín ang sirâ-úlong iyán.
  Don't mind that crazy person.

Tutà (literally, puppy) = one who blindly follows someone
Siyá ay tutà ng isáng pulítikó.
He is a blind follower of a politician.

Usad-pagóng (literally, moves like a turtle) = very slow
Ang kanyáng pag-unlád ay usad-pagóng.
His progress is very slow.

EVERYDAY TAGALOG EXPRESSIONS

In Lesson Three, an adequate number of everyday expressions—in addition to local versions of *Good day, How are you* and *Excuse me* as well as an introduction to **pô**, which is the Tagalog term for respect—were laid down as groundwork for succeeding lessons.

Listed in this lesson are more standard and common expressions in specific locations such as market and kitchen as well as instructions to children that would be more useful in interacting with native Tagalog speakers.

I. LOCATIONS AND DIRECTIONS

May I ask something?	**Puwédeng magtanóng?**
Where can I find a good restaurant?	**Saán akó makakakíta ng isáng magalíng na réstawran?**
Where can I find a Protestant church?	**Saán akó makakakíta ng simbáhang Protestánte?**
Where can I find a doctor?	**Saán may doktór?**
What is the name of this street?	**Anó ang pangálan ng kalsádang itó?**
Where does Mr. Cruz live?	**Saán nakatirá si Ginoóng Cruz?**
[Please] stop (at the corner)!	**Pára po (sa kánto)!**
Turn right/left.	**Kánan/Kaliwâ.**
Straight ahead.	**Dirétso lang.**
Does a bus stop here?	**Tumítigil ba ang bus dito?**
How long before the (next) bus comes?	**Gaáno katagal ang datíng ng (súsunod na) bus?**
Where is this bus going?	**Saán páparoón ang bus na itó?**
What time does this bus arrive in Manila?	**Anóng oras ang datíng nitóng bus sa Maynilà?**
How do I get to Ortigas Avenue from here?	**Paáno pumuntá sa Ortigas Avenue mulâ ditó?**
What is the name of this barrio?	**Anó ang ngálan ng báryong itó?**
Is this water safe to drink?	**Puwéde bang inumín ang túbig na itó?**
Where can we buy food?	**Saán makákabilí ng pagkain?**
Please show me the way.	**Pakiturò sa ákin ang daán.**
Let us take a taxi.	**Mag-táksi táyo.**
Wait here.	**Maghintáy ka rito.**

II. INSTRUCTIONS FOR CHILDREN

Come here.	**Halíka.**
Wash your hands and face.	**Maghúgas ka ng kamáy at mukhâ.**
Put on your shoes and clothes.	**Isuót mo ang iyóng sapatos at damít.**
Sit down and rest.	**Maupó ka at magpahingá.**
Go to sleep	**Matúlog ka na.**
Pick up your toy.	**Kúnin mo ang iyóng laruán.**
Put away your toys.	**Iligpít mo ang iyóng mga laruán.**
Do not cry.	**Huwág kang umiyák.**
Don't quarrel.	**Huwág kayóng mag-away.**
Go out and play.	**Lumabás kayó at maglarô.**
Do not wake up the baby.	**Huwág mong gisíngin ang sanggól.**

Be a good boy (or girl).	**Magpakábaít ka.**

III. TIME

What time is it?	**Anóng oras na?**
Today is Sunday.	**Ngayón ay Linggó.**
Tomorrow is Monday.	**Búkas ay Lúnes.**
Yesterday was Saturday.	**Sábado kahápon.**
It is now Holy Week.	**Ngayón ay Mahál na Áraw.**
This month is January.	**Ang buwáng ito ay Enéro.**
The date is April 20.	**Ang pétsa ay ika-20** (or **a bente**) **ng Abríl.**
The year is 2007.	**Ang taón ay dalawáng libo at pitó.**

IV. SPEAKING IN TAGÁLOG

I am learning to speak Tagalog.	**Nag-áaral akóng magsalitâ ng Tagálog.**
I speak only little Tagalog.	**Nagsásalitâ akó ng káunti lámang.**
Please talk to me in Tagalog.	**Kausápin mo akó sa Tagálog.**
How do you say ... in Tagalog?	**Paáno sinásabi sa Tagálog ang ... ?**
Please correct my pronunciation.	**Iwastô mo ang áking pagbigkás.**
We are studying your language.	**Nag-áaral kamí ng inyóng wikà.**
Do you speak Tagalog?	**Nagsásalitâ ka ba ng Tagálog?**
I do not understand.	**Hindî ko maintindihán.**
Please repeat.	**Paki-úlit nga.**
What did you say?	**Anóng sinabi mo?**

V. MAKING INTRODUCTIONS

My name is Jonathan.	**Ang pangalan ko ay Jonathan.**
What is your name?	**Anó ang pangalan mo?**
Who are you?	**Síno ka/kayó?**
Where do you live?	**Saán ka nakatirá?**
This is my friend Paolo.	**Itó ang kaibígan kong si Paolo.**
I am pleased to meet you.	**Ikínagagalák kong mákilala kayó.**
Please come and visit us.	**Dumálaw kayó sa ámin.**
I am Jolina's friend.	**Kaibígan akó ni Jolina.**
Who are your companions?	**Síno ang mga kasáma mo?**

Are you my sister's friend?	**Ikáw ba ang kaibígan ng kapatíd kong babáe?**
Do I know you?	**Kilalá ba kitá?**
I know you.	**Kilalá kitá.**
I do not know you.	**Hindí kitá kilalá.**

VI. DRESSING UP

What will you wear?	**Anó ang iyóng isúsuót?**
I do not know. I don't have a new dress.	**Ewan ko. Walá akóng bágong damít.**
That is an old one.	**Lumá na iyán.**

I have nothing to wear.	**Walá akóng máisuót.**
I will wear my Barong Tagalog.	**Isúsuót ko ang áking Bárong Tagálog.**
I like the Barong Tagalog.	**Gustó ko ang Bárong Tagálog.**
It is cool.	**Itó ay malamíg isuót.**
A coat is warm.	**Maínit ang amérikana** (refers to the formal coat and tie introduced by the Americans).

VII. AT A PARTY

The food is ready. Let's eat.	**Handâ na ang pagkain. Kumáin na táyo.**
Eat well.	**Kumáin kayóng mabúti.**
Do you like more rice?	**Gustó mo pa ng kánin?**
Please get some more.	**Kumúha pa kayó.**
Don't be shy.	**Húwag kayóng mahiyâ.** (This is a very common expression of hosts when they offer food to their guests and want to make the guests feel more welcome to their homes.)
Thank you. I am already full.	**Salámat. Busóg na akó.** (or **Húwag na. Salámat.**)

VIII. GOODBYES

It is late (at night). Let's go home.	**Gabí na. Umuwî na táyo.**
Thank you for coming.	**Salámat sa inyóng pagparíto.**
We enjoyed the party.	**Nasiyahán kamí sa inyóng handâ.**
Please come again.	**Pumaríto kayó ulî.**
We will return.	**Babalík kamí.**
Goodbye. Thank you very much.	**Paalám. Maraming salámat.**
Goodbye, until next time.	**Paalám, hanggáng sa mulî.**

IX. IN THE MARKET

Is the meat fresh?	**Sariwà ba ang karne?**
How much is this?	**Magkano ito?**
How much is a kilo of pork?	**Magkano ang isáng kílo ng baboy?**
Give me one kilo of beef.	**Bigyán mo akó ng isáng kílo ng baka.**
This is expensive.	**Ang mahál namán nitó.**
Do you have other things?	**Méron pa ba kayóng ibá?**
Is this made in the Philippines?	**Gawâ ba itó sa Pilipínas?**
Where can I buy souvenirs?	**Saán akó makakabilí ng mga subenir?**
The price is fair.	**Magandáng presyo** (or **Sulit ang presyo**).
This is not the correct change.	**Hindî táma ang suklî.**
Please wrap this item.	**Pakibalot ngâ ninyó itó.**

X. IN THE KITCHEN

The stove is hot.	**Maínit ang pugón.**
The pot is full.	**Punô ang kaseróla.**
The knife is sharp.	**Matálas ang kutsílyo.**
The pantry is empty.	**Waláng lamán ang páminggalan.**
The dishes are clean.	**Malilínis ang mga pinggán.**
The floor is dirty.	**Marumí ang sahíg.**
Let us cook the food.	**Lutúin nátin ang pagkain.**
Wash the vegetables thoroughly.	**Hugásan nang mabúti ang mga gúlay.**
Keep the cabinets in order.	**Iayos mo ang mga kábinet.**

XI. IN THE DINING ROOM

It is time to eat.	**Oras na para kumáin** (or **Kaínan na**).
What's for breakfast (or lunch or dinner)?	**Anó ang ulam?** (**Ulam** or viand goes with rice very meal time.)
Let us say our graces.	**Magpasalamat tayó [sa áting pagkain].**
Will you have meat?	**Gustó mo ng karné?**
Please pass the rice.	**Pakiabót ng kánin.**
Do you have tea?	**Méron bang tsa?**
I would like more tea.	**Gustó ko pa ng tsa.**
Please bring the bread.	**Pakidalá ng tinápay.**
We are through eating.	**Tapós na kamíng kumáin.**
A glass of water please.	**Isáng básong túbig ngâ.**
Please clear the table.	**Pakiligpít ang mésa.**
That was a good meal!	**Ang saráp ng pagkain!**

XII. IN THE LIVING ROOM

Please come in and sit down.	**Tulóy kayó. Maupô kayó.**
We are happy that you came.	**Natútuwâ kamí sa pagparito ninyó.**
This chair is comfortable.	**Ang úpúang itó ay komportable.**
Do you wish to listen to some music?	**Ibig ba ninyóng makiníg ng tugtóg?**
Would you like to read the newspaper?	**Ibig ba ninyóng magbasá ng diyaryo?**
Would you like some cold water?	**Ibig ba ninyó ng malamíg na túbig?**
How long have you been living here?	**Gáano katagál na kayóng nakatirá rito?**
We enjoy living here.	**Nasísiyahán kamíng tumirá rito.**
The people here are friendly and helpful.	**Ang mga tao dito ay mabubuti at matutulungin.**

CONVERSATIONAL TAGALOG

Below are given several examples of Tagalog conversations immediately followed by their English translations (enclosed in brackets). A vocabulary list as well as some cultural notes provide definitions and descriptions of words that have not been used or introduced in the previous lessons.

Pagtatatagpô at Pagpapakilala
Meeting Someone and Making Introductions

Dumating si Peter Smith galing sa Hong Kong. Sinalubong siya ni Linda Reyes, tagapamahala ng mga benta ng kanilang kompanya. (Peter Smith arrived from Hong Kong. He was met by Linda Reyes, sales director of their company.)

LINDA   : **Maligayang pagdating, Ginoong Smith.** (Welcome, Mr. Smith.)

PETER   : **Salamat, kumusta ka Martin?** (Thank you. How are you, Linda?)

LINDA   : **Mabuti po naman. Kayo? Kumusta ang inyong biyahe?** (I am fine. And you? How was your trip?)

PETER   : **Mabuti naman. Maayos ang lahat.** (It was all right. Everything was fine.)

LINDA   : **May reserbasyon kayo sa Manila Peninsula. Narito na ang sundo ninyo na magdadala sa inyo sa otel. Magkita po tayo mamaya doon sa otel para sa pulong.** (You have a reservation at the Manila Peninsula. Here's the person who will drive you to the hotel. I'll see you later at the hotel for the meeting.)

PETER   : **Maraming salamat.** (Thank you.)

Pinulong ni Peter Smith ang mga kawani ng kanilang kompanya sa otel. (Peter Smith met the personnel of the company in the hotel.)

LINDA   : **Ikinararangal kong ipakilala sa inyo ang ating pangulo, Si Ginoong Peter Smith.** (I have the honor to introduce to you our president, Mr. Peter Smith.)

PETER   : **Maraming salamat, Martin. Magandang umaga sa inyong lahat. Natutuwa ako sa muli nating pagkikita sa simula ng bagong taong ito. Binabati ko rin kayong lahat sa inyong magandang benta noong nakaraang taon.** (Thank you very much, Linda. Good morning to you all. I am happy to see you again at the start of this new year. I also congratulate you for the good sales last year.)

LINDA   : **Maraming salamat po. Talaga pong nagsikap ang lahat para maabot at malagpasan ang ating kota. Ginoong Smith, bago po tayo mag-umpisa ng miting, maari po bang ipakilala ko ang mga bago nating direktor?** (Thank you very much, sir. Everybody really tried hard to reach and go beyond our quota. Mr. Smith, before we start the meeting, may I introduce our new directors?)

PETER   : **Sige, ipagpatuloy mo.** (By all means, continue.)

LINDA   : **Ginoong Smith, si Ricardo Sandoval ang ating Katulong na Direktor sa Pagbebenta.** (Mr. Smith, this is Ricardo Sandoval, Assistant Director for Sales.)

PETER   : **Ikinagagalak kitang makilala, Ricardo.** (I am pleased to meet you, Ricardo.)

RICARDO : **Maraming salamat po.** (Thank you, sir.)

LINDA   : **At ito po naman si Binibining Delia Orosa, ang bago nating Direktor sa Pananaliksik.** (And this is Miss Delia Orosa, our new Director for Research.)

PETER   : **Ikinalulugod kong mapabilang ka sa ating pangkat, Delia.** (I am happy to have you in our group, Delia.)

DELIA   : **Salamat po.** (Thank you, sir.)

Vocabulary List

sundô = somebody who fetches	**pangulo** = president
pagbebenta = sales	**páliparan** = airport
pagpapakilala = introduce	**pulong** = meeting
pananaliksík = research	**magsikap** = to work hard
pangkát = group	**ipagpatuloy** = continue

Pagtatanong Ng Direksiyón
Asking Directions

Bagong dating ang mag-inang Aling Ana at Sally sa Quezon City. Galing sila sa lalawigan at bumaba sila sa estasyon ng bus sa Cubao. Pupunta sila sa Makati upang dalawin ang kapatid ni Aling Ana. Nagtanong sila sa isang lalaking dumaraan. (Aling Ana and and her daughter Sally had just arrived in Quezon City. They came from the province and got down at the bus station in Cubao. They are going to Makati to visit Aling Ana's sister. They asked a man who was passing by.)

ALING ANA :   **Mawalang-galang na po. Saan ba ang sakayan patungong Makati?** (Excuse me, sir. Where can we get a ride to Makati?)

LALAKI   :   **Dumiretso kayo riyan, tumawid sa Edsa at sumakay sa bus na may karatulang Ayala.** (Go straight ahead, cross Edsa and board the bus with the signboard Ayala.)

ALING ANA :   **Tanghali na kami. Marahil mas mabilis ang taksi.** (We're already late. Perhaps a taxi will be faster.)

SALLY   :   **Nay, bakit hindi natin subukan ang MRT?** (Mother, why don't we try the MRT?)

LALAKI   :   **Mas mabilis ang MRT. Madali kayong makararating sa Makati. Ang estasyon ng MRT Cubao ay nasa Farmers' Plaza. Bumili kayo ng tiket para sa Buendia Station. Pagdating ninyo roon, marami na kayong masasakyang jeepney o FX.** (MRT is faster. You will reach Makati easily. The Cubao MRT station is in Farmers' Plaza. Buy a ticket for Buendia Station. When you get there, you can take a jeepney or FX.)

ALING ANA :   **Maraming salamat po sa inyong tulong.** (Thank you for your assistance, sir.)

LALAKI   :   **Walang anuman po.** (You're welcome, madam.)

ALING ANA :   **Ibang-iba na ang Maynila ngayon. May MRT at FX na. Sa ating probinsiya ay marami pa ring karetela at traysikel.** (Manila is very different now. They already have the MRT and FX. In the province, we still have a lot of carriages and tricycles.)

Vocabulary List and Notes

bumabâ = to go down	**malapít-lapít** = nearer; a bit near
dirétso = straight ahead	**malayò** = far
dumalaw = to visit	**malayó-layô** = farther; a bit far
lalawigan = province	**tumawíd** = to cross
malapit = near	**MRT** = Metro Rail Transit

FX = an air-conditioned vehicle that can accommodate nine passengers. FX fare is more expensive than a jeepney's.

EDSA = Epifanio de los Santos Avenue, a major thoroughfare crossing several cities in Metro Manila.

Sa Bangko
At the Bank

Kagagaling lamang ni Nestor sa Saudi Arabia. Kailangan niyang magpapalit ng dolyar. Nagpasama siya kay Juan sa bangko. (Nestor has just arrived from Saudi Arabia. He needs to change his dollars into pesos.)

NESTOR :   **Magandang umaga. Maari bang magpapalit ng limang daang dolyar sa piso? Magkano ang palitan ngayon?** (Good morning. May I have my $500 changed into peso? What is the current exchange rate?)

TELLER :   **Kuwarenta y nuwebe po sa dolyar. Pakipunan po ninyo ang aplikasyon na ito.** (Forty-nine pesos to a dollar. Please fill up this application form.)

NESTOR :   **Salamat. Kung nais kong maglagak sa inyong bangko, magkano ang paunang deposito?** (Thank you. If I wish to deposit in your bank, how much is the initial deposit?)

TELLER :   **Sampung libong piso po ang unang deposito.** (The initial deposit is P10,000, sir.)

NESTOR :   **Ano naman ang mga kailangan para magbukas ng account?** (What are needed to open an account?)

TELLER :   **Kailangan ng dalawang ID tulad ng lisensiya ng drayber, pasaporte o SSS.** (Two IDs are needed like a driver's license, passport or SSS.)

NESTOR : **Kailangan rin ba ng litrato?** (Is a photo needed?)
TELLER : **Opo, puwede po kahit ano ang sukat.** (Yes, sir. Any size will do.)
NESTOR : **Maraming salamat. Babalik na lamang ako sa ibang araw.** (Thank you, I'll come back some other day.)

Vocabulary List

lisensiya = license
litrato = photo
magbukas = to open
maglagak = to deposit

magpalit ng pera = to change currency
pakipunán = please fill up
sukat = size

Sa Isang Pulong
In a Meeting

Ang pulong ng samahan ni Tessie ay tuwing ikalawang Martes ng buwan. Ito ay ginaganap sa isang restoran sa Malate. Ang layunin ng kanilang samahan ay tumulong sa mga maralitang kababaihan at kabataan sa Barangay 83 ng Sta. Ana. Noong Martes na iyon, pagkatapos ang pag-awit ng Pambansang Awit at ang panalanging pambungad, tinawag ng kalihim ang mga pangalan ng dumalo sa miting. (Tessie's club meets every second Tuesday of the month. It is held in a restaurant in Malate. The purpose of their club is to help the poor women and children of Barangay 83 of Sta. Ana. That particular Tuesday, after the singing of the National Anthem and the opening prayer, the secretary called the names of those who attended the meeting.)

TESSIE : **Magandang hapon sa inyong lahat. Kalihim Elsa, ilang kasapi ang dumalo sa pulong na ito?** (Good afternoon, everyone. Secretary Elsa, how many members are present in this meeting?)
ELSA : **May labinlimang kasapi ang naririto ngayon maliban kina Mary at Kris.** (There are 15 members present now excluding Mary and Kris.)
TESSIE : **Basahin natin ngayon ang mga tala ng nakaraang miting.** (Let's now read the minutes of the past meeting.)
TESSIE : **Salamat, Kalihim Elsa. Tatalakayin naman natin ang ating pangkabuhayang proyekto sa Tondo. May ulat ang tagapangulo ng lupon, si Pacita.** (Thank you, Secretary Elsa. We will now discuss our livelihood project in Tondo. Pacita, the chairperson of the committee will report.)
PACITA : **Sa ika-8 ng Pebrero, gaganapin ang ating proyekto na magtuturo sa mga kababaihan ng barangay ng iba't ibang paggawa ng longganisa.** (On February 8, we will conduct our project to teach the women of the barangay the different ways of making sausages.)
TESSIE : **Salamat, Pacita. At tungkol naman sa mga bata, ano ang ulat mo, Carol?** (Thank you, Pacita, Regarding the children, what is your report, Carol?)
CAROL : **Sa ika-16 ng Marso, dadalhin natin ang mga bata sa Museo Pambata sa Roxas Boulevard kung saan matututo sila ng maraming kaalaman tungkol sa kanilang paligid. Pagkatapos ay ipapasyal sila sa Rizal Park.** (On March 16, we will take the children to the Children's Museum on Roxas Blvd where they will learn a lot about their surroundings. Then we are taking them to Rizal Park.)
TESSIE : **Paano ang pagkain ng mga bata?** (What about the children's food?)
CAROL : **Isang kompanya ng gatas ang umako sa kanilang pagkain pati na ng kanilang transportasyon.** (A milk company will take care of their food as well as their transportation.)
TESSIE : **Binabati ko kayo, Pacita at Carol sa inyong magandang pamumuno. May iba pa bang bagay tayong tatalakayin? Kung wala na, tinatapos ko na ang miting na ito. Maraming salamat sa inyong pagdalo.** (Congratulations, Pacita and Carol for your fine leadership. Are there other matters to discuss? If none, the meeting is adjourned. Thank you very much for coming.)

Sa Palengke at Tindahan
At the Market and in a Store

Si Ginang Jones at ang kusinera niyang si Ada ay nagpunta sa palengke. Magkakaroon ng munting salu-salo si Ginang Jones para sa mag-asawang Thomas na galing sa Bangkok. Nais ni Ginang Jones na bumili ng mga sari-wang prutas at gulay sa palengke. Pumunta sila sa puwesto ng mga prutas kung saan nakakita sila ng mga mangga, saging, dalandan, papaya, tsiko at lansones. (Mrs. Jones and her cook Ada went to the market. Mrs. Jones will have a small party for the Thomas couple who arrived from Bangkok. Mrs. Jones wants to buy fresh fruits and vegetables in the market. They went to the fruit stand first where they saw mangoes, bananas, oranges, papaya, chico and lanzones.)

GNG. JONES : **Magkano ang mangga?** (How much are the mangoes?)

MALE VENDOR : **Sisenta po ang isang kilo.** (Sixty pesos per kilo.)

ADA : **Saan ba galing ang mga iyan?** (Where do they come from?)

MALE VENDOR : **Sa Pangasinan. Matatamis ang mga mangga na galing doon.** (From Pangasinan. Mangoes from that place are very sweet.)

GNG. JONES : **Bigyan mo ako ng dalawang kilo. Gusto ko rin ng saging na lacatan at isang piña.** (Give me two kilos. I also like **lacatan** and pineapple.)

ADA : **Bibili rin po ba kayo ng pakwan, madam?** (Are you also buying watermelon, madam?)

GNG. JONES : **Oo, gustong-gusto ni Ginoong Jones ang pakwan.** (Yes, Mr. Jones likes watermelon very much.)

MALE VENDOR : **Narito na lahat ng inyong pinamili.** (Here are all the things you have bought.)

GNG. JONES : **Salamat. Pakikuwenta lahat.** (Thank you. Please add up everything.)

Pagkatapos sa prutasan, nagtungo naman sila sa sa gulayan. (From the fruitstand, they went to the vegetable section.)

GNG. JONES : **Bumili tayo ng letsugas, kamatis at sibuyas para sa salad.** (Let's buy lettuce, tomatoes and onions for the salad.)

ADA : **Nais ba ninyong gumawa ako ng lumpiang sariwa?** (Do you want me to prepare fresh vegetable spring roll?)

GNG. JONES : **Oo, gusto ko iyon. Sarapan mo ang salsa.** (Yes, I like that. Make the sauce delicious.)

ADA : **Bibili ako ng petsay, karot, repolyo, abitsuelas at patatas. Hahaluan ko rin ng singkamas ang lumpia.** (I will buy Chinese cabbage, carrot, cabbage, beans and potatoes. I'll also mix turnips in the spring roll.)

GNG. JONES : **Sige, ikaw ang bahala. Pihadong magugustuhan ng ating mga panauhin ang lumpiang Pilipino.** (Okay, it's up to you. For sure, our visitors will like Filipino spring roll.)

Mula sa palengke, nagtungo si Ginang Jones at si Ada sa supermarket na malapit sa kanilang bahay sa Makati. Di kalakihan ang pamilihan pero maraming mga paninda, lokal man o galing sa ibang bansa. Pumunta si Ginang Jones at si Ada sa karnihan. Bumili sila ng lomo, giniling na karneng-baboy, lengua at manok. Nagtungo rin sila sa isdaan. (From the market, Mrs. Jones and Ada went to the supermarket near their house. The supermarket is not very big but it sells a lot of goods, both local and imported. Mrs. Jones and Ada went to the meat section where they bought sirloin, ground pork, ox tongue and chicken. They also went to the fish section.)

GNG. JONES : **Maganda at sariwa ang mga lapu-lapu dito. Pumili ka ng ilang piraso. Pumili ka na rin ng kaunting halaan at sugpo. Ayan, palagay ko nabili na natin ang lahat ng kailangan. Umuwi na tayo.** (The grouper here is good and fresh. Choose a few pieces. Also choose some clams and prawns. There, I guess we have all that we need. Let's go home.)

Sa Mall
At the Mall

Isa sa mga libangan ng mga Pilipino sa lungsod ay ang pagtungo sa mall tuwing Sabado at Linggo. Isang Sabado, ang mag-asawang Fidel at Dolor at ang kanilang mga anak na sina Boyet at Helen, ay nagpunta sa isang mall sa Quezon City. (One of the recreational activities of Filipinos in the city is going to the mall on weekends. One

Saturday, the couple Fidel and Dolor and their children, Boyet and Helen, went to a mall in Quezon City.)

DOLOR : **Tumingin-tingin muna tayo sa mga tindahan bago manood ng sine.** (Let's take a look around at the stores first before we watch a movie.)
HELEN : **Pumunta tayo sa tindahan ng mga plaka. May bagong labas ngayon ang bandang Hale.** (Let's go to the record store. The band Hale has a new release.)
BOYET : **Sa tindahan ng mga kompyuter ang gusto ko. May mga bagong labas na mga laro.** (I like to go to computer stores. There are new games.)
DOLOR : **Pumunta rin tayo sa loob ng department store. Bagsak-presyo sila sa maraming bagay. Baka ma-kabili ako ng sapatos.** (Let's go inside the department store. They have slashed prices on many items. I might be able to buy a pair of shoes.)
FIDEL : **Ay naku, lumalaki ang gastos!** (My! It's getting more expensive!)
HELEN : **Daddy, tignan mo. Napakaraming kainan dito. Parang masarap lahat.** (Look Daddy, there are many restaurants here. They all seem good.)
FIDEL : **Oo nga, pero mahal lamang ng kaunti.** (Yes, it's true, but it's a bit more expensive.)
DOLOR : **Fidel, bakit hindi ka bumili ng bagong pantalon? Luma na ang damit pampasok mo sa opisina.** (Fidel, why don't you buy a new pair of pants? Your office clothes are already worn-out.)
FIDEL : **Tignan natin.** (Let's see.)
BOYET : **Daddy, Mommy, may palabas pala ang mga artista dito. Manood tayo.** (Daddy, Mommy, there's a show by artists here. Let's have a look.)
DOLOR : **Baka tayo gabihin.** (It might be late by then.)
BOYET : **Sandali lamang po. Wala namang pasok bukas.** (It won't take long. Anyway, there are no classes tomorrow.)
DOLOR : **Siya, siya, sige na nga.** (All right, all right, let's go.)

Notes

It is never sufficient to translate the word *mall* into **tindahan** (or *store*) in Tagalog. The malls in the Philippines are multistory shopping centers that offer everything from food to entertainment to books and clothes. Also, the word *mall* has been adapted into the language of Filipinos, probably since the early 1990s. The word is also quite synonymous to a department store although it may be also found inside a mall.

Sa Oras ng Pagkain
At Mealtime

A. **ALMUSAL** (BREAKFAST)

Magkasabay nag-agahan ang pamilyang Aquino nang umagang iyon. Gaya ng dati, naghanda ng sinangag na kain si Aling Betty para sa pamilya. Nagprito rin siya ng tuyo at nagbati ng itlog. (The Aquino family had breakfast together that morning. As usual, Aling Betty prepared fried rice for her family. She also fried dried fish and scrambled eggs.)

ALING BETY : **Kumain kayo habang mainit pa ang sinangag.** (You better eat now while the fried rice is still hot.)
MANG JOSE : **Magdasal muna tayo bago kumain.** (Let's pray first before eating.)
DAUGHTER : **Nanay, paki-abot po ang binating itlog at kanin.** (Mother, please pass the scrambled eggs and rice.)
SON : **Gusto ko rin po ng binating itlog.** (I also like scrambled eggs.)
MANG JOSE : **Pakilagyan nga ng mainit na tubig ang tasa ko.** (Could you please pour hot water into my cup?)
ALING BETTY : **Mga bata, inumin ninyo ang inyong tsokolate.** (Children, drink your chocolate.)
CHILDREN : **Opô, inay.** (Yes, mother.)
ALING BETTY : **Kumain kayo nang mabuti para hindi magutom sa eskuwela.** (Eat well, so you won't get hungry in school.)

B. **TANGHALIAN** (LUNCH)

LORENZO : **Ano ang pananghalian, Manang?** (What's for lunch, **Manang**?)
MAID : **Nagluto ako ng paksiw na bangus at ginisang monggo.** (I cooked milkfish in vinegar and sauteed mung beans.)
LORENZO : **May kahalo bang bunga ng ampalaya?** (Does it have bittermelon fruit?)
MAID : **Oo, isinama ko na pati dahon.** (Yes, I also included the leaves.)
LORENZO : **Naku, masarap ang kain ko ngayon.** (My, I shall have a good meal today.)
MAID : **May minatamis din na saba.** (There is also sweetened **saba**.)

C. **HAPUNAN** (SUPPER)

Gabi na nang dumating si Mang Ignacio sa kanilang bahay. (It was already late in the evening when Mang Ignacio arrived home.)

MANG IGNACIO : **Masyado akong natrapik sa EDSA kaya ako ginabi.** (I was caught in a traffic along EDSA, that's why I'm late.)
ALING MAYA : **Siya, kumain ka na. Baka gutom na gutom ka na. Iinit ko lang ang ulam. Kumain na ang mga bata. Nag-aaral sila sa kanilang kuwarto.** (Well, you better eat now. I will reheat your food. The children had already eaten. They are studying in their room.)
MANG IGNACIO : **Salamat. Masarap ang ulam. Gusto ko ng ginataang tilapia.** (Thank you. The viand is delicious. I like tilapia in coconut milk.)

Vocabulary List and Notes

almusál = breakfast, also **agahan**
siya = colloquial term for *all right* or *okay*, do not confuse with the pronoun **siyá**
ulam = viand; dish of meat or vegetables that goes with rice in every meal
manang (for females) or **manong** (for males) = names used to address an older maid or any elderly person who serves in a household or sells commodities; **ate** (pronounced **a-te**) is frequently used to address a younger maid

---

Pagdalaw Sa Maysakít
Visiting an Ill Person

Dumalaw si Aling Lourdes sa kaibigang maysakit. May dala siyang isang dosenang dalandan. (Lourdes visited her sick friend. She brought a dozen oranges.)

LOURDES : **Tao po.**
PEDRO : **Aba! Si Aling Lourdes pala. Pasok kayo.** (Oh! It's Aling Lourdes. Please come in.)
LOURDES : **Kamusta ang asawa mo?** (How is your wife?)
PEDRO : **Mabuti-buti po ngayon. Pasok kayo. Narito siya.** (She's getting better now. Please come in. She is here.)
LOURDES : **Maria, kumusta ka na? Ano ba ang lagay mo ngayon?** (Maria, how are you? What is your condition now? How are you feeling now?)
MARIA : **Masakit ang aking dibdib at may lagnat ako sa hapon.** (My chest is painful and I have fever in the afternoon.)
LOURDES : **Maganda na ang kulay mo ngayon kaysa noong huli kitang dinalaw. May dala akong dalandan para sa iyo.** (Your color is better now than the last time I visited you. I brought some oranges for you.)
MARIA : **Naku, salamat, Lourdes. Nag-abala ka pa.** (Thank you, Lourdes. You shouldn't have bothered.)

LOURDES : **Mabuti'y patingin ka na sa doctor habang maaga nang gumaling ka.** (It's better for you to see a doctor this early so you can recover faster.)

MARIA : **Oo nga. Dadalhin ako ng aking anak sa PGH** (or Philippine General Hospital) **bukas. Wala raw bayad doon.** (Yes, that's true. My son will take me to PGH tomorrow. They say it's free there.)

LOURDES : **Siya, hindi na ako magtatagal para makapahinga ka na. At saka na ako paparito ulit.** (Well, I will not stay long so you can have some rest. I will visit you again.)

MARIA : **Maraming salamat sa pagdalaw mo.** (Thank you for visiting.)

LOURDES : **Adios.** (Goodbye.)

Notes

Tao pô = a set expression used to announce the presence of a person outside of somebody's house, especially if there is no doorbell

aling or **mang** = names used to address unrelated older persons, **aling** (for females) or **mang** (for males) is placed before the names; even those of the same age, especially the older people themselves, call each other this way.

Sa Páaralán
At School

Tapos na ang bakasyon sa tag-araw ng mga estudiyante. Muling pumasok sa kanilang paaralan sina Antonio at Roberta. May nakilala silang bagong lipat mula sa ibang paaralan at nagpakilala sila. (The students' summer vacation had ended. Antonio and Roberta went back to school. They met a transferee from another school and they introduced themselves.)

ANTONIO : **Ang pangalan ko ay Antonio.** (My name is Antonio.)

ROBERTA : **Ang pangalan ko naman ay Robert.** (And my name is Roberta.)

RICKY : **Ako si Ricky. Galing ako sa Bulacan.** (I am Ricky. I came from Bulacan.)

ANTONIO : **Bakit ka lumipat dito sa Maynila?** (Why did you transfer to Manila?)

RICKY : **Mas malapit ang trabaho ng ama ko dito kaysa sa Bulacan kaya lumipat na rin ang buong pamilya namin dito.** (My father's work is nearer here than to Bulacan so the whole family decided to move here.)

ROBERTA : **Ano ba ang taon at seksiyon mo?** (What is your year and section?)

RICKY : **Pangalawang taon, seksiyon 2.** (Second year, section 2.)

ANTONIO : **Magkaseksiyon pala tayo sa pangalawang taon. Halika, sumama ka sa amin. Tumunog na ang kampana.** (It seems we belong to the same section in the second year. Come, join us. The bell has rung.)

RICKY : **Salamat.** (Thank you.)

ROBERTA : **Maraming nag-aaral dito. May pang-umaga at may panghapon na mga seksiyon. Mahusay rin ang mga guro rito.** (There are many students here. There are morning and afternoon sections. The teachers here are also good.)

RICKY : **Nasaan ang aklatan?** (Where is the library?)

ANTONIO : **Nasa ikatlong palapag. Ipapasyal ka namin mamaya sa buong eskuwelahan, sa aklatan, sa gym at palaruan sa likod ng gusali.** (On the third floor. We will tour you later around the school, to the library, gym and playground behind the building.)

ROBERTA : **May kantina rin banda roon. Doon tayo mananananghalian.** (There's a canteen over there. We will have lunch there.)

RICKY : **May dala akong baon.** (I brought my own lunch.)

ANTONIO : **Hindi bale. Dalhin mo, doon ka na kumain sa kantina.** (It doesn't matter. Bring your lunch with you and eat it in the canteen.)

RICKY : **Salamat. Maraming salamat. Sana maging magkakaibigan tayo.** (Thank you. Thank you very much. I hope we would be friends.)

ROBERTA : **Siyempre naman.** (Of course.)

Magbakasyón Táyo
Let's Go on a Vacation

Ang mag-anak na Santos ay pumunta sa isang bakasyunan sa Batangas. Malapit ang bakasyunan sa dagat at maraming mga punong niyog sa paligid. (The Santos family went to a resort in Batangas. The resort is near the sea and has many coconut trees all around.)

SON : **Lumangoy tayo sa dagat mamaya.** (Let's swim in the sea later.)

MOTHER : **Teka, hindi pa tayo nakakapag-ayos ng mga gamit natin. Pumunta muna tayo sa kubo na inilaan sa atin.** (Wait. We have not fixed our things yet. Let's go first to the **nipa** hut reserved for us.)

DAUGHTER : **Inay, tignan mo. May bangka sa aplaya. Puwede tayong mamangka.** (Mother, look. There's a boat on the beach. We can go boating.)

FATHER : **Makikipag-ayos tayo sa katiwala tungkol sa pamamangka. Kailangang mag-ingat tayo. Kung minsan lumalakas ang alon sa lugar na ito.** (We will make an arrangement with the caretaker regarding the use of the boat. We have to be careful. Sometimes the waves in this place can be very strong.)

MOTHER : **Ibaba na ninyo ang mga gamit mula sa kotse. Iyong mga kaldero, mga plato, kalan, ihawan, kubyertos at ang lalagyan ng yelo.** (Unload the things from the car. The pans, plates, stove, griller, the silverware and the ice container.)

FATHER : **Narito ang lahat. Ano ba ang iluluto natin ngayon?** (Everything is here. What are we going to cook now?)

MOTHER : **Ihawin mo na ang dalag na nabili natin sa daan. At ilaga mo na ang mga alimango. Nagluto na ako ng adobong manok at gulay sa bahay kaninang umaga.** (Grill the mudfish that we bought along the road. Boil the crabs, too. I already cooked chicken **adobo** and vegetables at home.)

FATHER : **Hoy, mga bata. Tulungan ninyo ako rito. Pagkapananghalian ay maglalakad tayo sa aplaya. Makapamumulot kayo ng kabibe.** (Hey children. Give me a hand. After lunch, we'll walk along the beach. You can pick up shells.)

CHILDREN : **Tayo na, bilisan natin para makalangoy tayo kaagad.** (Come on, hurry so we can swim at once.)

Vocabulary Lists

ABBREVIATIONS

adj.	adjective	*conj.*	conjunction	*part.*	particle	*syn.*	synonym
adv.	adverb	*gr.*	greetings	*pr.*	pronoun	*v.*	verb
ant.	antonym	*interj.*	interjection	*pref.*	prefix	*vl.*	verbal
art.	article	*n.*	noun	*prep.*	preposition		

TAGALOG–ENGLISH

– A –

aba *interj.* exclamation of surprise, wonder, admiration

abala *adj.* busy, occupied

abo *n.* ashes

adiyos *interj.* Goodbye!

agad *adv.* at once, soon

ahas *n.* snake

aklatan *n.* library

alaala *n.* memory; gift

alaga *n.* someone under one's care

alahas *n.* jewelry

alam *vl.* to have knowledge of something

alat *n.* salty taste, **maalat** *adj.* salty

alikabok *n.* dust

alis *n.* depart

alisan *v.* to remove from

alisin *v.* to remove

aliwan *n.* entertainment, pastime

alon *n.* wave

ama *n.* father

amerikana *n.* a man's coat

amo *n.* master, boss, employer

amoy *n.* smell, odor

anak *n.* child; ~ **na lalaki** *n.* son; ~ **na babae** daughter

ani *n.* harvest

anino *n.* shadow

año *n.* year

anunsiyo *n.* advertisement, announcement

anyaya (*syn.* **paanyaya**) *n.* invitation

aplaya *n.* beach, seashore

aplikante *n.* applicant

aplikasyon *n.* application

apo *n.* grandchild

apoy *n.* flame

araro *n.* plow

araw *n.* sun; day

arte (*syn.* **sining**) *n.* art

artista *n.* performer; a person skilled in an art

asawa *n.* wife or husband

asim *n.* sour taste; **maasim,** *adj.* sour

asin *n.* salt

aso *n.* dog

aso *n.* smoke

aspile *n.* pin

asukal *n.* sugar

ate *n.* elder sister

awa *n.* pity; **kawawa,** *adj.* pitiful

away *n.* quarrel; a fight

ay! *interj.* exclamation of despair, sadness

ayaw *n.* dislike

ayos *n.* order, arrangement, appearance; *interj.* All-right!

aywan idiomatic expression, to not know. **Aywan ko** I don't know.

– B –

baba *n.* chin

baba *n.* lowness; **mababa,** *adj.* low

babae *n.* woman, female

baboy *n.* pork; pig

baga *n.* live charcoal

baga *n.* lungs

bago *adv.* before

bagong pasok *n.* new entry, newcomer

bagsak-presyo *adj.* slashed or discounted price

baha *n.* flood

bahagi *n.* a part, portion

bahala na! common expression meaning "Come what may."

bahay *n.* house

bahay kubo *n.* nipa hut

baitang *n.* grade; steps (of stairs)

baka *part.* used to express doubt

bakal *n.* iron, steel

bakasyunan *n.* a resort

bakod *n.* fence; **bakuran** *n.* yard

bakya *n.* wooden shoes

balak *n.* plan, aim, purpose

balikbayan *n.* a person who returns to his/her home-land for a visit

balita *n.* news

balon *n.* water well

balot *n.* wrapping; **balutan** *n.* package

bandila *n.* flag, banner

bangka *n.* boat, banca

bangko *n.* bank

bangus *n.* milkfish

banig *n.* buri mat

bansa *n.* nation, country; **pambansa** *n.* national

bantay *n.* watchman, guard

baon *n.* food or money provision

bapor *n.* ship

barangay *n.* smallest political unit in Philippine government

barbero *n.* barber; **barberya** (*syn.* **pagupitan**) *n.* barbershop

barkada *n.* peer, a circle of friends

baro *n.* dress

basa *adj.* wet

basag *adj.* broken

basag-ulo *n.* (idiom) fight; **basagulero** *n.* trouble-maker

baso *n.* drinking glass

bata *n.* child; ~**ng babae** girl; ~**ng lalaki** boy

batas *n.* law

bati *n.* greeting; *v.* to greet

bato *n.* stone; kidney

bawal *vl.* prohibited, not allowed

bawang *n.* garlic

bawa't *pron.* every, each

bayad *n.* payment

bayan *n.* town, country

bayani *n.* hero

bibig *n.* mouth

bigas *n.* rice

bigat *n.* weight, heaviness; **mabigat** *adj.* heavy

bigla *adj.* suddenly, at once

bilang *n.* number; *conj.* as

bili *vl.* amount paid for a thing

bilibid *n.* prison

bintana (*syn.* **durungawan**) *n.* window

binyag *n.* baptism

biro *n.* joke; **mapagbiro** *adj.* jester, full of jokes

bisig *n.* arms

biyahe *n.* trip, travel; **magbiyahe** *v.* to travel

bombilya *n.* electric bulb

boses (*syn.* **tinig**) *n.* voice

bote *n.* bottle

buhangin *n.* sand

buhay *n.* life

bukas *adv.* open; **buksan** *v.* to open

bukid *n.* field, farm

bukod sa *prep.* except, aside from, besides

– D –

daan (*syn.* **kalye, kalsada**) *n.* road, street; *adj.* hundred

dagat *n.* sea

dahon *n.* leaf

dakila *adj.* great; foremost

dalaw *n.* visit

dalawahan *n.* doubles

dalo *v.* to attend an event

daloy *n.* flow

damdamin *n.* emotion, feelings

damit *n.* cloth, dress

dangal (*syn.* **karangalan**) *n.* honor

dapat *pseudo v.* must, ought

dati *adj.* former; *adv.* formerly

daw *conj.* it is said

deposito *n.* money deposited in bank

dibdib *n.* breast, chest

dila *n.* tongue

dilaw *adj.* yellow

diligin *v.* to water, sprinkle water on

dilim (*syn.* karimlan) *n.* darkness

din *adv.* also, too

disgrasya (*syn.* aksidente) *n.* acccident

dito *adv.* here (near the speaker)

diyan *adv.* there (near the person spoken to)

diyaryo (*syn.* pahayagan) *n.* newspaper

Diyos (*syn.* Bathala, May-kapal) *n.* God, supreme being

doktor (*syn.* manggagamot) *n.* doctor of medicine

doon *adv.* there (far from the person talking)

dugo *n.* blood

dulo *n.* end

dumating *v.* to arrive; pagdating *n.* arrival

dumi *n.* dirt, refuse

dunong (*syn.* karunungan) *n.* knowledge, ability

duwag *adj.* coward

duyan *n.* hammock, cradle

– E –

eksamen *n.* examination; *v.* to examine

electrika *n.* electric, electrical

elegante *adj.* elegant, classy

eskuwela *n.* school

espesyal *adj.* good; special, extraordinary

estasyon *n.* station, waiting shed

estudyante *n.* student

– G –

gabi *n.* night, evening

galing sa *vl*, come from

galit *n.* anger; galit *adj.* angry

gamit *n.* use, usefulness; gamitin *v.* to use

gamot *n.* medicine;

gamutin *v.* to cure

ganda *n.* beauty

ganito *adv.* like this

ganyan *adv.* like that

gastos *n.* expenses

gatas *n.* milk

ginabi *v.* overtaken by nightfall

ginisa *n.* sauteed meat or vegetables

ginoo *n.* gentleman, mister

ginto *n.* gold

gising *adj.* awake; gisingin *v.* to wake up someone

gitna *n.* middle, center

goma *n.* rubber; rubber tire of cars

grado *n.* grade; class

gripo *n.* faucet

gugo *n.* refers to the bark from local gugo trees used as organic shampoo

guhit *n.* line

gulay *n.* vegetable

gulayan *n.* vegetable section in market; vegetable farm

gunting *n.* scissors

gupit *n.* haircut

gupitin *v.* to cut with a pair of scissors

guro *n.* teacher

gusali *n.* building

gusto *pseudo v.* like, desire

gutom *adj.* hungry; *n.* hunger

– H –

habâ *adj.* elongated

habà *n.* length

habang *conj./adv.* while, so long as

hagdan *n.* ladder

halaga *n.* cost, importance

halalan *n.* election

halamang gamot *n.* herbal plant

halik *n.* kiss

halimbawa *n.* example

handaan *n.* celebration, party

hangal *adj.* ignorant, stupid

hanggang *conj.* until

hangin *n.* wind, air

hapon *n.* afternoon

hapunan *n.* supper

harap *n.* front; sa harap *prep.* in front

hardin (*syn.* halamanan) *n.* garden, lawn

hatinggabi *n.* midnight

hatol *n.* judgment, decision

hawak *n.* hold

hawakan *v.* to hold

hayop *n.* animal

heto *adv.* here, here it is

hilaga *n.* north

hilaw *n.* unripe (fruit), uncooked (food)

hindi *adv.* no, not

hininga *n.* breath

hinlalaki *n.* thumb

hinog *adj.* ripe

hintay *v.* to wait for

hintayan *n.* a waiting place

hipon *n.* shrimp

hiram *adj.* borrowed; hiramin *v.* to borrow

hiya *n.* shame; mahiya *v.* to be ashamed

hukbo *n.* army; ~ng-dagat *n.* navy

huli *adj.* late

humiga *v.* to lie down

huminga *v.* to breathe

humingi *v.* to ask for, to request

husto *adj.* exact, fit, enough

huwag *adv.* do not

– I –

iba *adj.* other, another, different

ibabâ *n.* lower part; *v.* to lower the position; *prep.* under, below, down

ibabaw (*syn.* tuktók) *n.* above, on

ibig *v.* love; like; umibig *v.* to love

ibigay *v.* to give

ibon *n.* bird

ihawan *n.* griller, roaster

ilagay *v.* to put, to place

ilalim *adv.* beneath; sa ilalim *prep.* under

ilan *pron.* some; *adv.* how many

ilaw *n.* light, light fixtures

ilista *v.* to list down

ilog *n.* river

ilong *n.* nose

imbestigasyon (*syn.* pagsisiyasat) *n.* investigation

ina *n.* mother

ingay *n.* noise; maingay *adj.* noisy

inggit *n.* envy; mainggitin *adj.* envious

init *n.* heat, warmth, mainit *adj.* hot, warm

inúmin *n.* a drink; inumín *v.* to drink

isahan *adj.* single, singular

isama *v.* to take along; include

isara *v.* to close something

isauli *v.* to return something

isda *n.* fish

isdaan *n.* place where fish is sold

isip *n.* mind, thought; mag-isip *v.* to think

isuot *v.* to wear, to put on

itaas *adv.* above; *v.* to put up

itapon *v.* to throw away

itim *adj.* black

itlog *n.* egg

ituro *v.* to teach something, to show or point

iwan *v.* to leave behind

iyak *n.* cry; iyakin *adj.* cry-baby

– K –

kaagad *adv.* immediately

kaarawan *n.* birthday

kababayan *n.* fellow citizen

kabayo *n.* horse

kabibi *n.* empty clam shell

kabihasnan *n.* civilization

kabisado *v.* memorized

kabuhayan *n.* livelihood

kabutihan *n.* goodness; virtue

kagabi *adv.* last night

kagalang-galang *adj.* honorable; respectable

kagalit *n.* enemy

kagatin *v.* to bite

kaginhawahan *n.* relief from pain, consolation; luxury

kahapon *n.* yesterday

kahon *n.* box

kahoy *n.* wood, lumber

kaibigan *n.* friend

kailangan *pseudo v.* to need something; *adv.* necessary

kainan *n.* eatery

kakanin *n.* rice delicacies

kakilala *n.* acquaintance

kalabaw *n.* carabao

kalahati *n., adj.* one half

kalakal *n.* merchandise, goods

kalakip *adj.* included, enclosed

kalan *n.* clay stove

kalawang *n.* rust

kalayaan *n.* independence, liberty; **malaya** *adj.* free

kaldero *n.* cauldron, pot

kalesa *n.* two-wheeled vehicle pulled by a horse

kaligayahan *n.* happiness, contentment

kalihim *n.* secretary

kaliwa *n.* left (direction)

kalusugan *n.* health, well-being

kamag-anak *n.* relative

kamatayan *n.* death

kamatis *n.* tomato

kamay *n.* hand

kambal *n.* twin

kamisadentro *n.* man's shirt

kamiseta *n.* undershirt

kampana *n.* church bell

kanan *n.* right (direction)

kandila *n.* candle

kanin *n.* cooked rice

kanina *adv.* a moment ago

kanluran *n.* west; **kanluranin** *adj.* western

kanta (*syn.* **awit**) *n.* song; **mang-aawit** *n.* singer

kantina *n.* canteen

kapalaran *n.* fate

kapatid *n.* sibling, brother or sister

kape *n.* coffee

kapitbahay *n.* neighbor

karapatan *n.* right

karatula *n.* signboard

karayom *n.* needle

karne *n.* meat

karnihan *n.* place where meat is sold

kasama *n.* companion

kasapi *n.* member of an organization

kaserola *n.* caserole, cooking utensils

katas *n.* juice of fruits; **makatas** *adj.* juicy

katawan *n.* body

katulong *n.* helper, servant

kaunti *adj.*, *adv.* few, little

kawad *n.* wire; **~-elektrika** *n.* electric wire

kawani *n.* employee

kawawa *adj.* pitiful

kawayan *n.* bamboo

kay to (name of person), **sa kay** for (name of person)

kaya *conj.* so, *v.* can, be able to

kaysa *conj.* than

kayumanggi *n.* color of race of Filipinos; *adj.* brown complexion

keso *n.* cheese

kinatawan *n.* representative

klase *n.* class in school; kinds

klub *n.* club

konsulta (*syn.* **magpatingin**) *n.* consult; **konsultasyon** *n.* consultation

kuko *n.* fingernail

kulambo *n.* mosquito net

kulay *n.* color

kulog *n.* thunder

kumain *v.* to eat

kumot *n.* blanket

kumpuni *v.* to repair

kumuha *v.* to get

kumusta *gr.* How are you?

kundiman *n.* native love song

kung *conj.* if, when, as to

kuru-kuro *n.* opinion

kurtina *n.* curtain

kusina *n.* kitchen

kusinera/o (*syn.* **tagapagluto**) *n.* cook

kutsara *n.* spoon

kutsero *n.* calesa driver

kutsilyo *n.* knife

kuwadro *n.* picture frame

kuwarto *n.* room

kuwenta *n.* bill, account

kuwento *n.* story, fiction

kuwero *n.* leather

kuwintas *n.* necklace

– L –

laban *n.* fight, contest

labanan *v.* to fight someone or something

labas *n.* outside; **sa labas** *adv.* outside; **palabas** *n.* presentation, show

labi *n.* lower lip

labing- *pref.* means more than 10 when placed before a cardinal number from one to nine, **labing-isa** 11; **labingwalo** 18

labis *n.* surplus; *adv.* more than enough

lagay (*syn.* **kalagayan**) *n.* condition, state

lagda (*syn.* **pirma**) *n.* signature

lagi *adv.* always

lagnat *n.* fever

lagyan *v.* to put

lahat *pron.* all, everybody

lahi *n.* race of people, nationality

lakad *n.* walk; **lumakad** *v.* to walk

lakas *n.* strength, force

laki *n.* size; **lumalaki** *present v.* growing, increasing in size

lalagyan *n.* container

lalaki *n.* man, male

lalamunan *n.* throat

lamang *adv.* only

lambat *n.* fishing net

lamig *n.* coldness; **malamig** *adj.* cold

lamok *n.* mosquito

langaw *n.* housefly

langgam *n.* ants

langis *n.* oil

langoy *n.* swim; **lumangoy** *v.* to swim

lansangan *n.* street

lapis *n.* pencil

laro *n.* play, game

laruan *n.* toy

lasa *n.* taste

lasing *n.* drunkard

lasingan *n.* a noisy drinking party

lason *n.* poison

lata *n.* tin can

laway *n.* saliva

laya *n.* freedom; **malaya** *adj.* free, independent

layo *n.* distance; **malayo** *adj.* far; distant

layon (*syn.* **layunin**, **pakay**) *n.* aim, purpose

libangan *n.* recreation, entertainment

libro (*syn.* **aklat**) book

ligaya *n.* happiness; *adj.* **maligaya**

ligo *n.* bath; **maligo** to take a bath

liham *n.* letter

lihim *n.* secret

likas *adj.* native of; *adj.* natural

likha *n.* creation; product

likod *n.* at the back, rear

lindol *n.* earthquake

linggo *n.* week; *n.* Sunday

linis *n.* cleanliness; **malinis** *adj.* clean; **linisin** *v.* to clean

lipon *n.* group

lipunan *n.* society

listahan (*syn.* **talaan**) *n.* list

litrato (*syn.* **larawan**) *n.* picture

litson *n.* roasted pig; **litsunin** *v.* to roast

longganisa *n.* native sausage

loob *n.* interior; **sa loob** *adv.* inside

luma *adj.* not new

lumapit *v.* to come near, to approach

lumipad *v.* to fly

lumipat *v.* to move to another place

lumubog *v.* to sink

lungsod *n.* city

luntian *adj.* green

lupa *n.* earth, ground, land

lutò *n.* cuisine; *adj.* cooked food

– M –

maaari *v.* possible

maaga *adv.* early

mabaho *adj.* bad-smelling

mabait (*syn.* **mabuti**) *adj.* good (used with persons and animals)

mabangga *v.* to bump against, to collide with

mabango *adj.* fragrant

mabigat *adj.* heavy

mabuhay *interj.* Long live! *v.* to live

mabuti *adj.* good (character of an individual); well (mental and physical condition of an individual)

madalang *adv.* rare, infrequent

madalas *adv.* often, frequent

madali *adj.* easy; *adv.* fast

madilim *adj.* dark

magalang *adj.* courteous

magaling *adj.* good, excellent; free from sickness

mag-anak *n.* family

maganda *adj.* beautiful

mag-aral *v.* to study

mag-asawa *n.* husband and wife; *v.* to marry

magasin *n.* magazine

magdasal *v.* to pray

maghain *v.* to set the table

maghapon *adv.* all day long

maghugas *v.* to wash

magkano *adv.* how much?

magkapatid *adj.* a set of brothers or sisters

maglaba *v.* to wash clothes

maglaro *v.* to play; **manlalaro** *n.* player

magpaalam *v.* to bid goodbye

magpahinga *v.* to rest

magpalipas *v.* to while the hours away

magpareserba *v.* to have something reserved for someone

magpasyal *v.* to take a walk

magsasaka *n.* farmer

magsimba *v.* to hear mass, to go to church

magtanim *v.* to plant

magulat *v.* to be surprised

magutom *v.* to be hungry

mahaba *adj.* long

mahal *adj.* dear, precious, expensive

mahusay *adj.* efficient, exceptional

maingay *adj.* noisy

mainit *adj.* hot, warm

maitim *adj.* black

makabago *adj.* modern, up-to-date

makabayan *adj.* patriotic, nationalistic

makapal *adj.* thick

makina *n.* machine; sewing machine

makita *v.* to see

makiusap *v.* to plead, to make a request

makulit *adj.* annoying; wearisome

malamig (*ant.* **mainit**) *adj.* cold, cool

malapit (*ant.* **malayo**) *adj.* near

malayo *adj.* far

malinis (*ant.* **madumi**) *adj.* clean

maliwanag (*ant.* **madilim**) *adj.* clear, bright

malungkot (*ant.* **masaya**) *adj.* sad

malusog *adj.* healthy

mama *n.* a grown man, also a term used to address a man unknown to the speaker

mamamayan *n.* citizen

mamaya *adv.* by and by, later on (within the day)

mamulot *v.* to pick something

manalangin *v.* to pray

manang *n.* elder sister

manigo *adj.* prosperous

maniwala *v.* to believe

manok *n.* chicken

manong *n.* older person not related to speaker

mantika *n.* cooking oil

mantikilya *n.* butter

maputi *adj.* white

marami *adj.* much, many

marka *n.* grade; trade mark

marumi (*ant.* **malinis**) *adj.* dirty

marunong (*syn.* **matalino**) *adj.* intelligent, wise

masahe *n.* massage

masama *adj.* bad, wicked

masarap *adj.* delicious, tasty; pleasant

masaya *adj.* happy, cheerful

masipag *adj.* industrious

masunurin *adj.* obedient

masyado *adj.* excessive

mata *n.* eye

mataba (*syn.* **payat**) *adj.* fat

matamis *adj.* sweet

matamisin *v.* to make into dessert

matanda *n.* old person; *adj.* aged, elderly, old

matangkad (*syn.* **pandak**) *adj.* tall

matigas (*syn.* **malambot**) *adj.* hard

mayaman (*syn.* **mahirap**) *adj.* rich, wealthy

may-ari *n.* owner

maysakit *n.* patient, sick person

medyas *n.* socks, stockings

mesa *n.* table

minuto (*syn.* **sandali**) *n.* minute

misa *n.* religious mass

misang pasasalamant *n.* Thanksgiving Mass

miting *n.* pulong

mukha *n.* face

mula sa *prep.* from

mura *adj.* cheap

– N –

nakatira *v.* living in, a resident of

naku *interj.* an expression of surprise, shortened form of **Ina ko!**

naman *adv.* also, in like manner

namatay *v.* died

nang *conj.* when (for past actions); *adv.* any more, more

naparito *v.* came

naparoon *v.* went

narito *v.* here

naroon *v.* there

nasa *prep.* expresses position, location or direction

nasaan *adv.* where

negosyo *n.* business, industry

nerbiyos *n.* nervousness

nga *part.* please, really, truly

ngayon *adv.* now, today

ngipin *n.* teeth

ngiti *n.* smile

ngunit *conj.* but

nguso *n.* upper lip

ninang *n.* godmother

ningas *n.* flame

ninong *n.* godfather

ninuno *n.* ancestor

niyog *n.* coconut

noo *n.* forehead

noon *adv.* at that time

noong *conj.* when (for continuing actions)

nota *n.* musical note

nuno *n.* grandparent

– O –

o *conj.* or

oho (or **opo**) *interj.* yes sir/madam

oo *adj.* yes

oras *n.* hour, time

orasyon *n.* angelus

orihinal (*syn.* **likas**) *n.* original

ospital (*syn.* **pagamutan**) *n.* hospital

oyayi *n.* lullaby

– P –

paa *n.* foot

paalam *n.* farewell; *v.* goodbye

paano *adv.* how

paaralan (*syn.* **eskuwela**) *n.* school

pabuya *n.* tip, gratuity

pader *n.* wall

pag-asa *n.* hope

pagdadalamhati *n.* grief, extreme sorrow

pag-ibig *n.* love

pagkain *n.* food

pagkamatay *n.* death

pagkilos *v.* to act

pagód *adj.* tired, weary

pagod *n.* tiredness

pakinabang *n.* profit, gain

pako *n.* nail

pakpak *n.* wing

paksa *n.* subject, theme

palabas *n.* show

palad *n.* palm of hand; fate

palagay *n.* guess, personal opinion

palapag *n.* floor or story of a building

palaruan *n.* playground

palay *n.* rice plant

palayaw *n.* nickname

palayok *n.* clay pot

palengke *n.* market

paligid *n.* surroundings

palikuran *n.* toilet

pamahalaan *n.* government

pamantasan *n.* university

pamilya *n.* family

pampalamig *n.* refreshment

panahon *n.* time, season

pangalan *n.* name

pangalawang pangulo *n.* vice-president

panginoon *n.* master; **Panginoon** Lord

pangit *adj.* ugly

pangulo *n.* president

pantalon *n.* pants, trousers

papel *n.* paper

paraan, *n.* way

pareho *adj.* the same, similar

parusa *n.* punishment

pasaway *adj.* unconventional, stubborn

pasinaya *n.* inauguration

pasko *n.* Christmas

pasò *n.* burn (injury from fire or heat)

pasô *n.* flowerpot

pasó (*syn.* **lipás** or **pasado**) *n.* lapsed

pasok *v.* to enter

patay *n.* dead; *adj.* lifeless; extinguished as in light

patingin *v.* to take a look

patnugot *n.* director, editor

patong (*syn.* **susón**) *n.* layer

pawis perspiration, **anak-~** *n.* laborer

payak *adj.* simple

payat *adj.* thin

payong *n.* umbrella

pera *n.* money

pero (*syn.* **nguni't**) *conj.* but

pihado *adj./adv.* surely, certainly, certain, sure

pilak *n.* silver

pinggan *n.* plate

pinsan *n.* cousin

pinta *v.* to paint

pinto *n.* door

pintura *n.* paint

pipa *n.* pipe

piraso *n.* piece

pirmá *n.* signature

pirmí *adv.* always; fixed

pisngi *n.* cheek

piso *n.* peso

pista *n.* feast; **~ngbayan** town fiesta

plantsa *n.* flat iron

pluma *n.* fountain pen

posporo *n.* match

premyo (*syn.* **gantimpala**) *n.* prize, reward

probinsiya (*syn.* **lalawigan**) *n.* province

programa (*syn.* **palatuntunan**) *n.* program

proseso *n.* process

proyekto *n.* project

publiko *n.* public

pugon *n.* stove, oven

pula *adj.* red

pulbos *n.* powder

pulong *n.* meeting

pulubi *n.* beggar

punô *adj.* full

punò *n.* tree; leader, chief; source

punong-lungsod *n.* capital city

pusa *n.* cat

puso *n.* heart

putahe *n.* a dish or viand

putok *n.* blast

puwesto *n.* location; a stall or stand in a market

– R –

radyo *n.* radio

raw (or **daw**) *part.* it is said

regalo *n.* gift

rekado *n.* condiments for cooking

reklamo *n.* complaint

relihiyon *n.* religion

relo *n.* clock, watch

resibo *n.* receipt

riles *n.* railroad, specifically for trains

rosas *n.* a kind of plant or its flower; pink color

– S –

saan *adv.* where

sabaw *n.* broth

sabay *adj.* at the same time

sabi *n.* what was said; *v.* to tell, to say

sabon *n.* soap

sagana *adj.* abundant, plenty

sagot *n.* answer

sahod *n.* salary, wage

sakay *n.* passenger; **sumakay** *v.* to ride in

sakim *adj.* selfish

sakit *n.* sickness; pain

saksi *n.* witness

sala *n.* sin; living room

salamat *n.* thanks

salamin *n.* mirror; eyeglasses

salapi *n.* money; a fifty centavo coin (not in circulation)

salawal *n.* trousers

saligang-batas *n.* constitution

salita *n.* word, language

salop (*syn.* **ganta**) *n.* a unit of measurement particularly for rice approximately equivalent to two kilos

salu-salo *n.* party, banquet

samahan *n.* club, society

samahan *v.* to accompany

sama-sama *adv.* altogether

samba *n.* worship, **sumamba** *v.* to worship

sampaguita *n.* a shrub bearing fragrant white flowers, the national flower of the Philippines

sampu *adj. n.* ten

sandaan *adj. n.* one hundred

sandali *adv.* a moment

sanga *n.* branch

sapatos *n.* shoes

sarado *adj.* closed

sari-sari *adj.* of various kinds

sariwa *adj.* fresh

sarsa *n.* sauce

sasakyan *n.* vehicle

sayang *interj.* What a pity!

sayaw *n.* dance

seda *n.* silk

seksyon *n.* section (in class)

selyo *n.* stamp; dry seal

sepilyo *n.* toothbrush

serbidor *n.* server; waiter

serbisyo *n.* service

sero *n.* zero

sigarilyo *n.* cigarette

silangan *n.* east; the Orient

silid *n.* room; **~tulugan** bedroom; **~kainan** dining room

silya (*syn.* **upuan**) *n.* chair

simbahan *n.* church

simula *n.* beginning

sinangag *n.* fried rice

sinelas (or **tsinelas**) *n.* slippers

singil *n.* amount charged for services or sold goods

singsing *n.* ring

sinulid *n.* thread

sipon *n.* cold, runny nose

sira *n.* destruction, destroyed, torn, broken

siyudad (*syn.* **lungsod**) *n.* city

sobre *n.* envelope

sopas *n.* soup

subdibisyon *n.* subdivision

suka *n.* vinegar

sukat *n.* measurement

suki *n.* steady client

suklay *n.* comb

sulat *n.* letter; penmanship

sumama *v.* to go with

sumunod *v.* to follow

sundalo (*syn.* **kawal**) *n.* soldier

sunog *n.* fire

susi *n.* key

suskrisyon *n.* subscription

– T –

taas *n.* height; **mataas** *adj.* high

taba *n.* fat, **mataba**, *adj.* fat

tabak (*syn.* **bolo**) *n.* a native sword, shorter than a cutlass, that has everyday uses

tabako *n.* cigar; tobacco

tabing-dagat *n.* seashore

tabla *n.* wooden board, cut timber; **bahay na tabla** *n.* wooden house

tagapagsilbi *n.* server

tag-araw *n.* summer, dry season

taggutom *n.* famine

tag-ulan *n.* rainy season

tagumpay *n.* victory

tahanan *n.* home

tahi *v.* to sew; **pananahi** *n.* sewing; **mananahi** *n.* seamstress

tainga *n.* ears

takip *n.* cover

takot *n.* fear. **takot** *adj.* afraid; **matakot** *v.* to be afraid

taksi *n.* taxi

taksil *n.* traitor

talaan *n.* list, record

talambuhay *n.* biography

talì (*syn.* **panalì**) *n.* string, anything used to tie

tamad (*ant.* **masipag**) *adj.* lazy

tanawin *n.* view, scenery

tanga *adj.* stupid, irresponsible

tanghali *adv.* late at noon; *n.* noon

tanim *n.* plant

tanong *n.* question

tanyag *adj.* well-known; popular

tao *n.* person, human being

taon *n.* year

tapat *adj.* faithful, honest

tasa *n.* cup

tauhan *n.* personnel

tawa *n.* laughter

tawad *n.* bargain, reduction in price; pardon, forgiveness

tawagan *v.* to call

tela *n.* cloth

tíísin *n.* sufferings; **tiisín** *v.* to endure

tiket *n.* ticket

tila *adv.* it seems

timbangan *n.* scale, balance

timog *n.* south

tinda *n.* goods; **tindahan** *n.* store

tingnan *v.* to look

tinidor *n.* table fork

tinta *n.* ink

tiya (*syn.* **tita**) *n.* aunt

tiyo (*syn.* **tito**) *n.* uncle

totoo *adj.* true

trabaho *n.* job, work, livelihood

transportasyon *n.* transportation

tren *n.* train

tubig *n.* water

tubo *n.* pipe

tuhod *n.* knee

tula *n.* poem

tulay *n.* bridge

tulong *n.* help

tuloy *interj.* come in; *v.* to go ahead

tungkol sa *prep.* about; referring to

tunog *n.* sound

tuntunin *n.* rule

tuwâ *n.* gladness; **matuwa** *v.* to be glad

tuwalya *n.* towel

tuwid *adj.* straight

tuyâ *n.* sarcasm, irony

tuyô *adj.* dry; *n.* dried fish

– U –

ubo *n.* cough; **inuubo** *v.* coughing

ubod *n.* core; ~ **ng sipag** *adj.* very industrious
ugali *n.* custom; habit
ugat *n.* human vein; root of a plant; **salitang-~** *n.* root word
uhaw *n.* thirst; **mauhaw** *v.* to be thirsty
ulam *n.* viand
ulan *n.* rain; **maulan** *adj.* rainy
ulap *n.* cloud
ulat *n.* report
uli *adv.* once again
uling *n.* charcoal
ulit *adv.* again; *n.* repetition, number of times; **sampung ~** ten times

ulo *n.* head
umaga *n.* morning
umako *v.* to assume responsibility
umalis *v.* to go away
umawit *v.* to sing
uminom *v.* to drink
umisip *v.* to think
umpisa (*syn.* **simula**) *n.* beginning, start
umupo *v.* to sit
umuwi *v.* to go home
una *adj.* first
unan *n.* pillow
uod *n.* worm
upa *n.* pay; rent
upang *conj.* so, so that
upuan *n.* chair
uri *n.* kind; quality

usapan *n.* conversation
utak *n.* brain; **mautak** *adj.* intelligent
utang *n.* debt
utos *n.* command, order
uwi (*syn.* **pasalubong**) *n.* anything brought home by someone from a trip

– W –

wakas *n.* end; **at sa wakas** finally
wala *adj.* absent; *adv.* none
walang-hiya *adj.* shameless
walang-pagod *adj.* tireless
walis *n.* broom

wasto (*syn.* **tama**) *adj.* correct; appropriate
watawat *n.* flag, banner
welga *n.* labor strike
wika *n.* language

– Y –

yabag *n.* footstep
yakap *n.* embrace; **yakapin** *v.* to embrace
yaman *n.* wealth; **mayaman** *adj.* rich, wealthy
yari (*syn.* **gawa**) *adj.* style; finished product, structure; ready made; *adj.* finished
yelo *n.* ice

ENGLISH–TAGALOG

– A –

a (or **an**) *indefinite art.* ang isa, isang, sa isa
about *prep.* tungkol sa
above *adv.* sa itaas; sa ibabaw
abstract *n.* buod
abundance *n.* kasaganaan
abundant *adj.* sagana
accept *v.* tanggapin
accompany *v.* samahan, saliwan (sa pagtugtog)
account *n.* kuwenta
aching *v.* sumasakit
act *n.* gawa
adaptability *n.* pagbabagay, pag-aayon
addition *n.* dagdag. to add; *v.* dagdagan
adjustment *n.* pag-aayos
advertisement *n.* anunsiyo
advocate *n.* tagapagtanggol
after *adv.* pagkatapos
afternoon *n.* hapon
again *adv.* muli
against *prep.* laban sa
agreement *n.* kasunduan
air *n.* himpapawid; hangin
alive *adj.* buhay
all *pron.* lahat
almost *adv.* halos
alphabet *n.* alpabeto
already *adv.* na
also *adv.* din, rin
altar *n.* dambana
although *conj.* kahit
always *adv.* lagi, palagi
amount *n.* halaga; kabuuan

amusement *n.* libangan; aliwan
analysis *n.* pagsusuri
ancestor *n.* ninuno
and *conj.* at, at saka
angelus *n.* orasyon
anger *n.* gálit; **angry** *adj.* galít
anniversary *n.* anibersaryo
answer *n.* sagot, tugon
ant *n.* langgam
appropriate *adj.* bagay, naaayon, angkóp
arch *n.* arko
archipelago *n.* kapuluan
area *n.* lawak
argument *n.* pagtatalo
arm *n.* braso, bisig
army *n.* hukbo
art *n.* sining
as *adv.* katulad, kaparis, kagaya
ash *n.* abo
ask *v.* itanong
asleep *adj.* tulog
assimilate *v.* isama
assist *n.* tumulong
assistant *n.* katulong
at *prep.* sa
ate *v.* kumain
attack *n.* sumpong (in relation to sickness); **paglusob** (in relation to war)
attend *v.* dumalo
aunt *n.* sister of either parent, addressed as Tita
authority *n.* kapangyarihan
avoid *v.* iwasan

award *n.* gantimpala, pabuya

– B –

baby *n.* sanggol; also a term of endearment
bachelor *n.* binata
back *n.* likod; **at the back** *prep.* sa likuran
bad *adj.* masama
balance *n.* timbangan (or **weighing scales**); panimbang (or **steadiness**)
ball *n.* bola; sayawan
ballot *n.* balota
bamboo *n.* kawayan
banana *n.* saging
band *n.* banda ng musiko
baptism *n.* binyag
barber *n.* barbero
bargain *n.* baratilyo, pagkasunduan; *v.* tumawad sa halaga
basin *n.* palangana
basis *n.* batayan
basket *n.* buslo
bath *n.* paligo
bathe *v.* maligo
bathroom *n.* páliguán; banyo
beautiful *adj.* maganda
beauty *n.* kagandahan
become *v.* maging
bed *n.* kama
bedroom *n.* silid-tulugan
before *adv.* bago, dati, noong una

beggar *n.* pulubi
behavior *n.* ugali, gawi
belief *n.* paniwala
bell *n.* kampana, kampanilya
below *adv.* sa ibaba
belt *n.* sinturon
beset *v.* paligiran, lusubin
between *prep.* sa gitna, sa pagitan
big *adj.* malaki
bird *n.* ibon
birthday *n.* kaarawan
bite *v.* kagatin
bitter *adj.* mapait
black *adj.* itim, maitim
blanket *n.* kumot
blessed *adj.* pinagpala, masuwerte
blood *n.* dugo
blow *v.* hipan
blue *adj.* asul, bughaw
boat *n.* bangka
body *n.* katawan
boiling *v.* kumukulo
bolo *n.* itak, tabak
bone *n.* buto
book *n.* aklat, libro
boost *v.* itaas, tulak
borrow *v.* humiram
boss *n.* pinuno, hepe, tagapamahala
bottle *n.* bote
bottom *n.* ilalim
box *n.* kahon
boy *n.* batang lalaki; **house ~** *n.* utusang lalaki
brain *n.* utak
branch *n.* sanga ng tanim;

sangay isang opisina
bread *n.* tinapay
breath *n.* hininga
breathe *v.* huminga
bridge *n.* tulay
brief *n.* maikli; magtagubilin
bright *adj.* maliwanag (in relation to light); marunong
bring *v.* dalhin
broadcast *n.* pagbabalita; *v.* ibalita
broadsheet *n.* malaking pahayagan
broken *v.* sira, basag
broth *n.* sabaw
brother *n.* kapatid na lalaki; ~-**in-law** *n.* bayaw
brown *adj.* kayumanggi (in relation to color of race); kulay tsokolate, kulay kape
brush *n.* (**tooth~**) sepilyo; (**hair~**) brush sa buhok
building *n.* gusali
bulb *n.* bombilya
bullet *n.* bala
burn *v.* masunog. *n.* paso
burst *n.* putok
business *n.* negosyo
but *conj.* pero, nguni't
butter *n.* mantekilya
butterfly *n.* paruparo
button *n.* butones
buy *v.* bumili
by means of *prep.* sa pamamagitan ng

– C –

cake *n.* keyk
call *n.* tawag; *v.* tawagin
care *n.* alaga; *v.* alagaan
careful *adj.* maingat
carpenter *n.* karpintero, anluwagi
carry *v.* dalhin
cat *n.* pusa
catholic *n.* katoliko
cause *n.* dahilan
ceiling *n.* kisame
celebrate *v.* magdiwang
celebration *n.* pagdiriwang, pista
center *n.* gitna
century *n.* isandaang taon
certificate *n.* katibayan
chair *n.* silya, upuan
challenge *n.* hamon
chance *n.* pagkakataon
change *n.* sukli; pampalit
change *v.* suklian; palitan

character *n.* pagkatao, katangian
cheap *adj.* mura
cheerful *adj.* masaya, masigla
cheese *n.* keso
chest *n.* dibdib
chicken *n.* manok
chief *n.* puno
child *n.* bata, anak
chin *n.* baba
Christmas *n.* Pasko
chronicler *n.* taga-ulat, tagapagsalaysay
church *n.* simbahan
citizen *n.* mamamayan
city *n.* lungsod
civilization *n.* kabihasnan
class *n.* klase, uri
classroom *n.* silid-aralan
clean *adj.* malinis
clear *adj.* malinaw, maliwanag
climb *v.* umakyat
clock *n.* relo, orasan
close *v.* isara
cloth *n.* damit; tela
cloud *n.* ulap
coal *n.* uling; karbon
coat *n.* amerikana
coconut *n.* niyog; **coconut milk** *n.* gata
cold *adj.* malamig
collar *n.* kuwelyo
color *n.* kulay
comb *n.* suklay
come *v.* pumarito
comfort *n.* aliw; *v.* aliwin
committee *n.* lupon
communication *n.* pakikipag-usap
companion *n.* kasama
condition *n.* kalagayan, ayos
confidence *n.* tiwala
constitution *n.* saligang-batas
contemporary *n.* kapanahon; *adj.* magkapanabay
cook *n.* tagapagluto, kusinero/a
cook *v.* magluto
copy *n.* sipi, kopya; *v.* kopyahin
cork *n.* tapon
cotton bulak
cough *n.* ubo
courage *n.* tapang
courgeous *adj.* matapang
courteous *adj.* magalang
courtesy *n.* paggalang
cousin *n.* pinsan

cover *n.* takip; *v.* takpan
cow *n.* baka
coward *adj.* duwag
creative *adj.* malikhain
credit *n.* utang
cross *n.* krus
cruel *adj.* malupit
cry *v.* umiyak; *n.* iyak
cuisine *n.* lutó
culinary *adj.* tungkol sa pagluluto
culture *n.* kultura, kalinangan
cup *n.* tasa, kopa
curtain *n.* kurtina
custom *n.* ugali
customer *n.* mamimili; **regular ~** or **regular seller** *n.* sukì
cut *n.* hiwa; *v.* hiwain; putulin

– D –

damage *n.* sira; *v.* sirain
danger *n.* panganib
dangerous *adj.* mapanganib
dark *adj.* madilim
darkness *n.* karimlan
daughter *n.* anak na babae
day *n.* araw
dead *n.* patay
dear *adj.* mahal
death *n.* kamatayan
debt *n.* utang
deep *adj.* malalim
delicacies *n.* (refer to) minatamis, kakanin and other special or unusual foods
delicate *adj.* maselan
derive *v.* kunin, manggaling
describe *v.* ilarawan
description *n.* pagkakalarawan
develop *v.* painamin, paunlarin
dialect *n.* salita, diyalekto
diaper *n.* lampin
different *adj.* iba, magkaiba
digestion *n.* pagtunaw
diligent *adj.* masipag
diploma *n.* sertipiko ng pagtatapos
direction *n.* gawi, dako, banda
director *n.* patnugot
dirty *adj.* marumi
disaster *n.* sakuna
discipline *n.* disiplina

discussion *n.* pagtatalo, pag-uusap
disease *n.* sakit
distance *n.* layo, agwat
distant *adj.* malayo
divide *v.* hatiin
dizzy *n.* hilo; *v.* mahilo
do *v.* gawin
dog *n.* aso
doll *n.* manika
door *n.* pinto
doubt *n.* alinlangan
down *adv.* sa ibaba
drama *n.* dula
dress *n.* baro, damit (generic term)
drink *v.* uminom; *n.* inumin
driver *n.* (of car) tsuper; (of rig) kutsero
drop *v.* mahulog
drown *v.* malunod
drunk *adj.* lasing, lango
dry *adj.* tuyo
dub *v.* lagyan
dumb *adj.* pipi; hangal
dust *n.* alikabok

– E –

ear *n.* tainga
early *adv.* maaga
earning *n.* kita, suweldo
earth *n.* lupa, mundo
east *n.* silangan
eastern *adj.* silanganan
easy *adj.* madali
education *n.* pag-aaral
egg *n.* itlog
elbow *n.* siko
election *n.* halalan
electric *adj.* elektrika
embarrass *v.* hiyain
embarrassed *adj.* napahiya
employee *n.* kawani
end *n.* katapusan, wakas
enough *adv.* sapat; husto
enrich *v.* painamin, palaguin
equal *adj.* magkapantay; magkatumbas
eraser *n.* pambura
error *n.* mali, kamalian
even *adv.* pantay; kahi't; **even if** *adv.* kahi't na
evening *n.* gabi
event *n.* pangyayari
every *adv.* bawa't, bawa't isa; **everyone** *adv.* lahat
exact *adj.* husto, tama
example *n.* halimbawa

exchange *n.* palitan; *v.* magpalit; ipagpalit
expat (or **foreigner**) *n.* dayuhan, banyaga
expenses *n.* gastos
experience *n.* karanasan
eye *n.* mata
eyebrow *n.* kilay
eyeglasses *n.* (**spectacles**) salamin sa mata
eyelash *n.* pilikmata

– F –

face *n.* mukha; *v.* harapin
faith *n.* pananampalataya
fall *v.* mahulog
false *adj.* hindi totoo; hindi tapat
familiar *adj.* kilalá
family *n.* mag-anak, pamilya
far *adj.* malayo
farm *n.* bukid; kabukiran
farmer *n.* magsasaka
fast *adj.* mabilis, matulin
fat *adj.* mataba
fate *n.* kapalaran
father *n.* ama
father-in-law *n.* biyenang lalaki
faucet *n.* gripo
fault *n.* kasalanan, malî
favorite *n.* paborito
fear *n.* takot, pangamba
feather *n.* balahibo
feeble *adj.* mahina
feeling *n.* damdamin
female *n./adj.* babae
fence *n.* bakod; *v.* bakuran
festivity *n.* kasayahan, pista
fever *n.* lagnat
few *adv.* kaunti, iilan
fight *n.* away; *v.* awayin
finger *n.* daliri
fire *n.* sunog
first *adj.* una
fish *n.* isda
fix *v.* ayusin
flag *n.* bandila, watawat
flame *n.* ningas, apoy
flower *n.* bulaklak
fly *n.* langaw
fly *v.* lumipad; sumakay sa eroplano
follow *v.* sumunod
food *n.* pagkain
foot *n.* paa
for *prep.* para sa, para kay
force *n.* lakas
forehead *n.* noo
fork *n.* tinidor

formidable *adj.* mahirap talunin; mabigat na kalaban
fragrance *n.* bango
fragrant *adj.* mabango
free *adj.* malaya
freedom *n.* kalayaan
frequent *adj.* madalas
fresh *adj.* sariwa
friend *n.* kaibigan
from *prep.* sa, buhat sa, mula sa
front *adv.* harapan
fruit *n.* bungang-kahoy, prutas
fry *v.* prituhin
full *adj.* punô
furniture (or **appliances**) *n.* kasangkapan
future *n.* hinaharap; *adv.* sa darating na panahon

– G –

gain *n.* tubo, pakinabang
game *n.* laro
garage *n.* garahe
garbage *n.* basura, dumi
garden *n.* halamanan, hardin
general *n.* heneral; *adj.* lahat
genesis *n.* simula
get *v.* kunin
girl *n.* batang babae
give *v.* magbigay
glass *n.* (**drinking ~**) baso; *n., adj.* kristál
go *v.* umalis, lumakad, pumaroon, pumunta
goat *n.* kambing
godfather *n.* ninong
godmother *n.* ninang
gold *n.* ginto
good *adj.* mahusay, magaling, mabuti
government *n.* pamahalaan
grace *n.* grasya, biyaya
grain *n.* butil
grass *n.* damo
grave *n.* libingan
gray *adj.* kulay-abo
great *adj.* dakila
green *adj.* luntian, berde
ground meat *n.* giniling na karne
group *n.* pangkat, lupon; *v.* magtipon
guard *n.* bantay; *v.* bantayan
guide *v.* akayin, ituro
gun *n.* baril

– H –

hair *n.* buhok; balahibo
half *adj.* kalahati
hammer *n.* martilyo
hand *n.* kamay
happy *adj.* masaya, maligaya
hard *adj.* matigas; mahirap (similar to **difficult**)
harvest *n.* ani
hat *n.* sumbrero
hate *n.* matinding galit
have (or **has**) *v.* mayroon
head *n.* ulo, puno
headache *n.* sakit ng ulo
health *n.* kalusugan
healthy *adj.* malusog
heart *n.* puso
heat *n.* init
help *n.* tulong; **helper** *n.* katulong
here *adv.* dito
hero *n.* bayani
hesitant *adj.* nagaalanganin
high *adj.* mataas
history *n.* kasaysayan
hole *n.* butas
hope *n.* pag-asa
horse *n.* kabayo
hospital *n.* ospital, pagamutan
hospitality *n.* magiliw na pagtanggap sa panauhin
hot *adj.* mainit
hour *n.* oras
house *n.* bahay, tahanan
how *adv.* paano
humble *adj.* mababangloob; *n.* kababaang-loob
humor *n.* katatawanan, pagpapatawa
husband *n.* asawang lalaki

– I –

ice *n.* yelo
ice cream *n.* sorbetes
idea *n.* palagay; kuru-kuro
if *conj.* kung
important *adj.* mahalaga
in *prep.* sa, sa loob
indigenous *n.* katutubo
industrious *adj.* masipag
initial *adj.* pauna
ink *n.* tinta
insect *n.* kulisap
inside *prep.* sa loob
instruction *n.* turo
instrument *n.* kagamitan
insurance *n.* seguro

intention *n.* balak, hangarin
introduce *v.* ipakilala
invite *v.* anyayahan
iron *n.* bakal
island *n.* pulo, isla
itchy *adj.* makati

– J –

jail *n.* bilangguan, piitan
jaw *n.* panga
jealousy *n.* panibugho
jewel *n.* alahas
join *v.* pagsamahin, pagdugtungin
joke *n.* biro; *v.* biruin
journey *n.* paglalakbay
judge *n.* hukom; huwes
juice *n.* katas
jump *v.* tumalon, lumukso

– K –

keep *v.* itago
key *n.* susi
kick *v.* sipain
kind *n.* uri; *adj.* maawain; mabait
kiss *v.* halik
knee *n.* tuhod
kneel *v.* lumuhod
knife *n.* kutsilyo, lanseta
knot *n.* buhol; pusod (of hair); *v.* itali
know *v.* malaman
knowledge *n.* karunungan, kaalaman

– L –

laborer *n.* manggagawa
land *n.* lupa
language *n.* wika
last *adj.*, huli sa lahat
late *adj.*, huli
laugh *n.* tawa; *v.* tumawa
law *n.* batas
lawyer *n.* abugado; manananggol
lazy *adj.* tamad
lead *n.* tingga
leader *n.* pinuno, puno
leaf *n.* dahon
learn *v.* matuto, mag-aral
leather *n.* balat ng hayop
left *adj.* kaliwa (opposite of **right**)
leg *n.* binti
lesson *n.* aralin

letter *n.* sulat, liham; titik
level *adj.* patag, pantay
liar *adj.* sinungaling
library *n.* aklatan
lift *v.* buhatin
light *n.* ilaw, liwanag
light *adj.* magaan
like *adj.* katulad
like *v.* ibig, gusto
line *n.* guhit
linguist *n.* dalubhasa sa wika
lip *n.* labi
list *n.* listahan, talaan
listen *v.* makinig
literature *n.* panitikan, literatura
live *v.* mabuhay; nakatira (to **dwell**); *n.* buháy
lock *n.* kandado; ~**ed** nakakandado
long *adj.* mahaba
look *v.* tingnan
loose *adj.* maluwag
loss *n.* pagkawala
loud *adj.* malakas
love *n.* pag-ibig
low *adj.* mababa
lumber *n.* tabla, kahoy
lung *n.* baga

– M –

machine *n.* makina
mad *adj.* baliw
make *v.* gawin
male *n./adj.* lalaki
man *n.* lalaki
manager *n.* tagapamahala
map *n.* mapa
market *n.* palengke
marriage *n.* kasal
mat *n.* banig
match *n.* posporo
material, *n.* gamit
mature *adj.* (for fruits) hinog; (for man and animals) nasa hustong gulang
meaningful *adj.* makahulugan
measure *n.* sukat
meat *n.* karne, laman
medicine *n.* gamot
medium *n.* paraan
meeting *n.* pulong, miting
memorize *v.* isaulo; kabisahin
middle *n.* gitna
milk *n.* gatas
mind *n.* isip
mine *pron.* akin; minahan

minute *n.* minuto, sandali
mirror *n.* salamin
mixed *adj.* halu-halo
money *n.* salapi
monkey *n.* unggoy
month *n.* buwan
monument *n.* bantayog
morning *n.* umaga
mosquito *n.* lamok
mother *n.* ina, nanay
mother-in-law *n.* biyenang babae
mountain *n.* bundok
mouth *n.* bibig
move *v.* kumilos, gumalaw
movement *n.* kilusan
much *adv.* marami
music *n.* tugtugin, musika

– N –

nail *n.* pako; (**finger**~ or **toe**~) kuko
naked *adj.* hubad
name *n.* pangalan, ngalan
narrow *adj.* makitid
nation *n.* bansa, bayan
native *n.* taal
nature *n.* kalikasan
near *adj.* malapit
necessary *adj.* kailangan
neck *n.* leeg
needle *n.* karayom
negotiate *v.* pakikipag-ayos; pakikipagkasunduan
neighbor *n.* kapitbahay
new *adj.* bago
news *n.* balita
nickname *n.* palayaw
night *n.* gabi
no *adv.* hindi
noise *n.* ingay
none *adj.* wala
noon *n.* tanghali
north *n.* hilaga
nose *n.* ilong
note *n.* (of music) nota
now *adv.* ngayon
number *n.* bilang

– O –

obedient *adj.* masunurin
offer *v.* alukin
oil *n.* langis
old *adj.* matanda (referring to a person); luma (for things)
only *adv.* lamang
open *adj.* bukas; *v.* buksan

opinion *n.* palagay
opposite *adj.* kasalungat
orange *n.* dalandan
order *n.* utos, ayos
organization *n.* samahan, kapisanan
ornament *n.* gayak, palamuti, dekorasyon
other *adj.*, iba
out *adv.* sa labas
oven *n.* pugon
over *prep.* sa ibabaw
overeating *n.* sobrang pagkain
overtake *v.* lampasan
owner *n.* may-ari

– P –

page *n.* pahina
pain *n.* sakit
paint *n.* pintura
paper *n.* papel
parcel *n.* balutan
pardon *n.* patawad
parent *n.* magulang
past *adj.* nakaraan
paste *n.* pandikit; *v.* idikit
payment *n.* bayad, kabayaran
peace *n.* katahimikan
pen *n.* pluma
pencil *n.* lapis
people *n.* taong-bayan
perhaps *adv.* marahil
person *n.* tao
pet *n.* alagang hayop
picture *n.* larawan, litrato
pig *n.* baboy
pin *n.* aspile
pitiful *adj.* kaawa-awa
pity *n.* awa
plant *n.* tanim
plate *n.* pinggan
play *n.* laro; *v.* maglalaro
pleasure *n.* kasiyahan
plow *n.* araro
pocket *n.* bulsa
poison *n.* lason
poor *adj.* mahirap
popular *adj.* bantog, kilala
populated *v.* pinamamayanan
positive *adj.* tiyak
post *n.* haligi, poste ng bahay
pot *n.* pasô (for plant); palayok (for cooking)
potato *n.* patatas
powder *n.* pulbos
power *n.* kapangyarihan
precision *n.* kawastuhan

present *adv.* ngayon, kasalukuyan
present *n.* regalo, handog
price *n.* halaga
prison *n.* see **jail**
process *n.* paraan
proclaim *v.* ihayag
proof *n.* katibayan
property *n.* ariarian
protest *v.* lumaban; sumalungat; *n.* paglaban
public *adj.* pangmadla; *n.* madla bayan
publish *v.* ilathala
pull *v.* hilahin; batakin
punctuality *n.* pagdating sa oras
punishment *n.* parusa
purpose *n.* balak; layon
push *v.* itulak
put *v.* ilagay
puzzle *n.* palaisipan; *v.* tarantahin

– Q –

quality *n.* uri, klase
quantity *n.* dami
quarrel *n.* away; *v.* awayin
queen *n.* reyna
question *n.* tanong; *v.* magtanong
quick *adj.* madali
quiet *adj.* tahimik, walang kibo
quite *adv.* halos, tila
quiz *n.* pagsusulit

– R –

railroad *n.* riles
rain *n.* ulan
rat *n.* daga
rattan *n.* yantok
razor *n.* labaha
read *v.* bumasa
ready *adj.* handa
reason *n.* dahilan, katwiran
receipt *n.* resibo
receive *v.* tanggapin
recipe *n.* paraan ng pagluluto
record *n.* talaan
red *adj.* pula
reflection *n.* pagdidili-dili
regional *adj.* panrehiyon
religion *n.* relihiyon
remember *v.* alalahanin
remove *v.* alisin
request *n.* kahilingan

respect *n.* paggalang; *v.* igalang
rest *n.* pahinga; *v.* magpahinga
revision *n.* pagbabago
revolution *n.* paghihimagsik
reward *n.* gantimpala
rhythm *n.* kumpas
rice *n.* bigas; **cooked ~** *n.* kanin
rich *adj.* mayaman
right *adj.* tama, wasto; kanan; karapatan
ring *n.* singsing
river *n.* ilog
road *n.* daan, kalye
roadside *n.* tabi ng daan
roasted *adj.* inihaw
roof *n.* bubong
root *n.* ugat (of plants)
rope *n.* lubid
rough *adj.* magaspang
round *adj.* bilog
run *v.* tumakbo
rust *n.* kalawang

– S –

sad *adj.* malungkot
safe *adj.* ligtas
salad *n.* ensalada
salt *n.* asin
salty *adj.* maalat
same *adj.* pareho, tulad
sand *n.* buhangin
scale *n.* timbangan
school *n.* paaralan
science *n.* agham, siyensiya
script *n.* iskrip, manuskrito
sea *n.* dagat
seal *n.* tatak
seat *n.* upuan, silya
second *adj.* ikalawa
secret *n.* lihim
secretary *n.* kalihim
see *v.* makita, tingnan
seed *n.* buto, binhi
send *v.* ipadala
sentence *n.* pangungusap
separate *adj.* hiwalay; *v.* maghiwalay
shallow *adj.* mababaw
shame *n.* hiya, kahihiyan
shameless *adj.* walang-hiya
sharp *adj.* matalas, matulis
sheep *n.* tupa
ship *n.* bapor
shirt *n.* kamisadentro
shoe *n.* sapatos
short *adj.* maikli
side *n.* tagiliran, tabi
signage *n.* tanda, marka

signature *n.* lagda, pirma
silk *n.* seda
silver *n.* pilak
sin *n.* kasalanan
sister *n.* kapatid na babae
size *n.* laki
skin *n.* balat
skirt *n.* palda
sky *n.* langit
sleep *b.* matulog
slow *adj.* mabagal, mahina
slowly *adv.* dahan-dahan
small *adj.* maliit
smile *n.* ngiti
smoke *n.* usok
smooth *adj.* makinis
snake *n.* ahas
sneeze *v.* magbahing
snore *n.* hilik; *v.* maghilik
soap *n.* sabon
society *n.* lipunan
socks *n.* medyas
soft *adj.* malambot
some *adj.* ilan
son *n.* anak na lalaki
song *n.* awit, kanta
soul *n.* kaluluwa
sound *n.* ingay, tunog
soup *n.* sopas, sabaw
sour *adj.* maasim
south *n.* timog
special *adj.* katangi-tangi; di-pangkaraniwan
spoon *n.* kutsara
square *n.* parisukat
staff *n.* tauhan
stage *n.* entablado
staircase *n.* hagdanan
stamp *n.* selyo sa sulat
star *n.* bituin, tala
starch *n.* gawgaw
station *n.* himpilan
steam *n.* singaw
step *n.* hakbang
sticky *adj.* malagkit
stiff *adj.* matigas
stingy *adj.* maramot
stomach *n.* tiyan
stone *n.* bato
story *n.* kuwento
stove *n.* kalan, pugon
street *n.* daan, kalye
strength *n.* lakas
strong *adj.* malakas
stubborn *adj.* matigas ang ulo, makulit
study *v.* mag-aral
succulent *adj.* makatas
sudden *adj.* bigla, kaagad
sugar *n.* asukal
summer *n.* tag-araw
sun *n.* araw
supper *n.* hapunan

surname *n.* apelyido
sweet *adj.* matamis
swim *v.* lumangoy
synonym *n.* magkasingkahulugan
system *n.* paraan, sistema

– T –

table *n.* mesa
tail *n.* buntot
tailor *n.* sastre, mananahi
take *v.* kunin
talented *adj.* matalino
talk *v.* magsalita
tall *adj.* matangkad (person); mataas
taste *n.* lasa; *v.* tikman
tax *n.* buwis
teach *v.* magturo
teacher *n.* guro, maestro/a
tear *n.* luha; *v.* punit
tell *v.* sabihin
than *conj.* kaysa
that *pron.* iyan, iyon
there *adv.* doon, diyan
thick *adj.* makapal
thief *n.* magnanakaw
thin *adj.* payat, manipis
thing *n.* bagay
this *pron.* ito; **these** ang mga ito (plural)
though *conj.* kahit na
thought *n.* akala, isip
thread *n.* sinulid
throat *n.* lalamunan
thumb *n.* hinlalaki
thunder *n.* kulog
ticket *n.* tiket
tight *adj.* masikip
time *n.* panahon, oras, sandali
tin *n.* lata
tired *adj.* pagod
today *adv.* ngayon
toe *n.* hinlalaki ng paa
together *adv.* magkasama
toilet *n.* palikuran, banyo
tomorrow *adv.* bukas
tongue *n.* dila
tooth *n.* ngipin
top *adv.* sa ibabaw
touch *n.* hipo; *v.* hipuin
town *n.* bayan
trade *n.* kalakalan
tradition *n.* kaugalian
train *n.* tren
trait *n.* katangian
translate *v.* salin
travel *n.* paglalakbay; *v.* maglakbay
tray *n.* bandehado

treasurer *n.* ingat-yaman
tree *n.* punong-kahoy; punò
trial *n.* pagsubok
trouble *n.* ligalig; basag-ulo
trousers *n.* salawal
true *adj.* totoo
twice *adv.* makalawa
twin *n.* kambal
typhoon *n.* bagyo

– U –

ugly *adj.* pangit
umbrella *n.* payong
under *prep.* sa ilalim
understand *v.* intindihin, unawain
until *adv.* hanggang
up *prep.* sa itaas
upright *adj.* tuwid
us *pron.* sa atin, tayo
use *v.* gamitin
useful *adj.* mahalaga

– V –

vacation *n.* bakasyon
value *n.* halaga
variety *n.* pagkaiba-iba
vegetable *n.* gulay
vehicle *n.* sasakyan
verdant *adj.* luntian
verse *n.* tula
very *affix; adj.* napaka-
victory *n.* tagumpay
view *n.* tanawin
vinegar *n.* suka
visit *n.* dalaw; *v.* dumalaw
voice *n.* boses, tinig
vote *n.* boto; *v.* iboto
voyage *n.* paglalakbay

– W –

wage *n.* sahod
wait *v.* maghintay
walk *v.* lumakad
wall *n.* dingding; tabike
wallet *n.* pitaka
war *n.* digmaan, giyera
warm *adj.* mainit
wash *v.* maghugas; hugasan (except clothes)
waste *n.* dumi, basura
watch *n.* relo; *v.* bantayan
water *n.* tubig
wave *n.* alon
weak *adj.* mahina
weather *n.* panahon

week *n.* linggo
weight *n.* bigat
well *n.* balon; *adj.* mabuti, walang sakit
west *n.* kanluran
wheel *n.* gulong
when *adv.* kailan. *conj.* kung
where *adv.* saan
while *conj.* samantala
whip *n.* pamalo
whisper *n.* bulong

whistle *n.* sutsot; pito
white *adj.* puti
who *pron.* sino
why *adv.* bakit
wife *n.* maybahay, asawang babae
wind *n.* hangin
window *n.* bintana
wine *n.* alak
wing *n.* pakpak
wire *n.* kawad, alambre
wise *adj.* matalino;

marunong; **wisdom** *n.* katalinuhan; karunungan
woman *n.* babae
wood *n.* kahoy
word *n.* salita
work *n.* gawain; hanapbuhay
worm *n.* bulate, uod
wound *n.* sugat
write *v.* sumulat
writer *n.* manunulat
wrong *adj.* mali

– Y –

yard *n.* bakuran; yarda
year *n.* taon
yellow *n.* dilaw
yes *adv.* oo, opo/oho
yesterday *adv.* kahapon
young *adj.* bata
youth *n.* kabataan

Review Exercises

PART I

A. Use the following words in sentences.

Words that name	Words that describe	Action Words (in any tense)
táo	magandá	umalís
báhay	lálong malakí	lumákad
katúlong	mayáman	bumása
ikáw	maíngay	kumáin
iyán	palatawá	maglarô
Maynilà	pinakámabaít	pumuntá
pagkáin	mabúti	maglínis
kayo	nápakaínit	basáhin
bíbliya	malínis na malínis	daláwin
bulaklák	masaráp	kánin

B. Write a paragraph of about 100 words describing anybody or anything.

C. Translate the following active sentences into passive.

1. **Ang batà ay kumákain ng tinápay.**
2. **Ako ay bumilí ng sapatos sa Makati.**
3. **Ang katúlong namin ay naglutò ng gúlay.**
4. **Tumáwag ng doktor ang maysakít.**
5. **Kumúha ng lapis ang batà sa báhay.**

D. Translate the following paragraph into Tagalog.

The Lord Jesus and His friends were in a small boat (**bangkâ**) on the sea. A storm (**bagyó**) came up quickly. The waves were big. The wind was strong. The water was filling the boat. The men called to the Lord Jesus. They said, "Do you not care if we drown?" The Lord Jesus stood up in the boat. He spoke to the wind and the sea, saying "Quiet, be still!" It was calm (**tahimik**) at once.

PART II

A. Write five words to describe each of the following:

pagkáin	bulaklák	simbáhan	batá
1.	1.	1.	1.
2.	2.	2.	2.
3.	3.	3.	3.
4.	4.	4.	4.
5.	5.	5.	5.

B. Translate the following words and phrases into Tagalog.

1. my mother
2. our church (including speaker and listener)
3. his love
4. their study
5. your hope (singular)
6. her cooking
7. our planting
8. his poverty
9. my happiness
10. your work (plural)
11. John's plan
12. baby's laugh
13. man's anger
14. Mary's name
15. March wind
16. father's letter
17. cat's eye
18. priest's sermon
19. child's food
20. animal's feet

C. Answer the following questions.

1. **Kaníno bang aklát ito?**
2. **Ilan buwán na kayo sa Pilipinas?**
3. **Anu-anó ang inyóng ginágawa ngayón?**
4. **Bakit kayo nag-áaral ng Tagalog?**
5. **Anong mga wikà ang inyóng alám?**

D. Fill in the blanks with the correct answer.

Synonym	Antonym
magandà	_____
masípag	_____
madilím	_____
banal	_____
malínis	_____

E. Tick (√) the letters of the appropriate anwer to the sentence on the left.

1. **Ako ay naíinitang mabúti.**
   a. **Ako ay maglúlutò**
   b. **Ako ay malíligò.**
   c. **Ako ay mag-áaral.**

2. **Ang anák nilá ay payát na payát.**
   a. **Siya ay dapat uminóm ng gamut sa ubó.**
   b. **Siya ay dapat malungkót.**
   c. **Siya ay dapat kumain nang marámi.**

3. **Ang klase ay maíngay.**
   a. **Paalisín ang mga batà.**
   b. **Pagalítan ang mga batà.**
   c. **Bigyán ng maráming gáwain.**

4. **Ang gurò ay marunong at mabait.**
   a. **Siya'y kinayáyamután.**
   b. **Siya'y kinatútuwaán.**
   c. **Siya'y dapat tulúngan.**

5. **Ako ay nasa Pilipinas**
   a. **Dapat akong magsalitâ ng Ingles.**
   b. **Dapat kong matúlog sa hapon.**
   c. **Dapat akong mag-áral ng Tagalog.**

PART III

A. Fill in the blanks with the correct pronouns:

1. Ang kapatíd ko ay marúnong. _____ ay nag-áaral na mabúti.
2. Ang mga batà ay kumákain. _____ ay nagúgutom.
3. Maráming pera si Ramon. Iyón ay ibinigáy ng _____ amá.
4. Halíka, Helen. Sumama _____ sa amin.
5. Kúnin _____ ang aklát sa mesa.
6. _____ lahát ay ináanyayáhan niya.
7. Mayróon ba kayong pagkáin para sa _____?
8. Hindi isináma si Peter sa sine. Umíiyak _____.
9. Isáng aráw, _____ ay nagpasyál sa Luneta.
10. Nákita _____ ang maráming bapór sa dágat.
11. Kúnin _____ ang inyóng aklát.
12. Isáma ninyó ako kung púpunta _____ sa Baguio.
13. Ang báhay _____ ay nasa Pandácan.
14. Nákita _____ na ba ang Tagaytáy?
15. _____ ay mga tunay na kaibigan.
16. Sila ay magbábakasyon sa _____ baháy.
17. Gabí na nang _____ ay umalis.
18. Huwág _____ magágalit sa akin.
19. Nalúlungkot ba _____?
20. Marámi _____ bang kaibígan sa Maynila?
21. Magsalitâ _____ ng Tagalog sa áting kláse.

B. What are the missing words in the following sentences?

1. Ang papél at plúma ay gámit sa _____.
2. Sina Tom at Mary ay _____.
3. Ang _____ ay para sa mga nagúgutom.
4. Ang _____ ay mabangó at magandá.
5. Si Mang Tomas ay nagtátanim. Siya ay _____.
6. Si Gng. Cruz ay nagtúturo. Siya ay _____.
7. Tayo ay umíinom ng _____ kapag naúuhaw.
8. Maráming nábabasa sa mga _____.
9. Ang bátang _____ ay nakatútuwâ.
10. Ang bátang _____ ay nakagágalit.

C. Fill in with the appropriate adjective.

1. Si John ay bása nang bása. Siya ay maraming nálalaman. Nasásagot niya ang lahát ng tinátanong ng gurò. Si John ay _____.

2. Ang dálaga ay laging naglílinis ng kanilang baháy. Siya ang naglúlutò ng pagkáin. Siya ang naglálabá ng mga damít. Ang dalága ay _____.

3. Ayaw niyáng magtrabáho. Gusto niya ay matúlog lamang. Siya ay hindî tumútulong sa kanyáng iná. Kung may gágawin sa báhay siya ay umáalis. Bumabalik lamang siyá kung kákain. Siya ay _____.

4. **Hindi niya mákita ang kanyang kaúsap. Ang lahát ay madilím. Ang mga bulaklák ay waláng kúlay para sa kanyá. Siya ay _____.**

5. **Mahírap si Peter. Walâ siyáng pagkain. Walâ siyáng damít. Walâ siyáng mga magúlang. Si Peter ay _____ .**

D. Write five examples for each of the following categories.

mga hayop	mga pagkain	mga gawain	mga hanapbuhay
1.	1.	1.	1.
2.	2.	2.	2.
3.	3.	3.	3.
4.	4.	4.	4.
5.	5.	5.	5.

PART IV

A. Answer the following questions in complete sentences.

1. **Pumunta ba kayo sa palengke kahapon?**
2. **Nagsasalita na ba kayo ng Tagalog?**
3. **Umiinom ka ba ng kape sa umaga?** (in the morning)
4. **Aalis na ba kayo? Hindi pa ako aalis.**
5. **Sumulat ba kayo sa inyong kaibigan sa Amerika?**

B. Translate the following sentences into Tagalog.

1. I bought a big house in Quezon City.
2. We read (or are reading) in the class.
3. We shall go to your house tomorrow.
4. Peter's clothes are clean.
5. My dress is not clean.

C. Fill in the blanks with **ang**, **ng**, **sa** or their plural forms.

1. _____ bisita _____ bagong kasal ay mga kaibigan at kamag-anak _____ kanilang bayan.
2. Kami ang sumakay _____ kotse, kasama _____ katulong at _____ anak ko.
3. _____ bahay _____ aming kaibigan ay nasa Nueva Ecija.
4. Umalis kami _____ Maynila nang ika – 10:00 _____ umaga.
5. Maraming pagkain _____ mahabang mesa.
6. Maganda _____ asawa _____ aking kaibigan.

PART V

A. **-UM-** AND **MAG-** VERBS

1. Fill in the blanks with the **-um-** and **mag-** derivatives of the following words.

takbó (-um-)	alís (-um-)	salitâ (mag-)	alagà (mag-)
_____	_____	_____	_____
_____	_____	_____	_____
_____	_____	_____	_____
_____	_____	_____	_____
_____	_____	_____	_____

2. Translate the following sentences into Tagalog.

a. Mary wrote a book.   _____

b. He walked to school.   _____

c. Peter and his friends left early.   _____

d. Mary cannot cook rice.   _____

e. Why didn't you clean your hands?   _____

f. Do you sell mangoes?   _____

g. I want to buy two mangoes.   _____

h. He reads well.   _____

i. You should write to your mother every week.   _____

j. He who studies well will speak Tagalog.   _____

k. Did you eat your breakfast?   _____

l. Did Peter leave this morning?   _____

m. Don't you like to swim?   _____

3. Create sentences using the tenses and forms of the following verbs.

umáwit   _____

dumatíng _____

magbíhis _____

gumawâ   _____

pumások   _____

bumalík   _____

lumákad   _____

B. -IN VERBS

1. Form the **-in** derivatives of the following words.

sabihin	**awitin**	**dalhin**	**sirain** (to call)	**tawagin**
_____	_____	_____	_____	_____
_____	_____	_____	_____	_____
_____	_____	_____	_____	_____
_____	_____	_____	_____	_____
_____	_____	_____	_____	_____

2. Change the following sentences from active into passive by using **-in** verbs.

a. **Kumain sila ng isda.**   _____

b. **Sumulat siya sa akin ng liham.**   _____

c. **Bumabasa si Juan ng pahayagan.**   _____

d. **Ang aking katulong ay nagluluto ng pagkain.** _____

e. **Si Jesus ang nagsabi nito.**   _____

f. **Bumati kayo kay Juan para sa akin.**   _____

g. **Nagmamahal ka ba sa Diyos?**   _____

3. Give the future tense of the following active verbs and place the appropriate stress marks.

a. to read   _____   f. to wet   _____

b. to bring   _____   g. to say   _____

c. to wake   _____   h. to cure   _____

d. to change _____   i. to leave   _____

e. to play   _____   j. to remove _____

C. **Saan** and **Nasaan**

1. When do you use **saan**?   _____

2. When do you use **nasaan**?   _____

3. Translate the following questions and sentences into Tagalog.

a. Where is your home?   _____

b. Where is your friend?   _____

c. Where is your friend going? _____

d. Where is your church?   _____

e. Where did you eat?   _____

f. John is in the city.   _____

D. Look for the wrong words in the following questions and sentence. If there are any, give the correct ones.

1. **Dito siya nakatira.**   _____

2. **Saan ang iyong nanay?**   _____

3. **Nasaan ang kaibigan niya?**   _____

4. **Sa bahay ba si Maria?**   _____

5. **Nasaan sila pumaroón?**   _____

PART VI

A. Translate the following time, words and phrases.

	Tagalog		English	
1. today	_____	7. **kanina**	_____	
2. tomorrow	_____	8. **mamaya**	_____	
3. last week	_____	9. **noong Enero**	_____	
4. day before	_____	10. **bukas ng hapon**	_____	
5. yesterday	_____	11. **sa Linggo**	_____	
6. next year	_____	12. **sa isang taon**	_____	

	Tagalog		Spanish
13. 5:00 p.m.	_____	18.	_____
14. 2:00 p.m.	_____	19.	_____
15. 8:15 a.m.	_____	20.	_____
16. 10:30 a.m.	_____	21.	_____
17. 12:00 nn.	_____	22.	_____

B. Give the derivatives of the following words using the **ma-** and **maka-** affixes.

	makaalis	**makalakad**	**matúlog**
Infinitive	_____	_____	_____
Imperative	_____	_____	_____
Past	_____	_____	_____
Present	_____	_____	_____
Future	_____	_____	_____

C. Translate the following sentences into Tagalog

1. What did you see yesterday? _____
2. He was able to buy shoes. _____
3. He slept on the floor. _____
4. Don't be angry with him. _____
5. He was not able to pay. _____
6. He woke the baby unintentionally. _____

PART VII

A. Arrange the words and particles in the following sentences, and replace with correct ones.

1. **marumi ang bata ang raw ba** _____
2. **siya ay bata ba pa** _____
3. **siya ay kumain rin ay ba po** _____
4. **nakaalis nab a siya** _____
5. **nakapag-aral hindi siya pa** _____
6. **bakit siya hindi makatatakbo nang mabilis** _____
7. **ba ito ang aklat mo** _____

B. Give the Tagalog equivalent of the following words and phrases.

1. good _____
2. very good _____
3. how good _____
4. industrious _____
5. very industrious _____
6. most industrious _____

C. Translate these sentences into Tagalog.

1. Peter is brighter than John. _____
2. John is taller than his brother. _____
3. My house is as beautiful as his. _____
4. His child is small. _____
5. His child is smaller than my child. _____
6. His child is of the same height as mine. _____
7. His dog is not as bad as his neighbor's. _____
8. John and Peter are brothers. _____
9. Jack and his friend are of the same color. _____
10. My sister is more beautiful than I. _____

D. Create sentences using the following words.

1. **magandá** _____
2. **kay gandá** _____
3. **magandáng-magandá** _____
4. **nápakagandá** _____
5. **pinakamagandá** _____
6. **magkasintaás** _____
7. **hindî kasinggúlang** _____
8. **hindî kasimbaít** _____

E. Translate the following into Tagalog.

1. Don't eat now. _____
2. He cannot ride a horse. _____
3. Can you swim? _____
4. Yes, I can swim. _____
5. You should study Tagalog everyday. _____
6. Why don't you eat your supper? _____
7. Do you know his name? _____
8. What do you need? _____

PART VIII

A. Create sentences from the following root words using the prefixes on the left. Afterwards, give the English translation of your sentences.

1. **lambót** using **pa-in**   3. **upo** using **pa_in**
2. **kain** using **magpa-**   4. **inom** using **magpa-**

B. Translate the following sentences into English.

1. **Huwág mong sirain ang papel.**
2. **Pinasulat ko siya ng liham.**
3. **Siya'y pinaalis ng kanyang ama.**
4. **Ang kanyang tákot ay nagpatakbó kay Juan.**
5. **Pinabasa niya ako ng pahayagan.**

C. Give the plural form of the following adjectives in two ways.

magandá   _____   _____
mabuti   _____   _____

D. Translate the following phrases into English.

1. **ang mabaít** _____
2. **ang mabaít na tao** _____
3. **and bumábasa** _____
4. **ang binábasa** _____
5. **ang patakbó** _____
6. **ang maglabá** _____

E. Translate the following sentences into English using the passive voice of verbs.

1. **Kanyáng iniligtás ako.**   _____
2. **Siya'y pinalo ng kaibigan niya.**   _____
3. **Hindî niya ako sinulátan.**   _____
4. **Ako'y kanyang binigyán ng aklát niya.**   _____
5. **Ang iyong ibinigay ay akin na.**   _____
6. **Ang sa kanyá ay hindi magagámit ng ibá.**   _____

Answers to Review Exercises

PART I

C. 1. **Ang tinápay ay kinákain ng batà.**
2. **Binili ko ang sapátos sa Makati.**
3. **Naglutò ng gúlay ang katúlong namin.**

4. **Tináwag ng maysakít ang doktor.**
5. **Kinúha ng batà ang lapis sa báhay.**

D. **Ang Panginoóng Hesús at ang Kanyáng mga kaibígan ay nása isang maliít na bangkâ sa dágat. Isang bagyó ang dumating nang biglâ… Ang mga álon ay malalakí. Malakás ang hángin. Napúpunô ng túbig ang bangkâ. Tináwag ng mga laláki ang Panginoóng Hesús. Ang sábi nilá, "Walâ bang halagâ sa inyo na kami'y malúnod?" Tumayô ang Panginoóng Hesús sa bangkâ. Nagsalitâ Siya sa hángin at sa dágat at sinabi Niyá, "Tahímik!" Nagíng tahímik kaagád.**

PART II

B. 1. **ang áking ina**
2. **ang ating simbáhan**
3. **ang kaniyáng pag-íbig**
4. **ang kaniláng pag-aáral**
5. **ang kaniyáng pag-ása**
6. **ang kaniyáng pagluluto**
7. **ang ating pagtataním**

8. **ang kaniyáng kahirápan**
9. **ang áking kaligayáhan**
10. **ang inyóng trabáho**
11. **ang bálak ni John**
12. **ang táwa ng sanggol**
13. **ang gálit ng laláki**
14. **ang ngálan ni Mary**

15. **ang hángin ng Marso**
16. **ang súlat ng amá**
17. **ang matá ng pusà**
18. **ang sermon ng parì**
19. **ang pagkáin ng batà**
20. **ang paá ng háyop**

E. 1. b   2. c   3. c   4. b   5. c

PART III

A. 1. **siya**
2. **sila**
3. **kanyang**
4. **ka**
5. **mo**
6. **kaming**

7. **amin; akin; kanila**
8. **siya**
9. **kami; sila**
10. **namin; nila**
11. **mo; ninyo**
12. **kayo**

13. **ko; namin**
14. **mo**
15. **sila; kayo; kami**
16. **aming; ating; inyong**
17. (any nominative pronoun)
18. **kang; kayong**

19. **kayo; sila**
20. **ka**
21. **ka; kayo**

B. 1. **pagsúlat**
2. **magkaibígan; magkapatíd;** etc.
3. **pagkáin**
4. **bulaklák**
5. **magsasaká**

6. **gurò**
7. **túbig**
8. **páhayagan; aklát; mágasin**
9. **mabaít; magandá**
10. **masamâ**

C. 1. **marúnong**   2. **masípag**   3. **tamád**   4. **bulág**   5. **kaáwa-awà**

PART IV

B. 1. Bumili ako ng isang malaking bahay sa Quezon City.
   2. Bumabasa kami sa klase.
   3. Pupunta kami sa inyong bahay bukas.
   4. Malinis ang mga damit ni Peter.
   5. Hindi malinis ang aking baro.

C. 1. Ang mga bisíta ng bágong kasál ay mga kaibígan at kamag-ának sa kanilang báyan.
   2. Kami ay sumakay sa kotse, kasáma ang katúlong at ang anak ko.
   3. Ang bahay ng aming kaibígan ay nasa Nueva Ecija.
   4. Umalís kami sa Maynila nang ika-10:00 ng umaga.
   5. Maraming pagkáin sa mahábang mesa.
   6. Magandá ang asawa ng aking kaibígan.

PART V

A. 1.
Infinitive	tumakbó	umalís	magsalitâ	mag-alagà
Imperative	tumakbó	umalís	magsalitâ	mag-alagà
Past	tumakbó	umalís	nagsalitâ	nag-alagà
Present	tumatakbó	umaalís	nagsasalitâ	nag-aalagà
Future	tátakbo	áalis	magsásalitâ	mag-áalagà

2. a. Sumulat ng aklát si Mary.
   b. Lumakad siya papunta sa páaralán.
   c. Umalis nang maága si Peter at ang kanyang mga kaibigan.
   d. Hindi makapaglutò si Mary ng kánin.
   e. Bakit hindi ka naglínis ng mga kamáy?
   f. Nagbebenta ba kayo ng mga manggá?
   g. Gusto kong bumilí ng dalawáng manggá.
   h. Mahúsay siyang bumasa.
   i. Dapat kang sumúlat sa iyong ina linggú-linggó (or minsan sa isang linggo)
   j. Kung sino ang nag-áaral nang mabuti ay magsásalitâ ng Tagalog.
   k. Kumain ka ba ng almusál?
   l. Umalis ba si Peter ngayóng umaga?
   m. Ayaw mo bang lumangóy?

B. 1.
Infinitive	sabihin	dalhín	siráin	tawágin
Imperative	sabihin	dalhín	siráin	tawágin
Past	sinabi	dinala	sinirà	tináwag
Present	sinasabi	dinadala	sinisirà	tinátawag
Future	sasabihin	dadalhín	sisirain	tatawagin

2. a. Kinain nila ang isdâ.
   b. Sinulat niya ang liham sa akin.
   c. Binabasa ni Juan ang pahayagan.
   d. Niluluto ng aking katulong ang pagkain.
   e. Sinabi ni Hesus ito.
   f. Batiin ninyo si Juan para sa akin.
   g. Minamahal mo ba ang Diyos?

3. a. bábasa   c. gigising   e. maglalarô   g. magsasabi   i. áalis
   b. magdadalá   d. magbabago   f. magbábasâ   h. gágamot   j. mag-áalís

C. 1. **Saan** is used with an action word.
   2. **Nasaan** is used without. Both ask for location.

   3. a. **Nasaan ang iyong bahay?**   d. **Nasaan ang iyong simbahan?**
      b. **Nasaan ang iyong kaibigan?**   e. **Saan ka kumain?**
      c. **Saan pupunta ang iyong kaibigan?** f. **Si John ay nasa lungsod.**

D. 1. (no error)   2. **Nasaan**   3. (no error)   4. **Nasa**   5. **Saan**

PART VI

A. 1. **ngayon**
   2. **bukas**
   3. **noong isang linggo**
   4. **kamakalawa**
   5. **kahapon**
   6. **sa isang taon**
   7. a while ago or earlier in the day
   8. later
   9. last January
   10. tomorrow afternoon
   11. on Sunday or next Sunday
   12. next year

   13. **ikalima ng hapon**
   14. **ikadalawa ng hapon**
   15. **ikawalo at labinlima ng umaga**
   16. **ikasampu at kalahati ng umaga**
   17. **ikalabindalawa at kalahati ng tanghali**
   18. **alas sinko ng hapon**
   19. **alas dos ng hapon**
   20. **alas otso kinse ng umaga**
   21. **alas diyes y medya ng umaga**
   22. **alas dose y medya ng tanghali**

B.

Infinitive	**makaalis**	**makalakad**	**matulog**
Imperative	(none)	(none)	**matulog**
Past	**nakaalis**	**nakalakad**	**natulog**
Present	**nakaaalis**	**nakalalakad**	**natutulog**
Future	**makaaalis**	**makalalakad**	**matutulog**

C. 1. **Ano ang nakita mo kahapon?**
   2. **Nakabili siya ng sapatos.**
   3. **Natulog siya sa sahig.**
   4. **Huwag kang magalit sa kanya.**
   5. **Hindi siya nakabayad.**
   6. **Nagising niya ang bata.**

PART VII

A. 1. **Marumi raw ba ang bata?**
   2. **Siya ba ay bata pa?**
   3. **Siya rin pô ba ay kumain?**
   4. **Nakaalis na ba siya?**
   5. **Hindi pa siya nakapag-aral.**
   6. **Bakit hindi siya makatakbo ng mabilis?**
   7. **Ito ba ang aklat mo?**

B. 1. good - **mabuti**
   2. very good - **napakabuti**
   3. how good - **kay buti** or **mabuting-mabuti**
   4. industrious - **masipag**
   5. very industrious - **napakasipag** or **masipag na masipag**
   6. most industrious - **pinakamasipag**.

C. 1. **Lalong marunong si Peter kaysa kay John.**
    2. **Lalong mataas si John kaysa sa kanyang kapatid na lalaki.**
    3. **Ang aking bahay ay kasingganda ng kaniyang bahay.**
    4. **Maliit ang kanyang anak.**
    5. **Lalong maliit ang kanyang anak kaysa sa anak ko.**
    6. **Magkasintaas ang anak niya at ang anak ko.**
    7. **Ang kanyang aso ay hindi kasinsama ng aso ng kapitbahay niya.**
    8. **Magkapatid sina John at Peter.**
    9. **Si Jack at ang kanyang kaibigan ay magkasingkulay.**
   10. **Lalong maganda ang aking kapatid kaysa sa akin.**

E. 1. **Huwag kang kumain ngayon.**
    2. **Hindi siya marunong sumakay sa kabayo.**
    3. **Marunong ka bang lumangoy?**
    4. **Oo, marunong akong lumangoy.**
    5. **Kailangan mong mag-aral ng Tagalog araw-araw.**
    6. **Bakit hindi ka kumain ng iyong hapunan?**
    7. **Alam mo ba ang kanyang pangalan?**
    8. **Ano ang kailangan mo?**

PART VIII

B. 1. Don't tear the paper.
    2. I made him/her write a letter.
    3. His father made him/her leave.
    4. His fear made Juan run.
    5. He/She made me read the newspaper.

C. 1. **magaganda**; **mga maganda**
    2. **mabubuti**; **mga mabuti**

D. 1. the good one
    2. the good man
    3. the one reading
    4. the thing being read
    5. the manner of running or the running of (something such as a contest)
    6. the washing of clothes

E. 1. I was saved by him.
    2. He was hit by his friend.
    3. He had not written to me.
    4. His/her book was given to me by him.
    5. What you have given me is mine already.
    6. What is his/hers cannot be used by another.

Reading Materials

ANG PAGPAPANTAY-PANTAY SA LIPUNAN
Manuel A. Quezon (1878-1944)
President of the Commonwealth of the Philippines, 1935 to 1944

Talagang totoong ang Pilipinas ay may malaking pagsulong sa mga bagay tungkol sa bayan at sa kabuhayan sa loob ng huling 30 taon. Sa pagkamakabayan at puno ng pamahalaan, dumating tayo sa panahong nasa ating lahat ang mga karapatan ng isang pamahalaang malasarili at dahil dito'y masisiguro natin ang pagdating ng talagang kalayaan.

Sa kabuhayan, isang bansa tayong malakas sa kalakal ng Amerika; ang ating kalakal sa labas at loob ay dumarami at ang yaman ng bansa natin ay lumalaking mabuti. Gumagawa tayo ng pagsulong sa kalinisan, pagtuturo, at paggawa ng mga daan at lahat ng pahatiran.

Nguni't ang maraming may pakinabang dito ay ang mayayaman lamang. Ang mayaman ay maaaring mabuhay sa bigay ng salapi nila at pati mga anak nila ay lumalaki na palaging mayroon. Ang kanilang ibig ay mga ugaling mahalaga lamang ang lipunan at saya at iba pang ibig ng katawan nila. Talagang ugali nila ang sumunod sa kabuhayang masaya nang walang gawa at damdaming makatao.

Ang mga taong hindi naman mayaman at hindi naman mahirap ay mayroon ngayong mabubuting kabuhayan kaysa noong panahon ng Kastila. Ang mga kailangan para sa kabihasnan ngayon ay kanila nang kaya. Ang anak nilang lalaki at babae ay kumakain na ng mabuti, nagsusuot ng mabuting damit at nag-aaral ng mataas na karunungan.

Nakalulungkot sabihin, ngunit siyang totoo na ang kabuhayang iyan ay walang-wala sa bayang manggagawa. Lahat na ng mga gumagawa sa lupa, at pumapasok sa mga trabaho ay kaunti lamang ang ibinubuti ng lagay kaysa noong panahon ng Kastila. Totoo nga na ang sahod ngayon ay lumaki kaysa noong nasa kapangyarihan tayo ng Espanya at ang sahurin dito ay mataas kaysa alin mang bansa dito sa Silangan, bukod sa Hapon. Ngunit dapat nating isipin na ang pera noon ay maraming bagay at kailangan ang nabibili kaysa pera ngayon; at saka, sa samahan ng may patrabaho at manggagawa ay may palagayang hindi mababayaran ng salapi. Noon ang may paggawa at manggagawa ay malapit sa bawa't isa at ang ayos nila ay parang totoong magkapatid at mag-anak, kaya ang pagsasama nila at pagmamahalan ay malakas kaysa salapi. Ngayon ang samahan ay parang mag-ibang tao at lahat ay gumagawa para sa kanyang sarili, gaya rin sa ibang lupa na mayroong malalaking kalakal. Ang ating mga tao na man ay walang reklamo sa buhay na iyan mangyari'y ang palagay nila ay dapat tiisin ang lahat ng bigay ng Diyos para dumating sa atin ang awa ng langit.

Ngayon ang manggagawang Pilipino, hindi man nag-aral ay ayaw nang maniwala na ibig ng Diyos na ang iba ay mabuhay na mayaman at ang iba'y mabuhay sa hirap at pagtitiis. Ang manggagawang Pilipino ngayo'y naniniwala na siya rin ay mahal ng Ama sa Langit gaya rin ng ibang taong Kanyang ginawa; at dahil dito ang daigdig ay hindi ginawa ng Diyos para sa ilan lamang kundi para sa lahat.

Ang pagsulong ng Bansa sa pagpantay-pantay ng buhay sa lipunan ay talagang iniuutos ng Saligang Batas (Constitution) natin. Ang ating palatuntunan na tinanggap ng bayan sa paglagay sa inyo at sa akin man sa tungkulin natin, ay nagbibigay sa atin ng mabigat na tungkuling magkaroon at mag-alaga sa mga manggagawa. Dapat tayong maging masipag na sa alinmang batas ay huwag nating payagan na ang manggagawa ay gawan ng masama ng may paggawa, at huwag payagan ang anumang bagay na makasira sa layon ng pagkakapantay-pantay. Sa pagharap sa kinabukasan ng bagong bansa nating ito ay hindi dapat na tayo'y manghawak sa lakas ng batas kundi sa lakas ng tapat na pagsasama ng tao at ng pamahalaan ng naririto para sa layong sila'y alagaan para sa kanilang sariling buhay at kaligayahan.

Maging ang Kagawaran ng Katarungan (Department of Justice) o Kawanihan ng Paggawa (Bureau of Labor) ay parehong handang tumulong sa inyo sa paggawa ng mga kailangang batas para maitakip sa mga kulang ng mga batas na sinusunod ngayon at sa ganito ay maayos at magamot ang mga masamang nangyayari sa bayan at para magawa rin ang palatuntunang ipinasusunod ng ating Saligang Batas at gayon din ang mga inaantay nila sa atin na nasasabi sa palatuntunan nating panghalalan.

PAG-IBIG SA TINUBUANG LUPA (Excerpt)
Written in Barcelona, Spain, 1882
by Dr. Jose P. Rizal (1861-1896)
National hero, Philippines

Narito ang isang magandang paksa; at dahil din sa kanyang kagandahan ay napakadalas nang talakayin. Ang pantas, makata, makasining, manggagawa, mangangalakal, o mandirigma, matanda o bata, hari o alipin—ang lahat ay nakapag-isip na tungkol sa kanya, at nakapaghandog ng pinakamamahalagang bunga ng kanilang isip o ng kanilang puso. Buhat sa taga Europang mulat, malaya't mapagmalaki sa kanyang maluwalhating kasaysayan, hanggang sa negro sa Aprika, na hinango sa kanyang mga kagubatan at ipinagbili sa hamak na halaga; buhat sa matatandang bayang ang mga anino'y aali-aligid pa sa kanilang mga mapapanglaw ng guho, libingan ng kanilang mga kaluwalhatia't pagdurusa, hanggang sa mga bansang makabago't lagi ng kumikilos at punô ng buhay, ay mayroong isang pinakamamahal na dilag, maningning, dakila, nguni't walang habag at malupit, na tinatawag na Inang Bayan. Libu-libong dila ang sa kanya'y umawit, libu-libong kudyapi ang naghandog sa kanya ng kanilang mga makatang lalong matataas ang pangarap, ang naghain sa kanyang harap o sa kanyang alaala ng kanilang pinakamaningning na katha. Siya ang naging sigaw ng kapayapaan ng pag-ibig at ng kaluwalhatian, palibhasa'y siya ang laman ng lahat ng pag-iisip, at katulad ng liwanag na nakukulong sa isang malinis na bubog, siya'y tumatagos hanggang sa labas, na parang mga sinag na buhay na buhay.

At ito ba'y magiging sagwil upang siya'y pag-ukulan natin ng panahon? At tayo ba'y hindi maaaring mag-ukol sa kanya ng anumang bagay, tayong walang ibang kasalanan kundi ang pagkakahuli ng pagsilang sa maliwanag? Nagbibigay ba ang dantaong ika-labinsiyam ng karapatang huwag kumilala ng utang na loob? Hindi. Hindi pa nasasaid ang mayamang mina ng puso; sagana pa tuwina ang kanyang alaala, at bahagya man ang pagkakapukaw ng kanyang alaala, at bahagya man ang pagkapukaw ng ating kalooban, ay makasusumpong tayo sa kaibuturan ng ating kaluluwa na kung di man isang masaganang kayamanan, ay abuloy na bagaman dahop ay puspos naman ng kasiglahan. Katulad ng mga matatandang ebreong nangag-alay sa templo ng mga kauna-unahang bunga ng kanilang pag-ibig, tayong mangingibang lupain ay nag-uukol ng mga kauna-unahang tinig sa ating Inang Bayang nababalot ng mga panginorin at mga ulap ng umaga, lagi nang maganda at matulain, at sa tuwi-tuwina'y lalong sinasamba habang sa kanya'y nawawalay at nalalayo.

At ito'y hindi nararapat pagtakhan sa dahilang ang pag-ibig sa Inang Baya'y isang damdaming tunay na katutubo; sapagka't naroroon ang mga kauna-unahang alaala ng kamusmusan, isang masamang tulang awitin na ang kabataan lamang ang nakakikilala at sa mga bakas nito'y sumisibol ang bulaklak ng kawalang-malay at ng kaligayahan; sapagka't doo'y nahihimbing ang buong nakaraan at nababanaagan ang isang hinaharap; sapagka't sa kanyang mga kagubatan at sa kanyang mga kaparangan, sa bawa't punungkahoy, sa bawa't halaman, sa bawa't bulaklak, ay nakikita ninyong nakaukit ang gunita ng isang nilikhang minamahal ninyo, gaya ng hininga niya sa mahalimuyak na simoy ng hangin, ng kanyang awit sa mga bulong ng bukál ng ngiti niya sa bahaghari ng langit, o ng mga buntung-hininga niya sa magulong halinghing ng hangin sa gabi. Ang sanhi nito'y sapagka't doo'y nakakikita kayo, sa pamamagitan ng mga mata ng inyong gunita, sa ilalim ng tahimik na bubong ng matandang tahanan, ng isang angkang nag-aalaala at naghihintay sa inyo, nag-uukol sa inyo ng mga isipan at mga pagkabalisa nila; sa wakas, sapagka't sa kanyang langit, sa kanyang araw, sa kanyang mga karagatan at sa kanyang mga kagubatan ay nakakatagpo kayo ng tulain, ng paggiliw at ng pag-ibig, at hanggang sa libingan na ring pinaghihintayan sa inyo ng isang abang puntod upang kayo'y isauli sa sinapupunan ng lupa. Mayroon kayang isang kadiyusang nagtatali ng ating mga puso sa lupa ng ating inang-bayan, na nagpapaganda't nagpaparilag sa lahat, naghahandog sa atin ng lahat ng bagay sa ilalim ng isang anyong matulain at malambing, at nakararahuyo sa ating mga puso? Saapagka't sa papaano mang anyo humarap siya, maging nararamtan ng matingkad na pula, napuputungan ng mga bulaklak at laurel, makapangyarihan at mayaman; maging malungkot at nag-iisa, nababalot ng basahan, at alipin, nagmamakaawa sa kanyang mga anak na alipin din; maging anaki'y diwata sa isang halamang maalindog, naliligid ng mga bughaw na alon ng karagatan, nakahahalina at marikit, gaya ng pangarap ng napaglalalangang kabataan; maging natatakpan ng isang lambong ng yelo, nakaupong malungkot sa mga dulo ng daigdig, sa silong ng isang langit na walang araw at walang tala; maging anuman ang kanyang ngalan, ang kanyang gulang o ang kanyang kapalaran, siya'y lagi na nating minamahal, gaya ng pagmamahal ng anak sa kanyang ina sa gitna ng gutom at ng karalitaan.

TAPOK AT BANLIK (Excerpt)
First Prize, Essay in Filipino, 2005 Palanca Awards
Dr. Luis P. Gatmaitan
Physician and Writer of Children's Stories

"Putik pong malinis ang karaniwang putik. Pero ang banlik po ay putik na ubod ng dumi kasi'y galing sa bundok," gayon ang paliwanag sa akin ng isang nanay sa Infanta nang bisitahin namin ang lugar nila upang magsagawa ng art therapy sa mga batang nakaligtas sa landslide. Paulit-ulit kasing nababanggit ng mga bata ang salitang banlik kapag sila'y nagbabahagi ng kanilang kuwento. Akala ko, nakasanayan lamang nilang tawaging banlik ang putik. Gaya ng may iba-iba tayong katawagan sa isang bagay sa isang partikular na lugar.

May pagkakaiba pala ang putik at banlik. Akala ko, kasukdulan na ng dumi kapag sinabing putik. Naiisip ko ang kalabaw ng aking Tatang na nakaugaliang maglublob sa putikan kapag tapos na ang maghapong pag-aararo. Hirap na kinukuskos ni Tatang ang katawan ng kalabaw upang matungkab ang natuyong putik na nakakulapol dito. Pero may antas pa pala ng pagiging marumi. Mas marumi ang gumuhong lupa mula sa kabundukan sapagkat dala-dala nito ang mga ugat ng puno, damo, kulisap, itlog ng ahas, at kung anu-ano pang alamat at elementong matatagpuan doon.

Mula sa mga guho ng Real, Infanta, at Nakar (na mas kilala sa katawagang REINA) sa Quezon, di na mabilang ang mga kuwentong narinig ko. Mga salaysay ito ng pagkalubog at pagbangon mula sa banlik. Mga kuwentong marahil ay paulit-ulit na ikukuwento ng mga batang nakaligtas para di nila malimutan ang mga ama, ina, lolo, lola, amain, tiyahin, pamangkin, apo, kapatid, kaibigan, at kalaro na inangkin ng rumaragasang agos mula sa kabundukan isang gabing walang tigil ang pagbuhos ng ulan.

Aaminin ko, may daga sa aking dibdib nang una kong makaharap ang mga batang nakaligtas sa trahedya. Nandu'n ang pangamba ko na baka naiisip nilang 'kay lakas naman ng loob ng mamang ito na tumayo sa aming harapan gayong hindi naman niya talagang gagap ang tindi ng aming dinaanang tahedya.' O baka naman ganito ang nasa isip nila: 'hay naku, heto ulit ang isa pang grupo na pakukuwentuhin na naman kami nang nangyari sa amin hanggang sa kami'y maiyak!' Ewan ko ba pero noong una, parang nahihiya akong tumayo sa harap nila. Pakiramdam ko ba'y napapalibutan ako ng mga taong higit pa ang kakayahan kaysa sa 'kin. Ang mga batang kaharap ko ay mga batang nakayang lampasan ang kahindik-hindik na delubyong dumating sa Quezon! Hindi sila mga ordinaryong bata.

Sino nga ba kami para makialam sa kanilang buhay? Dumating na lang kami sa kanilang lugar nang walang kaabog-abog. Pero inari nila kaming mabuting kaibigan, waring mga piling panauhin sa isang magarang piging. Kapag ibinabahagi na sa amin ng mga bata ang kanilang naranasang sakit o takot, ramdam kong 'yun ang kanilang paraan ng pagsasabi ng 'mahalaga po sa amin na nandito kayo.' Sa pagbubukas nila ng loob sa amin, nasaksihan ko ang dakilang himala ng pakikipagkapwa-damdamin.

Sabi ng isang kaibigan ko, "ang mga bata raw ang nagsisilbing barometrong panukat ng isang komunidad. Kaya makabubuting pagmasdan ang kanilang hitsura't galaw, at mapakinggan ang kanilang sinasabi o di sinasabi."

Totoo 'yun. Dahil paano nga ba maitatago ang nararanasang paghihikahos ng pamilya kung ang kilik na bata ay maputla ang balat, malaki ang tiyan, litaw ang butuhing dibdib, at walang kislap ang mga mata? Paano nga ba mailililihim ang bunga ng nagdaang sakuna sa mga bata samantalang may mga gabing dinadalaw sila ng bangungot, pagihi sa banig, at pangangatal sa pagkaalala ng sakuna? Mahirap lurukin ang kalagayan ng isang komunidad kung ang pagbabatayan ay ang sinasabi ng kanilang tatay, nanay, at iba pang matatanda sa pamilya. Kayang-kayang kasing itago ng mga magulang ang lahat ng kanilang nararamdaman. Kaya nila kaming papaniwalain na ayos lang ang lahat kahit hindi. Iba ang mga bata.

Sa Real ko nakita ang batang kamukha ni Frankenstein. Nang makilala ko si Bunso, si Frankenstein ang unang pumasok sa aking isip. Paano kasi, punong-puno ng tahi ang kanyang ulo, batok, at leeg (para talagang 'yung karakter na si Frankenstein sa pelikula). Nangawit kaya ang kamay ng mga siruhano nang inoperahan nila ang batang ito? Sangkaterbang pilat ang iniwang alaala ng sakuna sa mukha at katawan ni Bunso.

"Nadaganan po siya nang gumuho ang Repador Building," paliwanag agad ng isang guro nang makita niyang waring nagtatanong ang aking mga mata sa hitsura ng batang kaharap ko. "Hindi po siya nakita agad. Akala nga po nila ay patay na si Bunso. Mabuti't nadala sa Maynila para maoperahan ang nabasag niyang bungo."

Mula noon, tuwing titingnan ko si Bunso, nahahabag ako. Kung ako kaya ang nasa katayuan niya, makakaya ko kaya ang sinuong niya? Walang sinabi sa mga tahing nasa mukha at ulo ni Bunso ang aking nag-iisang keloid bunga ng inoperahang sebaceous cyst sa aking likod. E, paano pa kaya ang mga pilat ni Bunso na di ko nakikita? Pihadong nag-iwan ng malalalim na pilat sa kanyang murang puso ang sakuna.

Kung nasa ibang lugar lamang si Bunso, pihadong panay tukso ang matatanggap niya mula sa ilang pilyong bata dahil sa kanyang kakaibang hitsura. Pero dito sa Real, walang nangahas bumiro kay Bunso. Siguro kasi'y ang karanasan ni Bunso ay karanasan din ng buong bayan. Ang bawat isang tahi sa mukha at ulo ni Bunso ay nagpapalutang lamang sa kanyang katapangan.

Hindi sinasadya'y naalala ko ang mga batang may kanser sa aming pagamutan. Sila man ay parang si Bunso rin sa maraming pagkakataon. Nasa isang sitwasyon sila na kahit tayong matatanda na ay mahihirapan din. Hindi birobiro ang diagnosis na kanser para sa sinumang kaanak. Ang aming mga anghel, di pa man nakababasa ng alpabeto, ay hindi rin ipinuwera ng sakit na ito. Sinong magulang ang hindi madudurog ang puso kapag nakita niyang tinitiis ng minumutyang anak ang hapdi ng turok ng karayom sa kemoterapi?

Pero kagaya ng mga batang nakaligtas sa trahedya ng Quezon, ang mga bata ring ito ay di nawawalan ng pag-asa na gagaling sila. Kapag nasimulan na ang kanilang kemoterapi, nagsisimulang malagas ang kanilang buhok kasabay ng pagpatay ng gamot sa mababagsik na cancer cells. Pagkatapos, mistulang isang komunidad na na-wash out ang hitsura ng ulo ng aming mga paslit. Pero nandun ang pag-asa na maaaring malampasan nila ang sakit na kanser.

Hitik sa kuwento, games, at activity ang tatlong araw na kasama namin sila. Nakatulong din na palagi kong bitbit ang aking digital camera. Manipis kasi ito at maliit lang kaya madaling ilagay sa bulsa. Sa tuwing pipindutin ko ito, una-unahang nagpo-pose ang mga bata para sa kodakan. Pagkatapos ay titingnan din kaagad ang picture nila, magtatawanan o magtutuksuhan ayon sa nakitang hitsura sa kamera. Minsan nga ay sila pa ang nagpiprisintang magpakuha ng litrato. Agad kong nakuha ang loob nila. Laking pasasalamat ko sa aking digital camera. Nakapasok ako sa mundo ng mga bata nang di sinasadya. Sa bawat klik ng kamera, palapit nang palapit ang loob namin sa isa't isa.

Noong unang araw, sinadya naming huwag munang sumalat sa trahedyang sinapit nila. Gusto lang naming magbukas sila ng kanilang mga sarili. At dahil mga lupa at banlik ang tumabon sa kanilang mga bahay at buhay, ninais namin na sa pagpapakilala nila sa kanilang sarili ay dumampot sila ng isang bagay mula sa paligid na kumakatawan sa kanila. Gusto naming bumalik ang tiwala nila sa bundok, lupa, puno, at bato.

"Kagaya po ako ng batong ito," pakilala ni Cynthia. "Ang ibig ko pong sabihin, matibay po ako, hindi kaagad madudurog. At saka, noong tumatakas po kami, mga matitigas na batong kagaya nito ang hinahanap naming tuntungan para hindi kami malubog sa banlik."

May mga dala rin kaming librong pambata para ikuwento. Subalit sa bawat kuwentong isinasalaysay ko, humuhugot sila sa nagdaang sakuna upang idugtong sa aming kuwento. Kung tutuusin, walang kinalaman sa bagyo o baha ang isang kuwentong isinalaysay ko. Tungkol ito sa pagmamahal ng isang sapaterong ama sa isang anak na ipinanganak na putol ang dalawang paa. Sa naturang kuwento, palihim palang gumagawa ng sapatos ang ama upang ialay sa anak niya. Kapag nalalapit na ang kaarawan ng bata, pilit na iniimadyin ng ama ang lumalaking sukat ng paa ng anak niya. Ngunit lingid sa kaalaman ng ama, napapanaginipan pala ng anak na walang paa ang mga sapatos na nililikha para sa kanya sa tuwing bisperas ng kaarawan niya.

Matapos ang pagkukuwento, hiniling ko sa mga bata na lumikha ng isang pares ng sapatos para sa bidang batang babae sa kuwento, at kailangang kumbinsihin nila ako na ang kanilang sapatos ang dapat kong piliin. Nagulat ako nang makitang karamihan ay bota ang iginuhit. Yung isang grupo ay nagdrowing ng botang may mataas na takong. Yung isang grupo pa ay gumuhit ng sapatos na convertible sa bota at ipinagdiinan pang ang sapatos nila ay waterresistant. Kasi raw, nang mga sumunod na araw matapos ang sakuna, mga bota na ang kanilang sapin sa paa. Natuwa ako na iginawa nila ng pambihirang bota ang batang bida sa libro. Ayaw raw nilang marumhan ng banlik ang bago nilang kaibigan.

Iniiwasan ko pa sanang banggitin ang nagdaang sakuna. Sa isip-isip ko, tatalakayin namin ito sa mga susunod pang araw. Pero ipinahiwatig na nilang handa na silang harapin ang kani-kanilang kuwento, katunayan ang mga iginuhit nilang sapatos na pambaha.

Tinanong namin ng kasama kong facilitator kung ano ang limang mahahalagang bagay na ililigtas nila sakaling may mangyaring sakuna. Maraming sumagot na ang ililigtas nila ay ang kanilang uniporme at gamit sa eskuwelahan (na para bang magkakalakas-loob pa ang mga prinsipal ng mga eskuwelahan na ideklarang may pasok kinabukasan). 'Yung iba, TV at pridyider ang gustong iligtas, na siyempre pa'y sinundan ng tawanan. Kahit yata sanrekwang adrenaline ang ipundar ng katawan, hindi kakayanin ng mga paslit na ito na buhatin ang kanilang pridyider!

Pero sa ilan, mga tao ang kanilang binanggit na ililigtas. Sa kanila, hindi mahalaga na "ano" ang tanong namin, kundi "sino" ang ililigtas nila. Mula sa mga sagot na damit, pagkain, notebook, telebisyon, at pridyider, lumabas ang pangalan ng kanilang lolo't lola, tatay, nanay, kapatid, at pamangkin.

Hanggang ngayon, hindi mawala sa isip ni May kung paanong nakabitaw ang lola niya sa kanyang kamay noong tinatangay sila ng rumaragasang agos. Hindi na nakita pa ang lola niya, nalibing sa natuyong banlik sa kung saan. At si May, hindi niya mapatawad ang sarili na hindi niya nailigtas ang lola niya. Di lang si May ang nagbahagi nito kundi ilan pang batang pipituhin o wawaluhing gulang na pawang nakangabitaw sa mahigpit na pagkakakapit sa mga kaanak nila. Nandu'n ang masidhing pagnanais na mailigtas ang kapamilyang minamahal. Kung tutuusin, kasama sa mga karapatan ng mga batang kagaya nina May ang unang mailigtas sa panahon ng trahedya. Pero para sa mga batang kagaya nila, higit na mahalagang nailigtas nila ang mahihina na nilang lolo't lola o ang mga nakababatang kapatid na karga-karga nila. Napag-isip-isip ko, sa panahon pala ng sakuna, nagbabagong-anyo ang mga bata. Gusto nilang maging tagapagligtas. Gaya ng napapanuod nilang cartoons sa TV na inililigtas ng superhero ang mga biktima.

Nang inaakala naming palagay na ang loob nila sa amin, hiniling namin sa kanila na isulat o idrowing ang naganap noong gabi ng Nobyembre 29, 2004. Naupod ang mga krayolang kulay-brown sa kanilang mga iginuhit. Nagkulay-tsokolate ang kanilang mga papel. Nagmistulang dagat iyon ng tsokolate, parang mga kumunoy na walang katapusan, inaangkin ang bawat batang nahuhulog doon.

Sabi ni Raymond, nagulat na lang sila sa napakabilis na pagtaas ang tubig. Wala na silang panahon pang makatapok (lengguwaheng Quezon para sa 'paglikas sa matataas na lugar'). Ang tanging nakita ng Nanay niya na mataas ay ang magkatabing puno ng abokado sa kanilang bakuran. Agad nila itong inakyat. Mahigpit na kumapit doon habang ginaw na ginaw, kasama ang isa pa niyang pamangkin. Sa kabilang puno, doon naman umakyat ang Nanay niya, ang ate niya, at isa pang pamangkin. Ngunit hindi naging mabait sa kanila ang mga punong ito. Nabali ito at sapilitang tinangay ang Nanay niya at dalawang pamangkin. Sila na lamang ng kanyang ate ang natira.

Nanlambot ako nang marinig ang kuwento ni Raymond. Hindi sila nailigtas ng matatayog na puno sa kanilang bakuran. Nag-uunahang pumatak ang luha sa mga mata ni Raymond sa pagkaalala sa ina at mga kalarong pamangkin. Paano pa ako kakain ng abokado gayong sa bawat pagbanggit ng prutas na ito ay ibinabalik sa aking gunita ang alaala ng pamilya ni Raymond?

Iisa ang hitsura ng kanilang drowing: mga bahay na nakalubog sa banlik at bubong lang ang makikita, mga taong nakatalungko sa bubungan, mga taong nakakapit sa mga sanga ng puno, mga bahay na inaanod ng rumaragasang banlik, mga nabunot na puno at troso, nalulunod na kalabaw, baboy, at aso. Nagulat pa ako dahil kahit stick figure lamang ang iginuhit ng karamihan, malinaw pa ring nakasaad doon kung ano ang kasarian o kung bata o matanda ang nakita nilang nalunod!

"Matandang babae po itong nalunod na ito," sabay turo sa drowing. "Ito naman po ay batang lalaki."

Sa narinig ay pilit gumagawa ng koneksyon ang aking naririnding utak. Magkaano-ano kaya ang matandang babae at batang lalaki? Maglola kaya ang dalawa? O baka wala naman talaga silang kaugnayan sa isa't isa. Sabay lamang silang nalunod.

Hindi rin nakaligtas sa drowing ng mga bata ang buwan, ulan, at kidlat. Napansin ko agad ang kakaibang hitsura ng buwan. Nilagyan nila ito ng mukha. Nakalabi ang buwan!

"Kasi po, sobrang lungkot noong gabing 'yon. Pulos hiyawan at iyakan ang maririnig. Maraming namatay. Maraming nawalan ng bahay. Nakakatakot ang mga troso at banlik. Parang umiiyak ang langit sa nangyari. Kaya naglagay po ako ng umiiyak na buwan."

Kakaiba rin ang sinulat na kuwento ni Jenny. Kapansin-pansin na magaling siyang humagod ng mga salita. Nang gabing 'yon, maaga raw siyang nahiga sa kama. Masarap daw matulog dahil malakas ang ulan. Makapal na kumot ang gamit niya. Akala niya'y panaginip ngunit nagising na lang siyang mistulang dagat na ang kanyang silid.

Nagkakagulo na ang kanyang buong pamilya. Nag-aapurang lumikas silang lahat patungo sa kanugnog na bundok, ingat na ingat na huwag madapa o malubog sa rumaragasang banlik. Tinapos niya ang maigsing sanaysay sa pagbanggit ng mga kaanak na nakaligtas.

"Mabuti naman at nakaligtas ang buong pamilya mo sa sakuna," sabi ko kay Jenny.

Hindi ko inaasahan ang tugon ni Jenny. "H-Hindi po."

Dito na unti-unting nanginig ang tinig ni Jenny. Sa paputol-putol na kuwento ay nalaman kong kasama palang inanod ang kanyang ina, at di na rin natagpuan pa. Pinalaya na niya ang luha na kanina pa pilit pinipigil.

Maingat ang pagkukuwento ni Jenny. Hindi niya binanggit ang kinahinatnan ng kanyang magulang. Kung ang pagbabatayan ko lamang ay ang sinulat na sanaysay ni Jenny, hindi ko iisiping may matinding nangyari sa pamilya ni Jenny. Sinadya niyang iwasan sa kanyang kuwento ang sinapit ng kanyang ina.

Sabi ng nanay ko, kapag sobrang masakit na raw ang nangyayari sa atin, di man sinasadya ay pilit tumatakas ang gunita. Gumagawa ito ng sariling paniniwalaan para malampasan niya ang personal na trahedya. Ayaw na ni Jenny na isiping may nawala sa kanya kaya hindi na niya ito ikinuwento pa. Pero nasukol si Jenny ng aking tanong kaya napilitan siyang magtapat. Noon lamang niya inamin ang pagkamatay ng nanay niya. Nang mga sandaling 'yun, pakiramdam ko, napakapakialamero ko. Nabulabog ko nang di sinasadya ang kanyang pananahimik.

Iyon din siguro ang dahilan kung bakit ang batang Frankenstein na si Bunso ay ayaw magbigay ng salaysay. Ayaw nitong magsulat ng kahit ano. "Baka puwedeng magdrowing na lamang," payo ko pa. Pero iniwasan din nito ang mga krayolang ibinigay namin. Hinayaan na lamang namin si Bunso na sumali sa lahat ng aktibidad namin: kasali sa larong "Open the basket", kasama ring umaawit sa kanilang "group cheer", kasabay na kumakain ng iba pang bata, nagtataas ng kamay para sa libreng kopya ng libro matapos ang aking pagkukuwento. Kapag makakasalubong ko siya, matipid siyang ngingiti kapag binabati. Pero ang kapansin-pansin sa kanya, kung ako'y nagpapahinga sa isang sulok, basta na lamang siyang tatabi sa aking kinauupuan, hahaplusin ang aking braso, o hahawakan ang aking palad. Minsan naman, napapansin kong nakakapit siya sa kamay ng iba pang nakatatanda sa kanya.

Iginalang ko ang pananahimik ni Bunso. Walang kaso kung wala siyang maalala sa nangyari. May kapangyarihan naman talaga ang ating isip na limutin ang mga pangyayari na hindi nakalulugod sa atin. Hanggang sa nakita niyang nagtapat ang lahat ng kanyang kasama sa nangyari sa kanilang buhay. Nakita niya kung paanong umiyak at humagulgol ang mga kapwa bata matapos ibahagi sa grupo ang kanilang isinulat o iginuhit. Noon nagkalakas-loob si Bunso na basagin ang pananahimik.

Siya ang pinakahuling batang pumunta sa harap at nagkuwento ng buhay. Wala siyang artwork o sinulat na sanaysay. Pero naikuwento niya, sa pagitan ng hikbi, ang nangyari. Nagpunta sila sa Repador building sa pag-aakalang ligtas dito kasama ang kanyang tatay, isang kapatid, at lola. Bigla na lamang daw may gumuho sa loob ng building, at basta na lamang siyang tumalsik. Naiwan sa guho ng Repador ang kanyang magulang at kapatid. Hindi na niya nalaman kung ano ang nangyari sa kanila.

Dinugtungan na lamang ng mga guro ang nangyari ky Bunso. Kung paanong ito'y natagpuang nakaipit sa mga guho. Kung paanong inilipad ito ng helikopter patungong Maynila para operahan ang bungong nabasag. Hindi na nahukay pa sa guho ang mga mahal ni Bunso, sama-sama nang nalibing doon. Masisisi ko ba si Bunso kung waring nabura na sa kanyang gunita ang sinapit ng mga kaanak?

PAMBANSANG AWIT NG PILIPINAS
Composed by Julian Felipe, Original Spanish lyrics by Jose Palma
Filipino lyrics by the Institute of National Language

Bayang magiliw
Perlas ng Silanganan
Alab ng puso
Sa dibdib mo'y buhay

Lupang hinirang
Duyan ka ng magiting
Sa manlulupig
Di ka pasisiil

Sa dagat at bundok
Sa simoy at sa langit mong bughaw
May dilag ang tula at awit
Sa paglayang minamahal

Ang kislaap ng watawat mo'y
Tagumpay na nagniningning
Ang bituin at araw niya'y
Kailan pa ma'y di magdidilim

Lupa ng araw ng luwalhati't pagsinta
Buhay ay langit sa piling mo
Aming ligaya na pag may mang-aapi
Ang mamatay nang dahil sa iyo!

SA AKING KABABATA
Dr. Jose P. Rizal (1861-1896)
National hero, Philippines
(sinulat noong siya ay walong taong gulang)

Kapagka ang baya'y sadyang umiibig
Sa kanyang salitang kaloob ng langit,
Sanglang kalayaan nasa ring masapit
Katulad ng ibong nasa himpapawid.

Pagka't ang salita'y isang kahatulan
Sa bayan, sa nayo't mga kaharian,
At ang isang tao'y katulad, kabagay
Ng alin mang likha noong kalayaan.

Ang hindi magmahal sa kanyang salita
Mahigit sa hayop at malansang isda,
Kaya ang marapat pagyamaning kusa
Na tulad sa inang tunay na nagpala.

Ang wikang Tagalog tulad din sa Latin
Sa Ingles, Kastila at salitang anghel,
Sapagka't ang Poong maalam tumingin
Ang siyang naggawad, nagbigay sa atin.

Ang salita nati'y huwad din sa iba
Na may alfabeto at sariling letra,
Na kaya nawala'y dinatnan ng sigwa
Ang lunday sa lawa noong dakong una.

PAG-IBIG SA TINUBUANG LUPA
Andres C. Bonifacio (1863-1897)
Philippine hero and Father of the Philippine revolution

Aling pag-ibig pa ang hihigit kaya
sa pagkadalisay at magkadakila
Gaya ng pag-ibig sa sariling lupa?
Aling pag-ibig pa? Wala na nga, wala.

Pagpupuring lubos ang palaging hangad
Sa bayan ng taong may dangal na ingat,
Umawit, tumula, kumata't at sumulat,
Kalakhan din niya'y isinisiwalat.

Walang mahalagang hindi inihandog
Ng may pusong wagas sa Bayang nagkupkop,
Dugo, yaman, dunong, katiisa't pagod,
Buhay ma'y abuting magkalagut-lagot.

Bakit? Alin ito na sakdal ng laki,
Na hinahandugan ng busong pagkasi,
Na sa lalong mahal nakapangyayari,
At ginugulan ng buhay na iwi?

Ay! Ito'y ang inang bayang tinubuan:
Siya'y una't tangi sa kinamulatan
Ng kawili-wiling liwanang ng araw
Na nagbigay-init sa buong katawan.

Kalakip din nito'y pag-ibig sa bayan,
Ang lahat ng lalong sa gunita'y mahal,
Mula sa masaya'y gasong kasanggulan
Hanggang sa katawa'y mapasa-libingan.

Sa aba ng abang mawalay sa bayan!
Gunita ma'y laging sakbibi ng lumbay,
Walang alaala't inaasam-asam
Kundi ang makita'y lupang tinubuan.

Pati ng magdusa'y sampung kamatayan
Wari ay masarap kung dahil sa bayan
At lalong mahirap. Oh, himalang bagay!
Lalong pag-irog pa ang sa kanya'y alay.

Kung ang bayang ito'y masasa-panganib
At siya ay dapat na ipagtangkilik,
Ang anak, asawa, magulang, kapatid;
Isang tawag niya'y tatalikdang pilit.

Hayo na nga, hayo, kayong nangabuhay
Sa pag-asang lubos ng kaginhawahan

At walang tinamo kundi kapaitan,
Hayo na't ibangon ang naabang bayan!

Kayong nalagasan ng bunga't bulaklak
Kahoy niyaring buhay na nilanta't sukat,
Ng bala-balaki't makapal na hirap,
Muling manariwa't sa baya'y lumiyag.

Ipahandug-handog ang buong pag-ibig
At hanggang may dugo'y ubusing itigis;
Kung sa pagtatanggol, buhay ay mapatid,
Ito'y kapalaran at tunay na langit!

ANO ANG PAGKAIBA NG FILIPINO SA TAGALOG? (Excerpt)
Isagani R. Cruz
Educator and Writer

Ngayon nama'y singkronik ang gagamitin kong pamaraan para pag-ibahin ang Filipino at Tagalog. Gagamitin kong texto ang orihinal sa Filipino at ang salin sa Tagalog ng unang pangungusap sa Seksyon 2.2.2 ng *Palisi sa Wika ng Unibersidad ng Pilipinas* (1992).

FILIPINO: Magiging boluntaryo ang pagturo sa Filipino.
TAGALOG: Ang pagtuturo sa Filipino ay kusangloob.

Pansinin ang balangkas ng pangungusap. Sa Filipino'y una ang panaguri, tulad ng napansin nina [Fe] Otanes. Sa Tagalog ay ginagamit ang panandang *ay*. Sa pormal na gamit ng Tagalog ay talagang ginagamit ang *ay*. Pormal ang gamit ng Filipino, dahil ito nga ang opisyal na palisi ng Unibersidad ng Pilipinas, pero hindi ginagamit ang ay. Ito ang unang pagkaiba ng Filipino sa Tagalog. Pormal o lebel-panulat ang karaniwang ayos ng pangungusap na walang ay. Pansinin ang pagkawala ng pag-ulit ng unang pantig ng salitang-ugat na turo. Ang salitang pagtuturo ay Tagalog; ang salitang pagturo ay Filipino. Ayon kay Teresita Maceda na naging Direktor ng Sentro ng Wikang Filipino sa Unibersidad ng Pilipinas, ang dahilan sa pag-alis ng pag-ulit ng unang pantig ng salitang-ugat ay ang impluwensiya ng mga wikang bernakular na tulad ng Cebuano. Nahihirapan daw ang mga Bisaya na mag-ulit ng pantig, kung kayat nagiging katawatawa o hindi istandard ang pagsalita ng Bisaya ng Tagalog. Pero sa wikang Filipino'y iba na. Hindi na kailangang mahiya ang Bisaya dahil tama na ang ugaling Bisaya sa paggamit ng panlapi at salitang-ugat. Ito ang ikalawang pagkaiba ng Filipino sa Tagalog. Inuulit ang pantig ng salitang-ugat o ang pantig ng panlapi sa Tagalog; hindi na kailangang ulitin ang mga pantig sa Filipino.

Pansinin ang paggamit ng hiram na salita mula sa Ingles sa pangungusap na Filipino. Sa halip ng kusangloob na taal na Tagalog ay boluntaryo mula sa voluntary ang ginagamit sa Filipino. (Sa totoo lang ay dapat na boluntari ang halaw sa voluntary, pero naging siokoy na boluntaryo, na hango naman sa voluntario, pero hindi sa Kastila kundi sa Ingles nanggaling ang pagkasiokoy ng salita.) Mas laganap kasi sa kamaynilaan ang salitang voluntary kaysa kusangloob. Madalas nating marinig ang salitang voluntary kung may humihingi ng kontribusyon o kung may naghahakot para dumami ang dadalo sa isang lektyur o kung may nagsisimula ng organisasyon. Bihira natin marinig ang kusangloob. Sa Filipino ay karaniwang ginagamit ang mas madalas gamitin. Ito ang ikatlong pagkaiba ng Filipino sa Tagalog. Mas hawak sa leeg ang Tagalog ng panulatan o matandang gamit ng salita; mas nakikinig sa talagang ginagamit o sinasalita ang Filipino.

Pansinin na hindi sa Kastila humiram ng salita kundi sa Ingles. Sa Tagalog, kahit na sa makabagong Tagalog, kapag humihiram ng salita'y unang naghahanap sa wikang Kastila, bago maghanap sa wikang Ingles. Ganyan ang mungkahi ni [Virgilio] Almario at ng maraming nauna sa kanya. Ito ang ikapat na pagkaiba ng Filipino sa Tagalog. Kahit na sa makabagong Tagalog ay Kastila pa rin ang wikang karaniwang hinihiraman; sa Filipino'y Ingles ang karaniwang hinihiraman, dahil nga Taglish ang ugat ng Filipino.

Samakatwid ay apat ang pagkaiba ng Filipino sa Tagalog batay lamang sa iisang pangungusap na hango sa palisi ng Unibersidad ng Pilipinas. Kung pag-aaralan natin ang buong palisi na nakasulat sa Filipino at ang buong salin nito sa wikang Tagalog ay sigurado akong mas marami tayong makikitang pagkaiba ng Filipino sa Tagalog. Iyon lamang pangailangan na isalin ang textong Filipino sa Tagalog ay patunay na na magkaiba ang dalawang wika.

Ngayon nama'y magbibigay ako ng ilang feature na sa palagay ko'y nagdidiferensyeyt sa Filipino at Tagalog. Dahil hindi naman ako linggwista'y hindi ko mapapatunayan na palatandaan nga ang mga ito ng pagkaiba, pero ibibigay ko ang mga ito para mairiserts ng ibang iskolar. Ipapaubaya ko na sa mga nag-aral ng lingguwistika ang pagpatunay o pagwalang-saysay sa mga natuklasan kong ibang feature ng Filipino sa Tagalog.

Una, sa Tagalog ay hindi ginagamit ang panghalip na **siya** para tukuyin ang hindi tao, pero sa Filipino ay karaniwan nang ginagamit ang **siya** para sa mga bagay. Halimbawa'y "Maganda siya." Maaaring hindi tao at hindi man lamang buhay ang tinutukoy ng **siya**; maaaring kotse o damit o kulay.

Ikalawa, sa Tagalog ay hindi karaniwang dinaragdagan ng **-s** ang isang pangngalang isahan para gawing maramihan ito. Sa halip ay gumagamit ng pantukoy, pamilang, o pang-uri na tulad ng napansin ni Santos. Pero sa Filipino ay madalas gamitin ang **-s** para gawing maramihan ang isang pangngalan. Ang una kong narinig na gumamit ng feature na ito ay ang mga taga-Davao noon pa mang 1969. Doon, ang dalawa o higit pang softdrink na coke ay cokes. Sa kamaynilaan ngayon, hindi ginagamit ang Tagalog na mga parent ko kundi ang Filipinong parents ko; halimbawa'y sa "strict ang parents ko."

Dapat kong banggitin dito ang pananaw ni Matute. Ang sabi niya tungkol sa salitang **barongs** ay ito:

Bakit **barongs** ang tawag namin, ang itinatanong mo, Kabataan? Hindi ba iyan ang dating tinaguriang barong Tagalog? Oo. Ngunit dumami na nang dumami ang allergic, pinamamantalan ng punong taynga sa salitang Tagalog. Gaya na nga ang Wikang Tagalog, hindi Wikang Filipino. Kaya, inalis na ang salitang Tagalog sa salitang barong Tagalog. Ginawang barong na lamang, ngunit sapagkat sa Ingles, kapag marami'y dinaragdagan ng titik **s**, kaya't ang barong ay naging barongs. Bakit bumilis ang bigkas? A, iyan ay sapagkat ang Pasay man ay naging Pasay (mabilis) na at ang Davao ay naging Davao (mabilis) na. Kaya bakit ang barongs ay hindi magiging barongs (mabilis)?

Mapapansin na pati si [Genoveva Edroza] Matute ay naniniwalang iba ang wikang Tagalog sa wikang Filipino. Hindi nga lamang siya kumikiling sa wikang Filipino, pero inaamin niya na iba ang wikang ito sa wikang kinagisnan niya bilang manunulat sa Tagalog. Siya na nga mismo, sa aking pagkaalam, ang unang nakapansin sa paggamit ng -**s** bilang palatandaan ng pagkamaramihan.

Ikatlo, sa Davao ko pa rin unang narinig ang paggamit ng **mag-** halip ng **-um-** sa mga pandiwa. Hindi karaniwang umaakyat ng bahay ang Davaoeños, kundi nag-aakyat o nag-akyat. Kung sabagay ay sa timog-katagalugan ay talaga namang napapalitan ang **-um-**ng **mag-**; sa Parañaque lamang, na napakalapit na sa Maynila, ay nakain sila sa halip ng kumain. Sa madaling salita, hindi nakakapagtaka na sa Filipino ay mas madalas gamitin ang **mag-** kaysa sa **-um-**. Gaya nga ng sinabi ni Ma. Lourdes Bautista sa isang papel na binasa niya noong 1989 sa kumperensya ng Language Education Council of the Philippines: "It is clear that the affix used for English verbs in actor focus is **mag-** and never **-um-** (perhaps because it is easier to use a prefix than an infix), and therefore this reinforces the predominance of **mag-** over **-um-**."

Ikaapat, at ito'y suhestyon ni Barry Miller. Sa Tagalog ay **i-** ang ginagamit sa tinatawag nina Otanes na benefactive-focus na pandiwa. Ang **-an** ay karaniwang directional focus. Ito ang dahilan kung bakit, sa libro nina Teresita Ramos at Bautista tungkol sa mga pandiwa ay ibili ang benefactive-focus at bilhan ang directional focus. Sa Tagalog, ang karaniwan nating sinasabi kung nakikibili tayo sa McDonald's ay "Ibili mo nga ako ng hamburger." Sa Filipino, ang karaniwan nating sinasabi ay "Bilhan mo nga ako ng hamburger." (Natural, kung dalawang sandwich ang ipinabibili natin, sa Tagalog ay sasabihin nating "Ibili mo nga ako ng dalawang hamburger." Sa Filipino ay sinasabi nating "Bilhan mo nga ako ng dalawang hamburgers.")

Ikalima, sa Tagalog ay laging inaalis ang sobra sa isang katinig sa isang klaster ng katinig kung inuulit ang isang pantig. Halimbawa'y nagpiprisinta ang sinasabi sa Tagalog dahil ginagawang **p** na lang ang klaster na **pr** sa inuulit na pantig na **pri**. Sa Filipino ay ginagamit ang buong klaster; samakatwid, nagpriprisinta o magprapraktis. Hindi na takot sa klaster ang Filipino, di tulad ng Tagalog na hangga't maaari'y umiiwas sa nagkukumpul-kumpulang katinig.

Ikaanim, dahil laganap na ang Filipino sa kabisayaan ay hindi na maaaring ibatay lamang ito sa Tagalog na tulad ng nais mangyari ng mga Tagalista. Napakarami ng mga Bisaya at hindi makatarungan na sila ang babagay sa mga Tagalog gayung napakaunlad na ng lunsod ng Cebu at lingua franca ng Bisayas at Mindanaw ang wikang Cebuano. Isang pagkaiba ng Cebuano sa Tagalog ay ang kawalan ng mga salitang panggalang na **po** at **ho**. Kung pag-iisahin tayo ng wikang Filipino at hindi paghihiwahiwalayin ay dapat huwag ipagpilitan ng mga Tagalog na gumamit ng **po** at **ho** ang mga Bisaya. Hindi naman nangangahulugan ito na walang galang sa matanda o sa kapwa ang mga Bisaya; sa katunayan ay kasinggalang ang mga Bisaya ng mga Tagalog sa kanilang mga magulang at iba pang karaniwang pinag-uukulan ng galang. Pero wala sa wika ng mga Bisaya ang mga salitang panggalang na **po** at **ho**. Hindi tao ang pinag-uusapan dito kundi wika. Sa wikang Cebuano ay hindi tanda ng paggalang ang paglagay ng **po** at **ho**. Samakatwid, sa wikang Filipino ay hindi dapat siguro isama ang **po** at **ho**. Gamitin na lamang ito sa Tagalog o sa diyalekto ng Filipino na ginagamit sa katagalugan.

Anim na pagkaibang estruktural ang naibigay ko para namnamin ng ating mga linggwista. Maliliit na bagay ang mga ito, pero makabuluhan kung mapatunayan. Ngayon nama'y babalikan ko ang malaking isyu tungkol sa relasyon ng Filipino sa Tagalog.

Diyalekto lamang ba ng Tagalog ang Filipino? Ito ang palagay ni Ma. Lourdes Bautista. Maaari, at ito'y hindi dapat problemahin dahil sa kasaysayan ng wikang Ingles ay diyalekto lamang ng Englisc ang East Midland nang ito'y ginamit ni Chaucer sa London. Pero ang diyalektong ito sa London ang naging kasalukuyang tinatawag nating Ingles. Kung diyalekto man ng Tagalog ang Filipino ng kamaynilaan ay pansamantala lamang naman ito. Sa susunod na mga dantaon ay tatawagin na itong Filipino at kakalimutan na ang Tagalog kung saan ito nagmula, gaya ng pagtalikod ng kasaysayan sa iba pang diyalekto ng Englisc. Samakatwid ay hindi ako sang-ayon kay Otanes na ang Filipino at ang Tagalog ay parehong wika kung estruktura at balarila ang pinag-uusapan at nagkakaiba lamang sila sa larangan ng sosyolinggwistika. Sa palagay ko'y iba ang Filipino sa Tagalog kahit na estruktura at balarila ang pag-uusapan. Ang kanyang diniscrayb sa kanyang libro'y Filipino at hindi Tagalog. Aksidente lamang ng kasaysayan na hindi pa naiimbento ang salitang Filipino noong panahong sinusulat ni Otanes ang kanyang gramatika, pero siya ang kaunaunahang nakapansin na may Educated Manila Tagalog na dapat seryosohin. Kaya nga, kapag isinalin ang Reference Grammar sa Filipino ay dapat tawagin itong Gramatika ng Filipino sa halip ng Gramatika ng Tagalog. Sa ganitong paraan ay lilinaw ang kasaysayan ng ating wikang pambansa. Kung si Lope K. Santos ang gumawa ng balarila ng Tagalog, si Fe T. Otanes naman ang gumawa ng gramatika ng Filipino.

May kongklusyon ba ako? Mayroon. Nagsimula ako sa pamagitan ng pagbanggit ng mga teoretikal na prinsipyong aking pinaniniwalaan, isa na nga ang ginawa ni Gonzalez sa Philippine English. Pagkatapos ay nagbigay ako ng ilang halimbawa ng totoong gamit ng wika ng ating mga tinitingalang manunulat, upang patunayan na hindi tama ang karaniwan nating akala ukol sa balarila. Pagkatapos kong magbigay ng kasaysayan ng Filipino na batay sa kasaysayan ng wikang Ingles ay pinuna ko ang ilang katangian ng wikang Filipino na iba sa wikang Tagalog. Ano ang patutunguhan ng lahat ng ito?

Sa aking palagay, ang perents sa larangan ng wika ay ang mga sikat na writer na tulad nina [Fren] Abueg, Almario, Lualhati Bautista at [B.S.] Medina [Jr.]. Kung totoo nga na ang ginagawa ng perents ay inaakalang tama ng kabataan, masasabi nating inaakala at nagiging tama ang talagang ginagawa ng ating mga batikang manunulat. Hindi ko ipinakita na ito rin ang ginagawa ng nakararaming Filipino sa kasalukuyan. Pero naipakita ko, sa palagay ko, na kung ang pinakamagandang gamit ang pagbatayan, ang wikang umiiral ngayon sa paligid natin, lalo na sa labas ng katagalugan, ay Filipino at hindi Tagalog. Naipakita ko na rin sana na may pagkaiba, maliit man o malaki, ang Filipino sa Tagalog.

(With permission from the author. Material is accessible at http://isaganircruz.blogspot. com/2006/10/ano-ang-pagkaiba-ng-filipino-sa.html.)